PATH WITHOUT DESTINATION

PATH WITHOUT DESTINATION

The Long Walk of a Gentle Hero

SATISH KUMAR

EAGLE BROOK

An Imprint of HarperCollinsPublishers

This book was first published in Great Britain in 1992 by Green Books as *No Destination*. A hardcover edition was published in 1999 by Eagle Brook, an imprint of William Morrow and Company, Inc.

HarperCollins books may be purchased for educational, business, or sales promotional use. For information please write: Special Markets Department, HarperCollins Publishers Inc., 10 East 53rd Street, New York, NY 10022.

First paperback edition published 2000.

Book design by Oksana Kushnir

The Library of Congress has catalogued the hardcover edition as follows:

Satish Kumar, 1936–
    Path without destination : an autobiography / Satish Kumar.
      p. cm.
    ISBN 0-688-16402-1
    1. Satish Kumar, 1936– . 2. Spiritual biography—India. 3. Spiritual life—Jainism.
    4. Jaina pilgrims and pilgrimages. 5. Jains—India—Biography. I. Title.
    BL1373.S29A3   1999
    294.4'092—dc21
    [B]   98-35572
                                                CIP

ISBN 0-688-16404-8 (pbk.)

00 01 02 03 04   10 9 8 7 6 5 4 3 2 1

FOR JUNE, MUKTI, AND MAYA

CONTENTS

1. Mother   1
2. Guru   14
3. Ashram   33
4. Benares   59
5. Wanderer   70
6. Escape   110
7. Floating   115
8. Mukti   128
9. E. F. Schumacher   135
10. Maya   140
11. Hartland   152
12. The Small School   160
13. Pilgrimage: Iona   168
14. Pilgrimage: Return   215
15. Japan   255
16. The College   270
17. Mount Kailas   275
18. Influences   283
19. Realization   308

————— ∞ —————

CHAPTER 1

Mother

BEFORE I WAS BORN, while my mother was still pregnant with me, she often had a dream—always the same one. A wise old man with a long beard was riding with her on the back of an elephant into a forest. He promised to take her to a land of gold and jewels. "Why are we on the back of an elephant?" Mother asked. "Let's go on horseback so we can arrive more quickly." The wise man said, "I don't know the way. Only the elephant knows the way." Mother argued, "This is stupid. A horse is much more intelligent than an elephant." The wise man replied, "It's not a question of intelligence but a question of going the right way." Mother's dream always ended with her and the wise man riding on the elephant, never reaching their destination.

On the ninth of August 1936 I was born in the town of Sri Dungargarh, at four in the morning: the time of Brahma, the god of creation, a time of complete stillness, calm, and peace. As the rays of the sun touch the earth, so the rays of knowledge come to the soul.

When Mother consulted the Brahmin who was the village astrologer about her dream, he said that I was the child of her unfulfilled wishes and that I would never have gold or jewels and that I would never reach my destination. Life for me would be an unending, continuous journey. Then, offering *ghee* (melted butter) to the fire, the Brahmin named me Bhairav Dan, which means "gift of Shiva."

I was four years old when my father died. My only memory of him, except for holding his index finger and walking, was of his body wrapped in a white cloth and heaped with marigolds and jasmine, only his face showing, his eyes closed as if in deep sleep. His body lay on a wooden stretcher in the courtyard of our home. Relatives and friends came from miles around, all the women wearing green saris as a sign of mourning. When they reached the beginning of our street, they started wailing loudly.

Mother retreated into her room in tears. One by one she removed the precious pieces of jewelry which Father had given her when they were married—golden chains, bracelets and rings, pearls, diamonds, and silver bangles. She took off the pendant from her forehead, the diamond stud from her nose, her diamond earrings, her gold armlet, her belt of gold wire studded with pearls, her silver anklets and silver toe rings. She removed her yellow sari embroidered with gold and put on a plain green one. She sat on the floor in the corner of the room. For days she didn't move, she didn't speak to anybody, she didn't take food. She just stayed in the corner of the room weeping. I came to her asking, "Why are you here, why don't you come out, why don't you come to the kitchen, why don't you . . ."

Four men took Father's body on to their shoulders and carried him in a funeral procession. Outside the town they laid him on the funeral pyre. Wood and coconuts were heaped over his body, and the fire was lit. Melted butter and sandalwood incense was poured onto the fire while the village priest chanted mantras. We stood in a circle around the pyre until the fire died. Next day the ashes were collected and then taken by my brother to Benares to be offered to the holy river Ganges.

I followed Mother like her own shadow. I went wherever she went. I was part of her body. She breast-fed me until I was two years old. She massaged my body daily with sesame oil. I slept in the same bed as Mother and always ate off her plate. She rose at four in the morning and meditated for forty-eight minutes, the prescribed period in the Jain religion, the religion of our family. She sat alone on the veranda with the glass sand timer, and meditated partly in silence and partly chanting the Jain mantra of Surrender:

I surrender to those who are Enlightened and therefore have no enemies
I surrender to the Released Spirits
I surrender to the Wise Gurus
I surrender to the Spiritual Teachers
I surrender to the Seekers of Enlightenment

She chanted it one hundred and eight times, counting with her bead necklace. After her meditation she took a daily vow to limit her needs. For example on one day she might say, "Today I will not eat anything other than the following twelve items: rice, lentils, wheat, mango, melon, cucumber, cumin, chili, salt, water, milk, and butter, and today I will not travel more than ten miles, and only towards the East."

At dawn she ground the flour by hand with a stone mill and churned butter from yogurt. At sunrise she milked our cows and the water buffalo. Then she would turn the animals out for the cowherd to take them to graze for the day. We were a large family—my three brothers, my four sisters, my uncle and great-uncle, their sons, wives, and grandchildren all lived in the house. If we were all together, the number of us would be about forty. Breakfast was generally a glass of milk—tea and coffee were never allowed.

The family would eat the midday meal from eleven o'clock onward. Mother would make sure that each member's taste was catered for too. Eating in our family was never a social occasion, it was an act of personal satisfaction. No conversation was allowed while eating. Though she limited her own appetite, Mother would prepare for each of us our favorite foods—but food was also her weapon to punish us for disobedience. For all of us Mother was the only mother, the head of the household: my cousins would call their own mother "Sister."

The family was strictly vegetarian—no meat, no fish, no eggs. About fifteen hundred years ago some wandering monks of the Jain religion had come to my ancestral village of Os. They taught complete adherence to the principle of *ahimsa* (not harming any living creature). My ancestors were Rajputs, belonging to the caste of *Kshatriya* (the warriors). They ate meat, they collected the taxes, and they were soldiers of the king. The monks awakened in them the desire to renounce all killing and converted the whole village into pacifists and vegetarians. The King granted the Oswals (the people of Os) leave from the army on the ground of conscience, but they had to change from the warrior caste to the trader caste. He appointed my ancestor as treasurer to the king, and since then we have borne the name *Sethias* (the treasurers).

Just before sunset, in common with Jain practice, we would eat the evening meal. While we were eating I would hear cowbells ringing, as our cows found their way home at "cow-dust time." Our two cows, a brown and a white one, would come into the courtyard, and I would run to prevent the cow going to her calf while Mother prepared the milk bucket. Mother would allow the calves to suckle a little before she milked the cow, and she would leave milk in the udder for the calves to finish. Then she would milk the water buffalo; they were harder to milk, but Mother always kept at least one because buffalo's milk makes richer butter. While she was milking she would let me feed the camel. The milk was always boiled, as she never allowed us to drink unboiled milk. She would give us some cow's milk to drink and also to anyone else who wanted it. The boiled buffalo's milk would be set for yogurt.

AFTER FATHER'S DEATH, Mother spent more and more time with the wandering Jain monks. She would leave the animals with a neighbor, and she and I would go off in our camel cart with pots, pans, food, and bedding. For several weeks we would accompany the monks, listening to their storytelling and readings from the scriptures, following them from one village to another. The monk's life is a life of continuous movement, a flow like a river. These monks have no permanent place: they walk from village to village, starting after sunrise and walking a few miles. Their rules permit them to spend only a few days in a village, begging their food and sleeping in houses which disciples vacate for them. It is only during the monsoon months that they may stay long in one place.

When I was seven, a group of monks came to spend the *chaturmas* (the four monsoon months) in our town. The news of their arrival traveled by word of mouth, and a group of people, including Mother and myself, went along the desert path to greet them, singing songs of welcome: "Today the sun is golden because our gurus are coming to our village with a message of peace . . ."

Suddenly out of the sand bushes, I saw three monks in their white robes, walking barefoot and carrying a few belongings on their backs. They were walking fast, their faces impassive to the crowds around them. I had to run to keep up. People had gathered in the courtyard of the house where the monks were to stay, to hear their first sermon. One of the monks, Monk Kundan, who was sitting on a table, gave the sermon. He spoke for a long time. One of the points he made was this: "Seekers, we have come to show you the path to liberate your soul. The soul is wrapped up in good and bad *karmas,* which imprison it. [*Karma* is the inexorable law of consequence for all and every human deeds.] You have to break out of the bonds of karma. In order to break free from karma, you have to leave everything you know and love; mother, father, wife, children. These relationships are the expression of possessive love rather than the expression of divine love that sustains the universe . . ."

At the end, men of the town went up to the monks, put their heads on their feet, and asked for blessings. I went up to Monk Kundan. He looked deep into my eyes and talked with me. I asked him if he would come to my home to receive food. He inquired the way. When I got home Mother said, "But don't expect him today because it is the first day and he will have been invited to many homes." I insisted we wait to eat and keep the doors open, since monks will only come into a house with an open door. I kept running out into the street to look for him. Nobody else thought he would come. After some time I saw him coming. He said to me, "We're going to spend four months here. Will you come every day to receive knowledge from us?"

At that time I was learning to read and write from our Brahmin-teacher during the day, so I could only go to the monks in the morning and evening. The early-morning encounter with the monks is called *darshan*—a glimpse of a holy face which is to purify and inspire. The monks would be in meditation, sitting on the veranda wrapped in their cotton shawls. In the evenings I went to hear them telling the story of Rama, which was told little by little over a period of about ten weeks. Fifty or sixty people from our town gathered to hear it every night. The narration of Ramayana was a combination of entertainment and religion. We sat listening in darkness—the monks did not use any kind of light; "Dark is beautiful, not to be burnt," they said.

One evening, cool after the monsoon rain, before the storytelling began, Monk Kundan talked to Mother. He said, "There is a line on your son's foot, the lotus line. We think he is the reincarnation of a spiritual soul. He looks and behaves like a spiritual person. For many generations no one from your family has offered himself as a monk. Out of eight children, surely you could contribute one?" It was dark. I couldn't see Mother's face.

Next day Kundan said to me, "If you become a monk, the people will come to listen to your preaching, they will bow their heads at your feet. You will go to heaven and after heaven to *nirvana*." "What is *nirvana?*" I asked. He said, "No birth and no death." That impressed me—no death. Father's death had created a deep question in my mind. I couldn't understand where he had gone and what had happened to him. Whenever I asked Mother about him, she said I asked too many questions and didn't answer me, so I used to ask the monks about what happened after death. Monk Kundan described human life as *samsara* (the everlasting round of birth and death) and the role of the monks who alone can free the individual from it. He showed me a picture.

A man lost in the forest was being chased by a wild elephant. The man climbed a tree and grabbed hold of a branch, but the elephant started to shake the tree with his trunk, trying to pull it out of the ground. Under the tree was a water hole in which there were poisonous snakes with their heads in the air, hissing. Sitting on the branch to which the man was clinging were two rats, a white and a black rat, symbolizing day and night. Just above the man was a wild bees' nest. When the elephant shook the tree, the bees flew out and started stinging the man all over, but from the beehive drops of honey trickled down into the man's mouth; the honey was deliciously sweet. Flying angels asked the man if he wanted to be rescued. He said, "Yes, yes, but could you wait for this drop of honey which is just coming, see it is coming, just wait . . ." The angels flew away. The man shouted after them. "It's coming, wait. I will come with you after this drop."

Kundan also showed me pictures of heaven and hell. Heaven was full of exotic flowers, beautiful men and women wearing rich clothes and fabulous jewelery, palaces, thrones, airplanes in which angels flew. He told me that those who didn't become monks went to hell for thousands and thousands of years. The pictures of hell terrified me—tortured bodies being cut up and boiled in caldrons of hot oil . . . Because he had been a businessman, I could see my father in hell being tortured, cut up, and fried. I could not eat or play—the pictures of hell made me shiver. If I went into business, I would go to hell too, I thought.

It was October, cool and dry, and the monsoon was over. The night before the monks left I couldn't sleep. After sunrise Mother was busy looking after the animals, but I went to see the monks. A crowd had gathered to see them off. Some people walked with them, and I also followed. At the next village they stopped. Monks went to beg food for themselves—it was considered wrong to give it to a nonmonk, and the other followers didn't know I had come alone, so nobody worried about me. I was very hungry. It was the first time I had been out of my town without Mother. At home Mother was worried. She searched everywhere. Eventually someone told her that they had seen me following the monks. She walked the ten miles to the village in the evening and found me. "Did you eat?" she asked. I said, "I haven't eaten, I'm hungry, give me some food." She said, "You're stupid. Why didn't you ask someone to give you some food?" I didn't tell Mother that I wanted to be like the monks.

MOTHER CAME FROM A PEASANT FAMILY and wasn't happy unless she did some farming. Every year when the monsoon came, she would hire about four acres of land, always on the west side of town so that when we walked to it in the morning that hot sun would be on our backs, and in the evening when we returned, the sun would again be on our backs. Just after the first rain of the monsoon, she employed a neighbor to plow with our camel, but all the other work she did herself. We planted maize, green beans, sesame, watermelons, sugar melons, marrows, horseradish, carrots, and gram peas. Mother prepared almond sweets for me and took them with us for our lunch. When the watermelons started to ripen, Mother and I would dig holes in the sand for them and cover them with sand, so that birds and animals didn't eat them and they could ripen on the plant. They would grow big and sweet and red inside, weighing up to thirty pounds. We would take them home on the camel cart and store them for the winter. Mother would dry most of the vegetables so that we had vegetables all the year round.

One morning Mother and I rode out on our camel to the land. The maize crop was ripe. We built a small hut with wood and rushes. There we could sleep and protect the crop while we were harvesting. Mother asked me why I looked so sad. I couldn't answer. She said, "You don't listen properly, you're not interested in playing anymore. Look at the other children, see how gay and cheerful they are, while you mope around, you miserable little soul!"

．　．　．

WHEN I WAS EIGHT, the head of our branch of the Jain order, the "guru" Acharya Tulsi, with his entourage of monks and nuns, spent the monsoon months in our town. Two rich families gave their homes to the guru for this period. Canvas tents were put up in the courtyards where people could go to hear him and receive his blessings. Mother took me to welcome the guru. I saw Tulsi walking toward us across the desert. He was plump and short, but his eyes were shining like big lights. His face was fair, calm, and peaceful. Three deep lines cut across his forehead. His brows were bushy and black. His ears were long, as I had seen on the statues of gods, and hair grew on the outer edge denoting wisdom. His arms were long too, which meant a man of many resources. His step was firm. He alone among the monks wore snow white clothes. All other monks carried bags on their backs; he alone was burden-free. He walked like a lion. He raised his hands to bless us. After the guru walked forty monks, then sixty nuns, then the male disciples, then the women. Men and women sang welcoming songs:

> *The sun is golden today*
> *The guru comes to our town*
> *O men and women, gather together*
> *And sing the songs of happiness.*
> *Now we can swim the ocean of* samsara

The monks and nuns walked with their eyes on the ground and remained silent. They looked like glorious angels in their robes. Through the clouds of dust I looked for any monk I might know. I saw Monk Kundan. He smiled and raised his hand. I felt as if the guru had come to rescue me from death.

A few weeks later Monk Kundan took me to the guru. Normally the guru remained aloof, beyond reach, and talked only at sermon times, but this day he looked at me with his kind and gentle eyes. I said, "The monks have told me that they feel something spiritual in me, a link with my previous life, and that I should become a monk." The guru replied, "A monk's life is very hard. You may have spiritual links from a previous life, but in order to continue these links in this life you have to gather strength and dedication." His words reverberated in my mind. I felt I belonged to the guru. He would take me to *nirvana* (enlightenment), he would give me light. I longed to put myself in his hands.

I stopped going to school and sometimes didn't even go home to eat. I no longer saw my friends and playmates. At night I walked in the desert, thinking of Tulsi. In the moonlight the sand shone like silver, and sometimes I slept on the sand. During the day I wandered around. The town was quiet. Near the well under a pipal tree sat a fat rich man smoking his hookah. Shepherd children rested under the trees with their goats and sheep. In the marketplace the women were buying monsoon fruits and vegetables, and chatting. But all this did nor attract me.

As every morning, Mother was making butter. She sat on the veranda by a pillar with the yogurt in a large clay pot in front of her. She pulled a wooden pestle backward and forward with a rope, gradually churning the yogurt, dividing it into butter and buttermilk. The beautiful sound of butter churning woke me up. I went to Mother and sat by her. I wanted to tell her of my meeting with the guru, but I just sat looking at the butter making, waiting for the butter to come, with a *chappati* (a flat bread) in my hand. Impatient, I interrupted Mother. "The butter is ready, it's coming, give it to me." She said, "It isn't ready—wait." I looked into the pot and pointed to some bubbles. "See, it has come." Feeling my anxiety, she gave me some butter, which was still not quite ready. After a while she said, "What's the matter with you, little one?" I said, "I want to become a monk!" Mother was shocked. There was silence. Then she said, "I was dreading the day you would say this. But, my son, you're too young. You can become a monk later on." She burst into tears. We didn't speak any more about it.

The Brahmin came to our house to ask why I wasn't going to school. Mother told him of a vow she had made when I had smallpox at the age of five. (Smallpox is a deity called *mata* [mother]. If someone has smallpox we say, "Mother has come into the body." Every year a special day is dedicated to her, when the family doesn't cook but eats the previous day's food and worships her. If mata is offended, she comes into the body in the form of smallpox.) When I had smallpox, Mother thought she had done something very wrong, and every day she prayed to mata, "Please leave my beloved son." In spite of herbal medicines, I became so ill that Mother feared I would die. She promised mata, "If you leave my son, I will never stand in the way of him leading a religious life." From the day she made this vow, I started getting better.

The Brahmin was angry with Mother, saying, "Your son is not an animal to be sacrificed. You'll regret it later on." Although the Brahmin was very close to our family, he was a Hindu not a Jain, and therefore Mother didn't trust him on religious matters. I listened to Mother and the Brahmin arguing. She said that if she broke her vow, mata might come again and this time to kill me. One day she said to me, "The thought of you becoming a monk grieves me, but I have given my word to mata. I will not interfere. You must decide for yourself." And then she burst into tears again. My decision was already made.

Together with Mother and some prominent people of the town, I went to the guru with a formal request that he make me a monk. The guru said, "You should wait. Think more. You're going to become a monk for your whole life, and there will be no turning back."

After a week I went to ask him again. Again he said, "Wait more."

After many pleas he said, "I accept to consider your request, and I will ask Monk Kundan to teach you and examine your intention properly." A few weeks later Kundan reported to the guru that I would make a good monk. I went to the guru with my final request. He pronounced, "On the last day of the monsoon I will make you a monk."

I was happy, but my family was in tears. The leading members of the Jain community made elaborate arrangements to celebrate my initiation into monkhood. There were dinner parties—at least one every day for the four weeks that were left till the end of the monsoon. Sometimes one hundred people would gather to eat with me. People gave me whatever I wanted to eat, to drink, to wear, to see. A white horse and horseman took me wherever I wanted to go. This horseman was famous in the community for his skill, and when he led the horse it would dance. We went to the main squares in the surrounding villages, and he would announce that I was the boy who was to become a monk and that everyone was invited to the ceremony, and the horse would dance for the people with me on its back. I wore pearl necklaces, diamond earrings, golden chains and rings. I was dressed in silk and satin. On my head was a silk turban and around it a jeweled band and pendant. One quarter of Mother's jewelery was made up into five hundred silver rings and a hundred golden rings, and on every ring my name was inscribed. I gave them away to people I met—friends, neighbors, and relatives—as a remembrance of my becoming a monk.

The family was required to give written consent and also to be present at the ceremony. My brothers and brothers-in-law were not convinced that a boy of nine should become a monk. My eldest brother said, "O Mother, have your wits left you? In your unstable emotional state you made a promise to mata, but you did not say that he would become a monk at such a tender age. It's not too late even now—we can at least postpone this event for a few years." Mother was upset and confused but still sure that she should not stand in my way. She put her trust in the guru.

The Brahmin came again, full of anger: his eyes were red, and he was biting his lips. I was frightened that he might make her change her mind. I sat outside the room praying, "O Lord Mahavir, give strength to my mother to stand up to him, and don't let this pagan Brahmin make trouble." I heard him shouting, "In your old age you have lost all sense. I have never seen you do anything which is not right, but now some demon possesses you, and you are letting this foolish child take this difficult decision alone. He is not destined to be a monk. I know his horoscope and I know his stars. I tell you that he cannot stay a monk, so stop him now."

When I heard his words my heart beat fast. I put my ear to the door to hear Mother's reply. "I have never gone against your advice. I have never said no to you, but in this matter I must follow my guru, and if he agrees to my son's wish then I dare not say no." The Brahmin stamped his foot. "Your guru is a fanatic to make children monks at the innocent age of nine. Go to hell if you wish to, but don't blame me that you were not warned." He walked out in a fury, and I heard my mother sobbing. I went in to reassure her. "Mother, don't cry. Our guru is kind and will look after me well. Monk Kundan said that I will have no difficulties, and you can come to have my darshan and hear my sermons, and I will bless you and the whole family will be blessed." Mother hugged me tight and said, "My son, I will not pull you back into the darkness of samsara. You have my consent."

On the day of my initiation, a message arrived to say that one of my brothers couldn't leave his business and be present to witness the initiation. The guru said, "All members of the family must be here to give their consent. If your brother cannot come, I cannot make you a monk."

It was a disaster. I suspected that this was a trick on the part of my brothers to prevent me from following my true path. Openly they did not dare to oppose my mother, but maybe this way they could stop me. Mother sent a telegram asking my brother when he could be present. He telegraphed back, "In two weeks."

I went with a special request to the guru, saying that all my family could be present in two weeks and could he wait till then to make me a monk. The monks ought to have left immediately after the end of the monsoon, but the guru agreed to extend his stay.

ON THE DAY OF THE CEREMONY, I got up just before dawn. My sisters and mother rubbed my body with a paste of turmeric powder, sesame oil, and lentil flour; then they washed me with flower-scented water. My head was shaved except for a tuft of hair in the middle. Mother and my sisters dressed me in a ceremonial silk costume.

An hour after sunrise the procession arrived at our house—fifteen horses, twenty camels, a band, singers, and more than a thousand people. The time had come to depart.

Mother put her arms around me and burst into tears. "I'll be alone, who will be with me?"

I climbed on the horse. Mother walked in the procession behind me, and we went around the town making it known that I was going to be made a monk that day and asking all the people to come and be witness to it. Three hours after sunrise we reached an open place in the center of the town. There on a high dais was the guru, surrounded by all his monks and nuns. They were wearing simple, white, seamless robes.

Sitting in the open space was an assembly of thousands of townspeople—women to one side and men to the other. In between the men and the women was a long pathway with a carpet over it. I stepped down from the horse and walked along the carpet path to the dais.

I bowed my head on the guru's feet and said, "I have come to you to receive knowledge, I have come to search for a new life, I have come to seek nirvana. I am ready, and I beg you to accept me. O my guru, will you lighten the darkness, will you purify my soul?" The guru answered, "I am here on this earth to help people find light. I am here to help people search for their soul and find liberation. If you want to do this, I am ready to help you."

I went behind a curtain to change my clothes. One by one, I handed over the jewelery, clothes, and shoes to my family, and they gave me three wooden bowls for begging food and water. My brother came forward with a white silk robe, which I put on. I went back to the guru and said, "Nothing belongs to me. I renounce everything. I am ready to leave this world, I am ready to follow you." The guru declared in a loud voice, "My disciple, I accept you. The first thing you have to practice is ahimsa [total nonviolence]. Respect all that is living and all creation. Do not hurt any person—neither plants, nor water, nor fire, nor air. Practice truth. Do not steal. Practice celibacy. Do not touch money nor think of it; have no possessions and live in poverty. Lastly, surrender your mind, your heart, your soul, and your will to the guru. Live in obedience."

"I accept."

The guru called to my relatives, "This member of your family has come to me to find light, to find truth and nirvana, freedom from the cycle of death and birth. I have accepted him to be my disciple. Do you agree?" Mother and my family said, "We have no more claim on him." The guru went on, "He is no more your son, your brother, your relative. He is no longer part of your society." My brother read out the written statement signed by all the family, which ended by saying, "We are fortunate that a member of our family has the wisdom and the understanding to accept this challenge and to search for a new life." The guru turned to my family and took the document. I climbed the steps and again put my head on the guru's feet. He held my head in one hand and with the other plucked the remaining hair from my scalp. A blaze of fire shot through my whole body. The guru said, "You have no past, you no longer belong to this world."

CHAPTER 2

Guru

THE NEXT MORNING the guru said to me, "O beloved of the gods, now you have become a monk, and therefore when you walk keep your eyes on the ground before you. Stand relaxed only on that ground which is devoid of living beings. Gently brush the earth to remove any creatures before you sit or sleep on it. Speak little and always in a language which is good and restrained. You will have no fixed abode. You will not possess more than thirty yards of cloth at a time. You will not use cushions or quilts. You will not drink water, eat, or take medicine at night. You will not sleep in the day. You will not travel by train or automobile or any other means of transport but your feet. You will not wear shoes or slippers. You will carry all your belongings yourself. You will not shave your head or chin with a razor but pluck out your hair and beard."

Then the guru called Monk Kundan and said to him, "You sowed the seeds of renunciation of the world in this young monk. Now I put him in your care to train him in the rituals so that he can follow the path of Mahavir, our Lord. Teach him the true meaning of the three cardinal principles: right knowledge, right vision, and right action." The guru turned to me and said, "Follow the instructions and commands of Monk Kundan. He is the wisest among our wise monks. His soul is pure and his life is humble." I placed my head on Kundan's feet, and from that moment I followed him.

My day began about two hours before sunrise with learning how to meditate. For one hour I remained sitting in the lotus position, silent and still. I wore a cloth folded eight times across my mouth to prevent any violent exhalation of breath which might hurt the air or any organisms in it. This cloth could only be removed to enable me to eat, and while I was eating, I could not speak. In the morning and evening I learned to inspect my clothes and belongings (blanket, begging bowls, and manuscripts), to see that no ants or insects had got into them and that I had not acquired anything which I did not need. I was instructed to walk slowly and gently, always being careful not to tread on any insects or plants. At night when I could not see clearly, I did not go outside, and if I walked within the house, I swept the floor in front of me with a broom of soft wool. The doors were always left open so that no creature could be trapped as they closed, and I slept on the floor wrapped in a blanket.

As a new monk, I was favored and did not beg for food. When the other monks brought food, the guru was the first to receive it, then myself and the other young monks. Every scrap of food had to be eaten. I would clean my bowl with a small piece of unleavened bread, wash it with some water, and then drink the water. In the evening the other monks ate the remainder of the morning meal, but someone would go out specially to beg a hot meal for the guru, and I was also allowed to take hot food with him. If the guru offered us some of his food, we all wanted it because he had touched it. If after drinking a little from a cup of milk, the guru passed it to me, I would feel that I was blessed. We all would wait for a kind look from the guru. After a meal a rug was put down on the floor on which the guru would walk. Sometimes he would rest his hand on my shoulder, but I had to be careful not to tread on the rug as I went along with him.

According to the rule of the monks, I didn't wash my clothes. I wore the same clothes until they wore out. I never took a bath nor cleaned my teeth. One day, sitting by the guru, I scratched my hair and fleas fell out. The guru looked at me and said, "You have fleas. It doesn't matter. You must remember that you have taken a vow that you will not hurt any creature, even a flea. Take the fallen fleas back and put them in your hair so that they will not die." "But they irritate me—I cannot bear them." "It is a test of your endurance," he said. "Don't think of the body at all." I accepted his command.

And so we lived, walking from village to village, staying sometimes one night, sometimes two or three. My feet were sore and blistered and full of splinters. The desert produces a thorn, sharp and strong as a needle, which I could carry to take out these splinters. The thorn was removed by a thorn.

The guru gave me daily teachings in the Jain scriptures. I was being trained to answer questions. People would come to discuss and debate with the guru, and I would listen. There was criticism of the practice of making young boys and girls into monks and nuns. The guru would present me as an example of a young monk who was totally committed to the spiritual life and understood it. When we went for morning walks, he would sit with me near a tree and say, "Start speaking now. Imagine you have two thousand people in front of you, and you have to convince them of your belief."

A FEW MONTHS AFTER I entered the monkhood, Monk Kundan came to the guru. He was in his midseventies, toothless with a pale and wrinkled face. After a few minutes' silence he said, "I am growing old. My body doesn't work anymore. I am unable to practice all the obligations and duties of a monk's life. I beg you to allow me to die." The guru said, "I understand your great desire. If a monk lives, he leads a good life; if he dies, he embraces a better life." "I wish to undertake the practice of *santhara,* to fast unto death." "The fast unto death is a path of pain and suffering." "I am ready for pain and suffering." "If that is your wish," said the guru. "This evening I will announce your decision to the disciples."

At sunset all the monks and lay disciples gathered to receive the guru's blessing. The guru asked Kundan to stand. There was a smile of happiness and the courage of conviction on Kundan's face. The guru spoke loudly. "Death is not something to be afraid of. It is the soul changing its garments. The soul leaves this body and takes a new one. But through santhara the monk prepares himself for *moksha* [ultimate salvation]. I am very glad to see Monk Kundan embracing death, and I bless him."

During his fast I went to Kundan and sat beside him. "The guru said that you will go to the land of angels." "It is true," said Kundan calmly. "No one has returned from there to tell us whether it exists or not." "Why do you have doubts, my young monk?" "Hundreds of monks have died and gone to heaven, but not one of them has returned. I want you to come and tell me whether heaven exists." "The angels of heaven live a very superior life. Heaven is very far from here, and this world is full of dirt, smells, and ugliness. Angels cannot bear the atmosphere of this planet—they cannot stand the filthy air of this earth." "Aren't angels powerful enough to break through the barriers and come for a few moments to tell us or even send us a message from heaven?" Kundan said, "I understand your desire, and I promise you that if I can I'll come to you." Kundan asked me to sing a song which he had taught me: "O Lord Mahavir, bless me with death at the moment when I am filled with the thought of you and when I have no worldly desires, no attachment to my body, and no fear of death."

He wanted me to sing this song again and again, which I did. He said, "Our guru is very kind. He kept me always with him. Only once did he send me away, and that was last year when I came to spend the monsoon months in the town of your birth. There I found you, a diamond in the sand. So I told our guru, and when you became a monk, I felt my last mission had been accomplished."

After twenty-three days of complete fast, Kundan died. The Jain community was happy to hear this news. I was sad. The monks said he had conquered the fear of death. I went to the room where his body had been placed. I looked at his face. I felt he had gone somewhere and might come back—in the night, in a dream, or could there be some signal that I might not recognize?

Dressed in yellow silk robes, Kundan was seated on a throne decorated with gold and red. He was carried on the shoulders of the lay disciples to the cremation ground, and on the way followers threw money for the poor. Then his body was burnt with dried coconuts, sandalwood, and butter.

MY HAIR WAS GROWING. Unwashed and uncombed, it stood on my head like a bush. Soon after sunrise on the appointed day, I prepared myself for the celebration of suffering. I went to the guru, and he told me that his own brother, who was very gentle, would pluck my hair. He told me a story: "Long ago, a young monk like you stood still in meditation in a cremation ground in the wilderness. While he was there his worldly father-in-law saw him and in anger wished to take revenge for the desertion of his daughter. So he took wet earth and made a crown on the monk's head, and within it he placed the burning embers from a fire. But the young monk did not move. He died standing and achieved moksha. In comparison to this," said the guru, "what you will suffer when your hair is pulled out is little, and I am confident that you will endure it bravely."

I bowed my head on the guru's feet, and he laid his hand on me. I went to his brother, who was waiting with a drink of ground almonds mixed with honey and milk. I drank it, then sat on the floor with my head between his knees. He gripped my head tightly and held my neck with his left hand, then with his right hand he took hold of some hair and tugged it out with a quick sweeping movement until every hair was removed from my head. Fellow monks stood near me and sang inspirational songs. My head was scarred and bleeding. My hair and its fleas were wrapped around my legs and tied and knotted tight so that the fleas could have their food from my body. They remained there until the fleas were dead.

One evening after the burning heat of the day, a few drops of rain had fallen, and people gathered in the village square to welcome the monsoon. We were on the veranda of a mud hut in meditation. I heard the sounds of drums and songs and, still sitting in my lotus position, I could see dancers passing in the distance. I tried to return to meditation but without success. Later a monk spoke of the dancers. The guru looked up with a blank face, and I realized that he had heard and seen nothing. His meditation had not been broken. I went to the guru as he was preparing to go to sleep and asked him what I should do to experience true meditation. He put his hand on my head. I felt a sense of relief in his touch. "Do you know why you are a monk?" the guru asked me. "Not clearly," I replied. "The monk's life is a way to achieve moksha— total liberation," he said. "My desire to achieve moksha is growing, but I am not sure of the path." The guru replied, "Do not doubt. As long as you are caught up in doubting, thinking, and questioning, you will not be able to experience the spiritual life. Submit your thoughts, your sorrows, your unhappiness to me. I am the ship to cross this wild sea of samsara. Pronounce the mantra of Surrender a thousand times a day; lose yourself in the deep sound of it. Fast on alternate days. This will give you better concentration. Only renouncing house, property, parents, and possessions is not enough. You must also renounce your own will."

ONE DAY AFTER the guru had given his morning sermon, he called me and said, "It is the holy duty of a monk to go and beg for food. We eat food not to build the body nor to satisfy the palate but to enable the body to practice *dharma* [the fulfillment of right action]. Today I send you to beg. Do not knock at the door of a house when the door is closed. Go to a house where the doors are open. Take only from people who are giving happily. The food should not be specially prepared for you, and you should not announce your going beforehand. You will meet many people who will refuse to give food, but do not take offense. Bless those who give and those who do not give alike. By begging you will learn humility. If a person offers you three chappatis, take one; if you are offered one, take a quarter. No one should be able to say that he has gone without because you have taken. Ask people to share their food with you, and only to give what they are able to be without, and not to cook more after you have gone. Fill your bowl from many places, but beg only once a day."

After a silence the guru went on, "Begging should not be easy. Often it may be necessary to make conditions which unless fulfilled prevent us from accepting the food. This enables us to practice endurance. Our Lord Mahavir, the founder of our religion two thousand five hundred years ago, made a vow that he would only accept food from a princess. This princess should have been sold and chained by the foot so that one foot was outside the house and one foot inside. There should be tears in her eyes, and she should offer soaked beans in a bamboo plate. For many days Mahavir fasted, going from house to house searching for someone who could fulfill his conditions. Six weeks had passed when at last he came to a rich man's house and, sitting in the doorway, he saw a woman whom he recognized as the daughter of a defeated king. She had been bought by this rich man, who had been called away on business and left her chained. When she saw Mahavir coming, she forgot her sorrows and smilingly said, 'O Lord Mahavir, in my pain and misfortune you have found me. Teach me the way to liberation. I have nothing but soaked beans to offer you. Accept them and give me your blessing.' All the conditions of his vow were fulfilled except that the princess was smiling, so Lord Mahavir turned away. Then the princess wept—'Everyone has deserted me, and even you refuse my offering. To whom can I look in this world?' Mahavir turned his head, and seeing tears in her eyes, he put both hands together and received the food. 'Now you must go and fulfill your dharma. Just as the honeybee goes from flower to flower and harms none, so you should go from house to house taking little.' "

The guru gave me a square of cloth with the four corners tied together. In it there were three bowls—one for liquids such as milk, one for vegetables, one for dry foods like nuts, rice, chappatis, or sweets. Then he told me and the other monks to which area we should go so that not more than one monk went to any one house.

I went to a house. There was a large family, and on my arrival all the members of the family gathered together. I checked that the food was not touching fire, that there was no unboiled water or raw vegetables, and that the people giving me the food were not wearing flowers or standing on grass or other plants. I made sure that the food had not been prepared for me.

One young man said, "You are strong and healthy. Why don't you monks work and produce food?" I didn't answer. The women told me not to listen. They were happy to share their food with me. They offered me cream, almonds, and milk sweets, and I took a little. I went to ten houses, and I brought sufficient food for several monks. First I offered it to the guru, and he took some, which made me happy, and the rest I shared with the other monks, and the other monks shared with me.

ONE COLD MORNING a monk complained to the guru that he had gone to bring water from a house. "I saw a begging bowl in front of a room. I couldn't understand how a begging bowl could be there, so I waited outside. After a few minutes this monk appeared, and a woman followed him. Therefore I believe that he has broken his vow of chastity."

The accused monk confessed, "I went for food to the home of a disciple. The husband of the woman was not there. She was beautiful. When I saw her smiling face, I forgot myself, and I forgot that I should leave her immediately after receiving food. I started talking, and during the talk I kissed her and asked her whether she would make love with

me. She said, 'How can I say no to a monk?' We started to have inter-
course, but I remembered my vow and stopped before ejaculation.''

The guru declared, "If you had discharged yourself, you would have
destroyed your whole monkhood and you would have had to become
a monk all over again. But I believe you, and therefore only six months
of your monkhood are destroyed, and all those who became monks
during that period will take precedence over you." The guru asked us
not to speak of this to anyone and said, "King Bhartrihari realized long
ago that the love of woman is part of the world of illusion." "Please,
guru, tell us how he came to this realization." "Listen, my monks. In
the kingdom of King Bhartrihari, there was a great yogi who practiced
self-mortification and meditation for many years. God Vishnu, being
happy to observe such a great act of purification, came and said, 'You
have purified your soul, and as a reward, take this fruit of immortality.'
For many days the yogi kept the fruit, not knowing how he could best
use it. Then he thought, 'What is the good of my body becoming immortal? I can do no good to anyone. But we have a king who is just
and kind, who follows the dharma and serves his people; if he lives
forever all the people will live in peace and harmony. Who knows who
will be king after Bhartrihari? And whether he will be as just and good.'

"So the yogi came to the king and said, 'O King, I give you this fruit
of immortality. By Vishnu's grace, death will not touch you ever. Take
it and eat it so that all living creatures may prosper under your eternal
rule.'

"The king kept the fruit. He said to himself, 'How could I bear to
live forever without my beloved queen? She is beautiful and devoted.
She is mother to all. She has no enemies. Let my love, Queen Pingla,
be immortal.'

"The queen received the fruit and thanked the king but did not eat
it at once. She had no desire to be immortal. She longed for the love
of the charioteer, who was strong and fresh. The queen spoke to the
charioteer in a soft voice. 'You are young, and there is no match for
your body. Eat this fruit and let your youth and beauty last forever.'

"The charioteer smiled and accepted the gift. He gave the fruit to a
beautiful courtesan with whom he was in love, thinking, 'If such a beautiful woman lives, that will be the greatest treasure for this kingdom—
beauty should never die.'

"The courtesan came to the king and said, 'I have got possession of this fruit of immortality, but I am a woman who lives by selling my body. What is the good of my living forever? But you, O King, are the greatest man on this earth, and if you live you will serve people, but if I live I will corrupt them. Take it and eat it.'

"Deeply shocked, the king took the fruit. His eyes were opened. His illusions were shattered. He realized that all that which he had called 'love' was merely a mirage. He said nothing, spoke to no one, stood up, left the throne, left the palace, renounced the kingdom, and did not look for one moment back to his beautiful women and the world of pleasures. He went to the forest, searched for the yogi, and when he found him, he surrendered himself at his feet. He became a wanderer, a *sadhu,* stopping at people's homes and begging his food.

"Once as he was passing his former palace he sang, 'O Mother Pingla, there is a yogi standing at your door, would you give him a piece of bread?' The queen was overjoyed to hear his voice and said, 'O my King, O my husband, remove those robes of a beggar monk and come back. Once again be my king, be my husband, and be my lover.' Bhartrihari replied, 'O Mother Pingla, truly there is no husband and no wife. In reality there is no mother, no father. We were born alone, and we shall die alone.'

"Never forget the last words of Bhartrihari," the guru concluded. " 'For whom I longed, she longed not for me, and whom she loved, he loved not her, and whom he desired, she desired someone else. Shame on me, shame on you, shame on him, shame on her. Shame on sexual desires.' "

One night not long after, a monk came and sat by me. He began talking about a beautiful woman and said that he went to the guru's morning sermon just to see this woman. "We're not supposed to look at women," I said. "There's nothing wrong in looking at women—I am not *doing* anything," he replied. I argued, "Our guru said that looking at women arouses passion and from passion comes desire, and desire leads to destruction of monkhood. Therefore, it is better not to see a beautiful woman."

Then the monk touched my face and caressed my back and took me in his arms. He rubbed his naked body against me. He took off my clothes. I didn't resist or say a word. I had an erection, but he didn't touch my penis. He just went on holding me in his arms, rubbing his body against me. There was tension. It was like playing with fire. He acted in a guilty way, afraid of breaking his purity but unable to control himself fully. I was angry at his interference with my celibacy and ashamed that I just let him have his way without resisting.

FIVE YEARS PASSED, learning scriptures and practicing rituals. I memorized ten thousand verses in Sanskrit and Prakrit (the language of the Jain scriptures). The whole Sanskrit dictionary was in my head. But was I any closer to *moksha* (salvation of the soul)? The monks were busy debating whether we should continue to follow the hard ascetic path laid down by the founders of the order, or adapt to modern ways and go to the cities and meet politicians, create centers, and publish books. The guru himself longed for modernization. So we walked hundreds of miles to spend the monsoon months in Jaipur, the capital of Rajasthan, to spread the Jain teachings.

When we arrived in Jaipur I fell ill. I was shivering as though I was in a sea of ice, but at the same time my temperature went up to 104 degrees, and my body was burning. In spite of all the monks' blankets over me, I was still cold. I had malaria. The guru came to my room and pronounced long mantras for my protection. But I didn't get any better. I became weak and frightened. I was convinced that I was going to die because of bad karma—either sexual indulgence with the monk or some other error. I was being punished. I was not allowed to be treated by a doctor, but monks went out and begged quinine, which I took with hot milk.

After I recovered I became friendly with one of our lay disciples, Keval, who was our guide and stayed with us all the time. It was the first time I had ever been to a big city. Keval felt it his duty to protect us by carrying a stick which contained a sword. My guru never objected, but one day I asked him about it. The guru said, "We don't carry the sword, and Keval isn't a monk. He lives in a world of compromise." Later I asked Keval himself. "You shouldn't concern yourself with the sword—it's my business," he answered. "But you stay with us all the time," I said. "This is a big city, and there are all sorts of people— anything might happen. Do you think I should stand by and let something happen to you or to the guru?" "But we believe in nonviolence," I said. "You couldn't live nonviolently unless we were here to protect you." I was confused and asked what he meant. "You don't produce any food because there is violence in producing and cooking it, but if we don't produce or cook food, can you live in this world? If monks are to live a life without committing violence or without accepting money, there must be some people to support them."

One day Keval walked with us to the fountain of Galta in the mountains. I had been born and brought up in a desert area, so when I went to Galta I sat down near the fountain and looked at it for hours. The flow of water was coming from the mouth of a stone statue of a cow. Keval had brought some cannabis leaves with him and prepared the drink *bhang* (cannabis and milk), which he then drank. The high peaks of mountains were touching the clouds, and hundreds of red-faced monkeys were playing around. I had never seen so many monkeys. "Monkeys have a special place in our life," said Keval. "They are our forefathers, and moreover the monkey-faced god, Hanuman, was the greatest devotee of Rama. Therefore, we worship monkeys." I laughed. "You seem devoted to us monks, Keval—why do you take bhang?" "It gives me an opportunity to forget about the world and be myself." "Drugs are forbidden by our religion," I commented. "Yes, but from personal experience, I know that when I am high with bhang I am extremely happy."

We came back quite late, and I told the guru about bhang, the monkeys, and the abundance of beauty at Galta. The guru said, "This is all illusion. We monks neither admire pleasing objects nor despise the unpleasant. A monk shouldn't indulge. We are like the lotus. Although its roots are in muddy water, the flower is always above the water. We are in the world, but we are above the world."

AFTER JAIPUR we set out for Delhi. As we were walking there from the north, Vinoba Bhave was walking from the south. Vinoba had worked closely with Gandhi in the independence movement. After the Telangana riot of landless against landlords, in which hundreds of people had been killed, Vinoba had solved the immediate problem by persuading the landlords to redistribute part of their land to the landless. He had begun by walking from village to village, saying he would not wait for the government in Delhi to bring changes; he would walk to every village in India for the abolition of private ownership of land. Within a very short time, Vinoba had collected fifty thousand acres for distribution among the poor and had been joined in his campaign by hundreds of young people—doctors, lawyers, teachers, and students.

Overnight Vinoba became a name on everyone's lips. Here was someone with a message of revolution in landownership, and people were voluntarily giving him their possessions and property. Nehru, then prime minister of India, invited Vinoba to Delhi, offering to fly him there in a private plane, but Vinoba replied, "I will come in my own time and on foot as always." So he walked to Delhi and stayed not in a hotel or official residence but in a bamboo hut near the place where Gandhi's body had been cremated, by the side of the river Jumna.

Here my guru and Vinoba met. They, the two saints, were sitting on the ground on blankets, facing each other. A hundred monks and lay disciples were gathered around them. I was sitting by my guru. I looked closely at Vinoba. He had a long white beard and no teeth; his face was scholarly and wise, his eyes half closed and peaceful. I saw this man wearing fewer clothes than I, but unlike me not claiming to be superior in any way—a man without a label. My guru asked me to stand up and briefly explain the fundamentals of the Jain religion in Sanskrit. I recited a passage from scripture, then spoke in Sanskrit. As I was talking, Vinoba looked at me and I at him. He smiled. I was touched.

DURING THE EIGHT years I had been a monk, I was always with my guru. He treated me as his son, and I treated him as my father. People thought I was being groomed as his successor. But I was beginning to feel overpowered by him. His answers no longer satisfied me. Ever since his decision to modernize the order, I felt he was trying to travel in two boats at the same time—denouncing the world and also seeking its recognition.

Usually monks traveled in groups of three and nuns in groups of five. I wanted to go in a small group with Monk Mohan, with whom I had studied and whom I knew I could trust. Both of us went to the guru to ask his permission. "We have come to ask you to bless us and permit us to travel independently. Please assign us someplace where we can spend the next monsoon months." "My young monks, time is not yet ripe for you to go by yourselves. You should stay with me and learn more." I said, "I have spent many years sitting at your feet, and now I want to spread the knowledge you have given me." "I give you twenty-four hours to think. Think and rethink," he said.

Next day we went back to the guru, saying, "We have thought a lot and still wish to go independently of you." "You have to travel through villages where there are no disciples living, and where there'll be hostility and opposition." The guru guided us in the words of the Buddha. "If people come and abuse you, think that they are only abusing you, not hitting you; if they hit you, think that they are only hitting you and not wounding you; if they wound you, think that they are not killing you; and if they kill you, think that they have liberated you from this body. If you are able to follow this path, then I give you my blessing to go by yourselves and spread the religion of self-denial."

After giving his blessing, the guru asked a third monk, Chandra, to join us on our journey, and he sent us to Ratangarh. The day of leaving was full of sadness. Some monks came to the outskirts of the town to see us off, then stood and waved their hands.

We traveled in the mornings and preached in the evenings. We walked for six months through beautiful desert villages to Ratangarh. During the monsoon months I preached every morning, and Mohan preached in the evenings.

The disciples, men and women, gathered together three hours after sunrise, and for forty-eight minutes they would become "time-bound monks." They removed their stitched clothing and put on a length of cloth and covered their mouths like we did. They would vow that during this period they would not think of worldly affairs nor family problems, they would commit no violence, touch no money, allow no sexual desires. It was mostly to these "time-bound" monks and nuns that I would preach, and among them was the woman who had been my mother. She had come from Sri Dungargarh.

I would sit on a low table, the lay disciples around me. Their minds were one-pointed, concentrated, and ready to receive. I would begin with the mantra of Surrender. I would read a passage from one of the thirty-two books of Jain *sutras*: the words of Mahavir.

> *All that is living wishes to live*
> *Nothing wishes to die*
> *Therefore killing is dreadful*
> *And the monks, free from all bonds, refrain from killing.*

Then I would elaborate with stories, analogies, and examples. In the afternoons individual disciples would come to talk about their lives and problems or to learn scripture. In the evenings Mohan would tell Ramayana (the story of Rama) episode by episode, so that it would take the whole of the monsoon months to tell.

One day a disciple, Kishor, offered me a book by Gandhi. I told him I wasn't allowed to read any nonreligious books. Next morning as I walked through the desert to find a place for my toilet, he followed and urged me to read the book. He said, "This book is religious in a deep sense, and therefore it is not wrong to read it."

What Gandhi was saying was that religion is not religion if it does not help to solve the problems of this world, here and now. If religion takes a person away from this life and this society, then it is escapism. The search for truth is a continuous daily experience. There is absolute or ultimate truth, and the search for truth never ends. Every person's life is a kind of laboratory, and every person should make experiments with truth.

Gandhi's ideas were in contradiction with my guru's teaching that as monks we should keep our backs to society and our faces toward God. According to the guru, people like Gandhi who involved themselves in the world and in politics were "living in darkness." Gandhi's words raised doubts in me about the monk's life. For me the rituals had become monotonous. I was thirsty for the joy of spiritual experience, but I wasn't achieving it.

When I read Gandhi's ideas, it was an awakening. I talked about his ideas with Mohan: whether it was possible for us to cut off totally from the outside world. As long as we were in the body, as long as we needed clothes, food, shelter, then we had to attend to these needs. It seemed that we were escaping from a reality we could not deny, shutting our eyes and pretending the rest of the world did not exist. I asked him if he was sure that we would reach heaven or nirvana. Mohan said, "Once you are a monk, you are a monk forever. There is no way out, we have to die as monks." "But when seedlings are small and tender, a gardener keeps them in pots and raises them till they have grown stronger. Then the plants have to be planted out in open fields for them to grow fully into trees. In the same way, we are grateful to our guru that he gave us guidance and training and laid a strong foundation for our growth, but now it is time for us to stand on our own feet." Mohan said, "I agree with you. I want to free my spirit and experience the world. But it would be a great blow to our families, and if we do leave the monkhood, what can we do and where can we go? Our parents are not going to take us back."

For weeks we argued and pondered these questions, spending many sleepless nights. Mohan and I were of one mind that nirvana could not be found by rigid adherence to a particular path, and we had to take courage in our hands.

We opened our minds to Monk Chandra. He had been a monk for a couple of years, and we found that he too was disillusioned. We all knew that by leaving the monkhood we would bring sorrow and pain to the guru, but we felt we could remain monks no longer.

IN THE TOWN OF RATANGARH, there were two hundred families who were followers of our religion, and they would be bound to make it impossible for us to break from our monkhood. So we needed a way to escape secretly and quietly. There was a woman living in the town who was beautiful, and a poet. She had a special relationship with the guru. For many years she had come to see him. When they talked together, I used to guard the door. So there was a strange bond between us, and I felt that I could trust her. I suggested to Mohan that we ask her to help us. We were afraid to speak to her openly, so we sat down and wrote her a letter.

> Dear Sister,
>
> This letter may upset you, but we are confident that you will understand our predicament. Over the past few months we have been going through profound heart searching. We have gained a great deal from the practice of Jain principles, but we have grown more and more disillusioned by the way a monk's life puts boundaries on the open search for truth. We wish to find nirvana in the midst of the world, and therefore we have decided to discard our monastic robes.
>
> We are writing to seek your help. Will you be kind enough to give us clothes and some money, which will enable us to take the train from Ratangarh to Madras?
>
> Please treat this letter in strict confidence. Yours with brotherly love . . .

I gave the letter to the woman in the morning.

That night I had a dream. I was standing upright in a yoga position on one leg. A cobra came and bound itself tightly around the leg I was standing on, from ankle to knee. Because I was standing in meditation with my eyes closed, I didn't see the snake coming, nor did I even feel it wrapping itself around my leg. Only when it started tightening its grip did I become aware of it. I opened my eyes to see the snake with its body bound around my leg, its head facing me. It opened its hood, swaying its head, ready to bite. Terrified, I woke up covered in sweat.

The next afternoon the woman came. Her first reaction on reading the letter was to say, "What will the guru think?" But eventually she said, "I don't want to know whether or not you are going to leave the order. However, what you have asked me to do I will do, but without being emotionally attached to my action. Come to my house for food."

I went to her home, and she gave me a small parcel of clothes and four hundred rupees in an envelope.

That evening we did everything as usual. At sunset we had one hour's meditation, then instead of Mohan, I preached. Since this was the last day of the monsoon months, a large number of people had gathered to hear us speak. As I sat down cross-legged, I caught the eye of the woman who had given me the parcel.

I told the assembled people the following story. A rich businessman received a call from his business a long way away and left his home and his pregnant wife, thinking he would be away for a short time. However, the business was doing badly and the man was forced to stay away longer and longer. Time passed. His wife gave birth to a son who grew up without his father. The son was always asking, "Where is my father? I want to see him." When the son was nine, he insisted that he should go and see his father, so his mother arranged for some bullock carts and servants to accompany him. Meanwhile the father had decided that he must leave his business and travel home to see his first and only son. He also set out with a large entourage of servants and bullock carts. One night the father arrived in a certain village and moved into the top floor of a guesthouse. A little later, the son arrived in the village and stayed in the ground floor of the same guesthouse. In the middle of the night, the little boy had a pain in his stomach which became so bad that he couldn't sleep. He was crying. The servants of the rich businessman came down and spoke angrily with the boy's servants, saying, "This crying is disturbing the sleep of our lord. Get the boy out of this place." So the boy's servants took him from the guesthouse and made a bed for him in a bullock cart. When the businessman got up in the morning, he asked, "Who was it in the night, crying? What was the matter?" He was told that it was just a little boy with a stomach pain. The businessman asked what had happened to the boy and who he was. His servants went to find out, and the boy's servants told them, "It is very unfortunate that this little boy has died. He was traveling to meet his father, whom he had never seen."

For me, the father represented a guru who ignored the cries of his disciple and allowed his spirit to die. I said, "We are all on a journey. It is a hard and dangerous journey. We must listen to the inner cry which disturbs the sleep. This inner cry is the source of salvation. Let me warn you that no outside authority can lead you to liberation. You must not be deceived by false prophets or external appearances. Even monks in their white robes can deceive themselves by blindly following the outer manifestations of the spiritual life, and by deceiving themselves they deceive everyone . . ."

When my sermon ended people came up, praised me for my words, put their heads on my feet, and asked for my blessings. By nine o'clock everyone had left except a watchman who used to sleep at the front gate of the house. I told him we would be retiring early. The three of us went into the room and put a curtain over the doorway. It was a cold night, and the curtain would keep the cold out. Also the watchman would think we had gone to sleep. We put our wool brushes by the door. This was the usual indication that we did not want any nonmonks to enter.

That night, shortly after midnight, we began our escape. Chandra crept out first, while Mohan and I watched him from behind the curtain. Mohan went second, and when I was sure that both of them had passed safely out of the courtyard without waking the watchman, I too left the room, treading softly. My heart was beating like a hammer, but all else was quiet. We met a short distance from the house and then, as we had decided, walked separately to the station to avoid any suspicion. It was twenty minutes' walk from the house to the station. We bought three tickets for Delhi and boarded the train.

The train slowly pulled out. There was some sense of relief mingled with a fear that we might be recognized; our heads were hairless, and where we removed the strip of cloth from our mouths, there were white bands across our faces. We went to a crowded third-class compartment and slept on the luggage racks so that if there were some disciples on the train they wouldn't see us.

At Ratangarh, unknown to us, someone had got off the train in which we were now heading for Delhi. This man had come with a message from some monks in another town. After getting off the train, he went straight to see us and told the watchman that he had a very urgent message, which he must deliver at once. He couldn't wait until the morning because he had to get back very early. He stood outside the door to our room calling out to us, but as there was no answer, he eventually poked his torch through the curtain and saw that no one was in. He ran back to the watchman and told him. They searched the whole house frantically, every room, but they could not find us. Realizing that perhaps the three of us had escaped, he went back to the station and asked the ticket clerk if he had seen three young people going somewhere. The clerk told him that he had sold three tickets for Delhi. Immediately the man made a telephone call to our disciples in Delhi, saying that the three of us had escaped.

As the train drew into Delhi, to our horror we recognized on the platform, a large number of disciples, who seemed to be waiting for us, carefully spaced out so they wouldn't miss us. They were important people, some of the leading disciples of our order. As the train pulled in, we jumped out of the other side of the carriage and onto the railway track and ran as fast as we could away from the train. Only now did we think that we should have got off one stop before Delhi. At the Delhi station there was no way out except through the ticket barrier where three disciples stood waiting. They caught us; there was no way of escape. One of them was shouting, "We cannot let you go." "We don't want to go with you," we said. "We are no longer monks, you don't have any control over us." They said on no account would they let us go, and we must explain why we had tried to escape. They said, "If you won't come with us, we will report you to the police for stealing books from the order or for running away; then you will be in trouble. Be quiet and come with us." We were violently arrested by the adherents of nonviolence!

We didn't know what to do. They took us to some other monks in the city, who told us that the Jain community would never accept us back. Nobody would give us a job, nobody would give us a home, and if we didn't come back to the monkhood, then we would be in great trouble. Again we said that we didn't want to go back to being monks. The disciples said they would put us on a plane to the guru in Bombay. They wanted us to confess to the guru that we had committed a great error without proper understanding and beg him to take us back. Again we were obstinate, saying that whatever happened we would not become monks again. We said to ourselves, "Let's face it now," and we started to gain confidence.

For a week the disciples kept us in confinement, interrogating us. Why did you escape? Is the monk's life too hard for you? Is there a disagreement with the guru which has caused your departure? Or have you developed doubts about the basic tenets of our religion? They argued against all our replies. There was no more meeting of minds. They wrote to our relatives, asking them to come and persuade us to return to the monk's life. The person who came to see me was my brother-in-law. He said that he couldn't take me to his house and that he couldn't take any responsibility for me. He had come to advise me to become a monk again, otherwise nobody would give me anywhere to live. Eventually he decided to send me to my mother, who might be able to persuade me.

I left Delhi feeling greatly relieved. I saw the world—the sky, the mountains, the earth, people—with new eyes, and they all held a new meaning for me. I felt a sense of independence too. It was as if I had come out from behind a mask. No longer did anyone bow to me in the street. No longer did anyone rush up to me to touch my feet. No longer did I carry my begging bowl. I was no longer a monk. I was just a man.

CHAPTER 3

Ashram

I GOT OFF THE TRAIN at Sri Dungargarh and walked three miles through the sandhills to the town. It was nine years since I had left the village. I passed the monsoon lake where I had played as a child, riding into the water on the backs of buffalo. I passed the sacred fig trees where I used to hide to watch the young women, dressed in their beautiful saris of red, yellow, and pink, carrying clay pots filled with water on their heads. At this moment meditation and Mahavir were not on my mind. I was returning to the alleys and streets of my childhood, where I had played my childhood games. For nine years I had had no home; now I was returning to my village and my home. I saw my playmates, Kanu, Moti, and Ramu; they looked at me with bewildered eyes. They were lost for words. They could not decide whether to welcome me or reject me, whether to call me brave or a coward. I myself was in a state of uncertainty. I waved at them and passed by. I got better smiles from Ali and Akbar and Aziz, our Muslim neighbors.

Mother wept when she saw me. "My fortune is broken. You have committed a great error. By coming back to this world which you renounced, you are eating your own vomit." I said, "Don't cry." My heart ached for her—I knew what she was thinking. If she took me back, she would be breaking the law of dharma, the Jain community would ostracize her, and other monks might be encouraged to leave the monkhood. "There is no room for you here," she said. "Go back to the guru. He is the only one who can make you happy. Don't come to me. For me you are dead."

I went to my sister-in-law. She said, "Let the old woman cry. It is not very cold. I'll give you a good blanket, and you can stay outside on the veranda of the guest room in the courtyard."

I spent the days in darkness and indecision about what to do next. Whenever Mother saw me she cried. Gone was the mother I remembered, sane and strong. My leaving the monkhood made her more unhappy than even my father's death. She walked about confused and disoriented. I could hear her murmuring.

In despair I sat on a bench opposite a tea shop with a sad face. A teacher from the local school came up and talked to me. He said he hadn't seen me before, which seemed strange since he knew all the boys in the town. I told him I was born here and later had become a monk. He wanted to know more. He invited me to his home and gave me some food to eat. In the two weeks since leaving the monkhood, this was the first person to accept me with some sympathy. He said, "Why don't you go to Vinoba?" "But do you think he will accept an ex-monk?" He replied, "I don't think it matters to Vinoba. You can go to an ashram, a community of his followers." Here was a little light in my darkness.

Kishor, who lived in the neighboring town of Ladnu, and who had sown seeds of discontent in me by lending me Gandhi's autobiography, came searching for me and found me once more sitting on the bench opposite the tea shop. I could not believe my eyes—without saying a word we fell into each other's arms. "What a brave act, well done." These were Kishor's first words; no one else so far had understood my action, let alone praised it. Meeting Kishor, I began to gather strength and pull myself out of despair.

He did not rest until he had dug out the whole story of my escape. He was amazed and amused and frequently laughed at it. Talking about my future, he also thought that I should join the work of Vinoba. He gave me a wonderful piece of news: Sadhak, who had been a monk and had also escaped, was living in a Vinoba ashram in Bodh Gaya, Bihar.

Why didn't I go there? Kishor promised to write to Sadhak and advised me to go there without waiting for his reply, as Sadhak was bound to sympathize with my predicament.

That gave me hope. At home I was depressed; Mother wouldn't speak to me. I had spent all the money the woman in Ratangarh had given me. I had bought a pair of trousers and a small camera. I had also bought a sweater, and some good shoes. I asked my sister Suvati, who was living off a little money her late husband had left, to give me enough to buy a train ticket. Although she was poor, Suvati gave me twenty-five rupees.

I STOPPED IN DELHI on my way to the ashram. I went to see a man who had promised to give me food and a place to stay for the night. He was a kind man; a businessman. He said, "Why go so far to an ashram in Bihar? You can stay with me, and I will find you a job." But after five days he found it impossible to get me a job: I had no education, no degree, no languages, no mathematics, no salesmanship, no typing nor any craft. I knew nothing. No one in the Jain community would give a job to an ex-monk. "You are an outsider, a misfit," he said.

By this time I had just enough to buy a ticket to Bihar. When I asked the man if he could lend me some money, he said, "What guarantee do I have that you will be able to pay me back?" I discovered that giving a few days' hospitality was part of his dharma as a businessman, but giving actual cash was not!

I was to leave the following morning. All night I worried and worried . . . I couldn't sleep. The train, the Calcutta Mail, was due to leave at 8:00 A.M. I had to be at the station by 7:00 to find a place and buy a ticket. I got up at five, while the others were still sleeping. As I got up I noticed a coat. I went over and put my hand in the pocket and pulled out one hundred rupees. I thought—I don't need one hundred rupees, I need about fifty rupees to keep me going. So I took fifty.

My host woke up. "Are you leaving now?" he asked. I said, "Yes, I am leaving. Thanks very much for your hospitality and all your help. Good-bye." But my host had decided to come with me to the station. He came to the platform and helped me find a good place. After that he went back. There was still an hour before the train left. Meanwhile the owner of the coat had got up, found the fifty rupees missing and started searching everywhere. My host mentioned that I had got up very early and thought that I might have taken the money because I had spoken of having very little the day before. He also remembered that I had several notes in my purse after buying the ticket, which confirmed their suspicions. They both came to the station, found me, and threatened to call the police if I didn't return the money. I gave the fifty rupees back, which meant that I had to travel without money.

I arrived in Gaya early in the morning of the next day. It was too dark to go anywhere, so I slept on the platform. When I asked for directions to the ashram, I discovered it was about seven miles from Gaya in another small town—Bodh Gaya. I went to a rickshaw man and asked if he would drive me in exchange for my cap, because I didn't have any money. He agreed.

As we were traveling, the rickshaw man said, "Bodh Gaya is a holy place. Here Buddha received enlightenment. For fifteen years I have been taking pilgrims from all over the world to the temple of the Buddha. My dharma is to bring people to the Buddha." I said, "I am so grateful to you for taking me without money." "Don't worry about money or even about giving your cap. Many travelers and especially pilgrims pay me very well."

When we reached Bodh Gaya, we found the ashram. I asked the rickshaw wallah to wait a few minutes while I found out if I was in the right place. There were a few people, a few small huts, and a well for water. The man in charge was wearing white clothes and had a small beard and shaved head. I asked for Sadhak. He told me that Sadhak was working in the village of Shekhwara, six miles away. I said, "I have come from Rajasthan to see him, and also I want to work and live in the ashram. Could you let me rest for a while? Then I could walk to the village where Sadhak is." He asked me if I had any letters or references. I said, "No, but I am a friend of Sadhak." He said, "It would be better if you go to Sadhak straight away." When I asked him if I could leave my bag, again he said no. I was shy to tell him that I hadn't any money, because it might have created suspicion in his mind. I went back to the rickshaw man and told him the man I was looking for was in another village. I gave him my cap, and I said, "Now I will walk to that village. I cannot waste any more of your time and prevent you from earning some money." The rickshaw man said, "Don't worry. I will take you there, and you need not pay any money. But first get the proper name of the village and its location, so we don't get lost."

When we arrived, I wanted to give him my sweater. I said, "It will make me happy—it is not for you, it is for me." He was happy. He took the sweater and left. I stood and watched him go. The day before in the house of the rich businessman I had become a thief. But the rickshaw man, who had so little, made me feel generous.

On a low table in the sun, two women were sitting and spinning cotton, and a man with no clothes on except a small loincloth around his hips was also there. I told them that I had come to see Sadhak. The man said that Sadhak was out but would be back soon. He motioned me to sit down, and we began talking. He didn't stop his spinning. The women brought some breakfast to me. I hadn't eaten anything for twenty-six hours, so I was very hungry. They brought me bananas, milk, and porridge. After a while Sadhak came. He had left the Jain order but hadn't changed his dress—he was still wearing a white robe but without the cloth over his mouth. I was wearing Western trousers and shirt, and the village people and children gathered to stare at me because I looked like a young modern city boy.

Sadhak received me warmly and said, "I heard from Kishor that you had left the monks. I am glad that you have come. Let's go to the village well, where we can bathe and talk." After nine years of not having a bath, buckets and buckets of water being splashed over me was beautiful, washing away all the dirt from my body, and the past. We laughed and threw water over each other. We spent a long time there, with the open rice paddy fields all around.

Sadhak said, "It will be good for you to have some experience of ashram life and the philosophy behind it. I think you should live for a while at Bodh Gaya ashram." I said, "If a few minutes' encounter is anything to go by, I doubt if I can be happy there. Particularly with the old man." "Don't worry, he's not the only person there, and later you'll find that he is a very gentle person. Perhaps he didn't understand you."

The next evening we both walked to the ashram. Across the fields it was only three miles. It was prayer time, so we joined all the members gathered together sitting on blankets on the ground. They recited a passage from the second chapter of the Bhagavad Gita, then chanted the name of Rama and pronounced the eleven vows of ashram life:

nonviolence, adherence to truth, nonstealing, chastity, poverty, manual labor, right diet, fearlessness, religious tolerance, use of locally made produce, and rejection of untouchability. After the prayers, someone reported on the work that had been done that day. Then Sadhak introduced me and asked me to speak. The old man, whose name was Surendra, was impressed with my story and told me I had come to the right place. I was accepted to stay at the ashram for a trial period.

THE ASHRAM IS A COMMUNITY where people live and work in harmony. The word *ashram* means "a place where people live by their own labor." Surendra explained, "In ancient times a sage or scholar lived with his or her disciples to study the spiritual nature of the universe. Students came to learn and share the knowledge and wisdom, but everybody was required to take part in the daily activities. Whether it was gathering wood or food, or producing shoes or books, all the activities were performed by the ashram dwellers."

As the influence of a traditional way of life diminished during the Muslim and British rule, the number of ashrams diminished as well. There were a large number of ashrams in the foothills of the Himalayas and along the banks of the Ganges. A few hundred of them still continue. Mahatma Gandhi revived the ashram life in the early part of this century. He established a score of new ashrams, where his friends and followers practiced the simple way of living, combined with manual labor on the land and crafts. He combined political and social work with spiritual and religious practices; self-reliance and consumption of only homegrown and locally made produce became the key concept of the ashram way of life.

The next day and every day, activity at this ashram started at dawn. Brother Dwarko beat the gong, and Surendra could be heard singing Vedic mantras. We all gathered for the morning meditation followed by a reading from a Upanishad. After the meditation, I was asked if I would prepare breakfast. Although I had watched my mother cooking in my early childhood, I had never touched fire or a cooking pot in the nine years I had lived the life of a begging monk, but I was too shy to admit my inability to cook, and I cut my finger with a knife, burnt the food and pot, depriving the ashramites of their proper breakfast. I could see signs of discontent on some of their faces, and I felt extremely ashamed, but Dwarko said to me, "You will also prepare lunch, but this time I will help you."

Dwarko taught me how to cook. I gradually learned how to mix and make dough of whole meal wheat flour, to make *parathas* and *puris,* and I cooked rice and vegetables and curry. Dwarko also taught me how to spin. I liked the beautiful musical sound of spinning, which made meditation easier. After six months I had made enough thread to make my own shirt and *dhoti* (a long piece of material used as trousers). I got rid of all my machine-made clothes, feeling happy to have my own handspun clothes on my body.

During the morning I joined the eight other ashram members in cleaning the building and went to dig land to make a garden. For the first time in my life I experienced the weight of a pickax and spade. About four acres of land had been donated to Vinoba for the purpose of starting this ashram. He suggested that the main work of the ashram should be "to find a synthesis between the intellectual and the manual, between the head and the hands, between contemplation and action, and between science and spirituality."

In order to achieve this integrated way of life, the day was divided into two parts. Before noon was devoted to manual work—digging, planting, spinning, weaving, et cetera. All the ashram members were required to spend at least four hours doing these tasks. We were to earn our livelihood by working with our hands, thereby satisfying our physical needs. The afternoons were devoted to writing poetry, painting, music, community work, political and social action—anything could be done, according to the members' personal interests.

Dwarko said, "When you were a monk you were using your mind in meditation but never your hands to produce things. Now you must aim at integration of mind and body, hand and head, serving mother earth. Working on the land is the path to spiritual enlightenment. You should live by three new mantras; cooking, digging, and spinning."

In the ashram itself, I wasn't using money at all. Only when I had to go into the town and use a bus or a train did the ashram give me a little money. My total living expenditure could not exceed thirty rupees per month. If I needed medicine, we grew some medicinal plants and roots. The emphasis was on prevention rather than cure.

Slowly, as weeks and months passed, I discovered that ashram work was not only to dig land, cook food, and spin clothes. The ashram was a center for a large number of workers engaged in the area to bring about an equitable distribution of land. As long as land was not available to those who lived by it, as long as landless laborers were exploited by a few rich landlords and moneylenders, a cozy, self-sufficient, introverted ashram life could not be a right way of living. Therefore, most of us spent a lot of time and energy in helping the Land for the People (Bhoodan) Movement.

Dwarko wrote to Vinoba to inform him that I was now living in the ashram. Vinoba was very happy that two ex-monks had come to join the ashram. When my guru heard that Vinoba had given me sanctuary, he was angry and persuaded the chief minister of Rajasthan to write to Vinoba, saying that if he went on providing shelter to ex-monks, there would be no monks left in the order. Vinoba laughed and said, "Let all the monks come and join the ashrams. They will lead much more useful lives."

I lived in a small mud hut with a wooden couch near the window on which I did everything: sitting, reading, writing, spinning, and sleeping. Every afternoon when I looked out of the window I would see a young Tibetan lama sitting on my veranda meditating. He wore a robe of deep brown, and his head was shaven. His eyes were closed, and he sat silently; after a while, he would begin chanting Tibetan mantras. I too closed my eyes and meditated with his sound.

A few evenings a week, he would come to lead the ashram members in meditation, which would be followed by a talk on the Buddhist dharma. As Surendra was a Hindu, myself a Jain, and our lama teacher a Buddhist, we always had a lively discussion! I felt a sense of continuity with my Jain meditation, yet I felt more open to new approaches and more relaxed within myself. I warmed to the lifestyle of the lama: he always seemed to go with the flow. He acted like a counselor to the ashram. When any ashram member had emotional, psychological, or personality difficulties, the lama would spend long hours sorting them out. Coming from outside the ashram, he was like a breath of fresh air. He became a substitute for my guru without the formal ties. He personally taught me the Buddhist approach to the nature of mind and the nature of suffering and the way out of mind and suffering. Often I would accompany him to the temple and sit with him under the banyan tree where Buddha had sat.

. . .

AMBADAS WAS one of the more eccentric members of the ashram. Vinoba had assigned to him the duty of keeping the ashram and the village of Bodh Gaya clean. Every morning after breakfast he would put his enormous broom on his shoulder. Sometimes he would smile and call to me, "Hello, Satish, let's go and sweep the streets of Bodh Gaya," and I would go with him. If he found much rubbish outside a house, he would knock on the door and speak in a gentle voice. "My brothers and sisters, please don't make the street a dustbin." If he found excrement he would say, "Streets are not toilets, please can you dig a hole and put your excrement in the hole and cover it with earth so that it can return to the earth and not cause disease. Excrement left in the open air brings ill health and ill luck, but buried under the earth it brings good fortune and fertility." Often he would say, "The broom is my only friend." When we came back, we would go to the well and pull out buckets of water, and he would always scrub himself thoroughly with Lifebuoy soap. Then he would go back to his room, and for the rest of the day he would do very little.

One day he disappeared. We went out looking for him, and people from the village came to ask what had happened to him, because he had never missed a single day of work. Later we found a letter among his clothes saying, "I have decided to offer myself to the mother river and let her take me in her arms and absorb me in herself." Someone had seen him walking toward the river near the ashram, but we never discovered the body—the river flowed very fast, and he must have been swept quickly away.

I was sent for two months to the town of Gaya, to a craft school to learn spinning with the Ambar wheel, which has four spindles. I was given one hundred rupees to live on for the two months.

The town was on one side of the river and the craft school on the other. On the town side of the bridge, there was a narrow street. This street always blossomed in the evening: it was full of the sound of music, and the air was heavy with the sweet smell of perfume. Here lived the women dancers and singers of the town. The atmosphere was gay and relaxed. Men wandered through in their light evening dress, chewing betel leaves and buying jasmine for their ladies. As I walked through, I looked up at a young woman, sitting on a balcony, decorated with red and blue lights. We caught each other's eyes, and she smiled at me invitingly. Her lips were red with lipstick and betel leaves, her cheeks were rouged and her eyes darkened with *kajal*. Her hair hung loose, and she wore a red sari with a golden border. Her breasts were round and youthful.

I was with my craft teacher. I asked him if we could go to her. I was feeling a little afraid. He agreed, and both of us went upstairs to this young woman. My young craft teacher, more used to the ways of the world, said to the woman, "My friend wants to meet you." Having introduced us, he walked through the room and sat on the veranda overlooking the street. There were two rooms, a sitting room for talking and drinking and a bedroom. She came to me and put her arm on my shoulder, and stroked my hair. She kissed me. My body started shaking and shivering. I thought of being naked with her in the bedroom, lying beside her body. She pulled me toward her. I was frightened. I said, "I have been a monk and have never been with a woman, but I feel drawn to you." She said, "You are young, and it is quite natural that you should feel attracted to me. Come here." I said, "I want to talk to you, tell me about yourself."

Then we sat down on a large, low couch and reclined on a bolster, our shoulders touching. The woman said, "At the time of the Partition of India, my father, mother, and many of my family were killed. I was left alone. I couldn't find a job or anywhere to live. People suggested that since I was a Muslim I should go to Pakistan, but I didn't know anyone there, and I was too frightened to go. Then I met a man who introduced me to a woman who taught me singing, dancing, and making people happy."

I was more and more terrified. I got up to go. She asked, "Why are you going? Will you come again?" "Yes, I will." She said, "Come again, I like you. If you want, we can go to the cinema together." I couldn't answer her. I gave her ten rupees and left.

I FINISHED MY COURSE at Gaya and came back to the ashram. That evening Dwarko said, "You have been with us over a year now. It is time for you to go to the villages and work with the poor. You should go to Shekhwara, where a community of untouchables is being hard-pressed by the landlord. This is the village where Sadhak and other Gandhians have been engaged in distributing land to the landless. They need your help."

This seemed to be a new challenge and an opportunity. I made a small bundle of my belongings and walked through the fields of paddy and wheat. As I approached the village, I found a community of untouchables clustered together in small and shabby huts at one end of the village. As I walked through this cluster for the first time, I saw people the likes of whom I had never seen before. These were men, women, and children who were the victims of corrupt and misguided caste systems; in fact here there was neither caste nor system—these people were *outcastes*. I stood in stunned silence, gazing at them. Their eyes were bloodshot with weariness, their bodies and limbs taut with lack of nourishment. Upon these people lay generations of suffering—the cruelty of nature, which gave them a searing sun and no water; conditions which bred smallpox, malaria, and dysentery, and above all, exploitation. They had been flogged and whipped and robbed of their minds, these lowest of the low, the *harijans,* whom Gandhi called the "children of God." All that they produced—even their children—went to the cities. They lived without hope, and there was no one to speak for them. They were the forgotten people.

Bewildered and shocked, I arrived at the place where the three Gandhian workers, Bharat, Lakshmi, and Sushila, lived. They were expecting me. I was shown my hut, given food, and made welcome. This was to be my home for the next few months. That evening we were visited by a young harijan. He crouched in the doorway, anxious and unsure what to do. I asked him to come in and sit down. He was hesitant. "I am a poor man, not worthy to sit with you." "I am a man and you are a man," I said. "I am poor. I was born in poverty, and I will die in poverty." I replied, "Poverty is not something ordained by God. Poverty exists because you accept the exploitation of yourself. It is your right to live as a human being. What can we do for you?" "I have been given two acres of land, but I am as poor as before because I have no bullocks to plow with. I have a wife and two children to feed, so I have come to ask for help. Like the other harijans in the village, I am forced to work as a laborer on the temple land for only four pounds of rice a day. We are all hungry. What can we do?" After a lengthy conversation I suggested, "You and your fellow recipients of Bhoodan land get together tomorrow, and let us talk over these problems." He seemed pleased with this suggestion, and he came for me the next day. I went with him to the fields. The landless were all gathered there. At first they were reserved; then the complaints started to flow: "The landlord who gave us land has taken it back," someone said. "My homestead is on the temple land, and they are asking me to leave," another said. "I have six children and four adults at home, but the temple only allows one person to work from each home . . ." We talked for several hours. They explained that most of the land around Shekhwara was owned by the Hindu temple in Bodh Gaya and was managed by an unjust agent. I had not realized that the temples were among the worst landowners. This was a disagreeable surprise. I recalled that their feeling of inferiority and helplessness was so deeply rooted that they felt incapable of doing anything. I suggested that we should go immediately to talk to the agent of the temple.

As we drew near the agent's house, I could feel the harijans' fear and apprehension. They walked more and more slowly, looking at the ground. "We shall go on strike!" I shouted in an effort to revive their spirits. They shouted in response, "Rich give land—poor give labor." By the time we reached the agent's house, we had managed to create an atmosphere of some strength and confidence.

In the courtyard, sheaves of paddy were stacked high and a team of bullocks were shuffling around and around on the threshing floor. The agent was eating his lunch. I could see his back through the doorway. He was a large man. I went in and told him that we had come to talk with him about wages. He nodded curtly and continued eating, ignoring me. When he had finished his meal, he came out onto the veranda. There was a hush and an atmosphere of suspense and expectation. Before I had a chance to speak, a young harijan jumped up boldly. "The land which now belongs to the temple once belonged to the village. We are very poor, but you take away all the grain and we don't see any of it. You stand over us from seven in the morning till three in the afternoon. I think we should go on strike until you pay us more."

The crowd murmured; they were excited now. The agent shouted, "I will hire laborers from other villages to harvest the land." He glared angrily at me. "If the villagers had come to complain on their own, without you Vinoba workers, I might have conceded. But you stir up trouble. You don't know these people as I do. They are lazy, good-for-nothing bastards. If they had a day's supply of food at home, they wouldn't work. They cheat and steal. Anyway, what do you think they do with their own land? Giving them land is like throwing gold onto the garbage heap." I replied, "It is amazing the harijans have put up with these conditions for so long." The agent, ignoring my remarks, said, "You laborers are always grumbling. Go on strike if you wish to. There is no shortage of hungry men who will come on their knees, begging for work." He turned on his heel and went into his house.

Everyone was angry. We divided ourselves into groups of two or three and went to the neighboring villages to spread the news. "The harijans of Shekhwara are on strike, and no one else should work on the Shekhwara temple land."

Hungry or not, the laborers of the surrounding villages were impressed to see that the harijans of Shekhwara were standing up for their rights, and no one came to break the strike. We ourselves were amazed to see such solidarity.

The harvest went uncut, and the grain was in imminent danger of rotting. Then the agent came to talk to us and agreed to double the harijans' wages to eight pounds of rice per day. The offer was accepted, and every harijan family went out to get the harvest in. The agent was pleased.

This whole episode, which happened within the first month of my arrival, provided the basis of a trusting relationship between me and the harijans.

After the harvest comes the traditional time for celebration and weddings. I was invited to a harijan marriage. I learned that the father of the bridegroom had to take a ton of grain from the temple agent to provide food for the marriage feast. As was the custom, he had to feed all his caste folk. Since he had nothing, he had no means of paying for the grain except by bonding his son to the temple for the rest of the son's life. For the son it would be a double marriage—to his wife and to lifelong slavery to the landlord.

I argued against this practice. "You don't want to sell your son, do you? Why not have a small party that you can afford?" But the father would not budge. "If I do not have a proper feast, inviting all my family and friends, no one will respect me in the village. This is the one occasion when everyone must be invited to the party. When I was married no one was forgotten, even though as a consequence I have been bonded to the temple land ever since. My family honor is at stake." I suggested, "Let every harijan family contribute a pound of grain to make the feast." But the father replied, "How can I ask them to bring their food to my feast?" I said, "If the bonding of your son is part of the price of the marriage feast, then I cannot come to the marriage." He was sorry, but he could not act otherwise.

The land of the harijans was barren because there was no means of irrigation. We started to dig a well. The villagers gave their labor as a gift one day a week, and a Vinoba admirer in Gaya gave the bricks and cement to build it. This was typical of how things were organized by the ashram: everything was based on *dan,* or "gift": *bhoodan* (land gift); *shramdan* (gift of labor); *sampattidan* (gift of wealth); *sadhandan* (gift of tools); *budhidan* (gift of knowledge).

I went every day at sunrise. There was a minimum of ten men digging and five women carrying the earth. As we dug down into the earth, we left a spiral of earthen steps up which the women carried the basketfuls of soil on their heads. On a good day, we had thirty or forty of us laboring, and then we would stand in a line from the digging point to the place where the earth was to be deposited. We would pass the baskets of soil along the line from hand to hand. When we went deeper we erected a pulley to take the earth up. People came from other villages, students came from the college in Gaya, to give their labor.

When the first bubble of water appeared, we rejoiced and broke co-conuts for the God Shiva. "The water is the gift of the gods," the people exclaimed. We distributed pieces of coconut with a lump of raw sugar to everyone present. When the village bricklayer completed the well, another Vinoba admirer in Gaya made a gift of four pairs of bullocks with plows to be owned and worked collectively by the harijans. Soon the landscape was transformed. The harijans grew wheat in the spring and summer, rice in the monsoon rains, and vegetables, sugar, and to-bacco for their home use. Of course, seventy acres of land with one well, shared among seventy-five families, did not make them wealthy, but it made a huge improvement in their material lives and a great in-crease in their self-confidence.

WHEN I WAS DIGGING THE WELL, one of the young women who came every day was Sita, the daughter of a harijan. I would dig, putting soil into a basket, and when it was full, Sita came and stood close to me, and I would lift the basket onto her head. How could I not notice her beautiful face, her black eyes, her dark skin and firm breasts through the thin, tattered sari she wore? She walked fast up the steps out of the well to throw the earth so that she could stand beside me, waiting while I filled the next basket. We laughed and talked for those two months. Afterward, I used to see her occasionally, and I always felt attracted to her. One day I asked Wasudev, a local supporter of our work who employed Sita's father, if he thought it possible for me to marry Sita. He said, "A high-caste man like you marrying an untouchable, an outcast! Such a thing has not been heard of in this village." I said, "If I am ready for it, then it is up to me. Moreover, breaking of caste barriers is an important part of my beliefs." Wasudev said, "I doubt if Sita's father would agree to it." "Will you do me this favor? Will you be my messenger and ask him on my behalf?" I asked.

The next day Wasudev came with Sita's father, Hari. Hari looked reserved but cheerful. He wore a white turban and a silver earring in one ear, and carried a stick in his hand. He was relatively well off among his caste folk. He had a large family, so he had been given two acres of Bhoodan land. His wife worked on road construction, and one of his sons worked in Gaya, so they were an enterprising family. I gave Wasudev and Hari some sherbet. Then Hari opened his mind and said, "I am very honored to hear that you wish to marry my daughter, but, sir, please do not make me break the customs carefully preserved from our forefathers. If by some temptation we break the custom once, then nobody knows where it will end. Therefore I pray you not to entertain this idea any further." I said, "Hari, you are a wise man, but you know that the tradition of untouchability has kept you and your people down. Will you not let us make a hole in this inhuman barrier?" Hari said, "We are very grateful to you and your leader Vinoba for the concern you have shown for us. If we can have land, jobs, and houses, then the caste barrier is no problem to us. What we need is mutual respect between the castes, not the mixing of castes. My daughter in your community will be like a fish out of water. We have our own values and our own traditions. We must follow our dharma. You will find many young, attractive women within your own caste who will be very happy to marry you. And as for Sita, it is my duty to find her a suitable husband within my caste."

I heard Hari's answer with amazement. Although my heart and my body longed for Sita, I suddenly realized how little I understood the mind of the harijans. Hari did not approve of these patronizing politics. For him, many more important issues were at stake.

After this encounter with Hari, I was unsettled on many levels. It was impossible to concentrate on anything while the beautiful Sita was around the corner, so near and yet out of reach. Moreover, my presence in Shekhwara was of very limited value. The harijans did not want us to interfere in the fabric of their society. I learned a great deal by being in Shekhwara, but it was not a place for me to stay.

The followers of Vinoba were to meet together in the South, in Kerala. This was to be the annual *Sarvodaya* conference, where large numbers of people who try to follow the teachings of Mahatma Gandhi and Vinoba Bhave come together. I had been living the ashram life for about three years, and here was an opportunity to get away and to meet Vinoba himself—the absent master of the ashram.

I left the ashram on a four-day journey by train, through Calcutta and Madras. I arrived in the town of Kalari, where the conference was to be held. A whole new tent city to accommodate ten thousand people had been erected there. People were arriving from every corner of India, but Vinoba was still two days' walk away. So I took a local bus to the village where he was.

When I arrived, there was an atmosphere of a large number of people on the move. Mahadevi, who had been with Vinoba for thirty years and looked after his health, took me to him. He was sitting on a couch in a small hut, naked above the waist, wearing a simple loincloth. On his head was his distinctive green cap with earflaps tied under his chin. Many people gathered round him, and he was reading. Vinoba greeted me and said, "Tomorrow at four A.M. we start our march from this village to the next. Come and walk with me, and we can talk."

Next morning, Vinoba started out while it was still dark with someone walking in front of him with a lantern. A few minutes later he inquired where I was. Mahadevi sent someone to fetch me—I was still sleeping. Luckily, the Jeep which collected the sleeping rolls and other luggage had not left to join the group. The driver took me to Vinoba. Vinoba said, "This is the best part of the day to talk together. We have open skies, woods and mountains and fresh air. This is the time for fresh thoughts."

There were about thirty people walking. Many villagers lined the way to receive darshan from Vinoba. Women stood with decorated earthen water pitchers on their heads. Over the mouths of the pitchers were banana leaves held in placed by coconuts—a sign of welcome. Occasionally Vinoba acknowledged them by bowing his head. Vinoba said to me, "By leaving the monk's life, you may find a real monk in you. Exclusive spirituality is not spiritual. And remember—as you did not get stuck in the monk's life, don't get stuck in anything else. Keep flowing. We should learn from the river, which keeps itself pure and healthy by continuing to flow. If a river gets blocked and the flow is hindered, it stagnates, produces a stink, and the mosquitoes breed. We should be like the flowing river."

I was quite touched to hear this—he spoke exactly to my own predicament. I said to myself, "I do not need to return to Shekhwara, I should flow on."

After walking for about an hour, Vinoba sat on a hill to rest. We gathered around him. He always used this time for dialogue and discussion. He called it his "walking university." He spoke on a passage from the Upanishads, "Ishawashyopnishad is my favorite. Its first verse encapsulates the entire Hindu philosophy of nonduality. It says that everything we can imagine and also everything we cannot imagine is the home of God. In fact the creator and the creation are not separate, as the dance and the dancer are not separate. That is why we have the image of dancing Shiva. The whole universe is the dance of Shiva." I had never heard this kind of explanation of *advaita* (nondualism) before. If Vinoba teaches these kinds of ideas every day, I must stay and walk with him for some time, I thought.

After speaking on the Upanishads, he answered questions. One of the group asked Vinoba, "In Kerala we have a strong socialist movement. We are trying to get government power. You and your followers should join the socialists, then the work of land reform will be speeded up." Vinoba said, "*Gramdan* (village cooperative) is a different concept from that of socialism. We want to bring the realization of their power to the people. Then they will withdraw their support from existing governments and become their own government. If I were to enter politics directly, it would be impossible for me to walk as I do today, a free man, with nothing to hinder me from speaking the truth as I see it. I should no longer feel the inward spiritual strength which I experience now. I could no longer roar like a lion. Politics and service do not go together; authority and power are not conducive to service. My aim is to build up a new kind of politics, and in order to do so, I keep myself aloof from the old kind. This is the politics of the people, as opposed to the Politics of the State."

When we arrived in the next village, there was an atmosphere of festivity. People greeted us with drums and flutes. We passed under bamboo archways laden with leaves, fruits, and flowers. Banners proclaimed, "Long live Vinoba, long live Gandhi." In the village square Vinoba spoke. "My plea—that every son of the soil has a right to Mother Earth—is not my own. The Vedas proclaimed it. No brother should prevent his brother from serving his mother earth. Land, like air, sun, or water, is a free gift of God, and what I am looking for, on behalf of the landless, is no more than justice. Though my own stomach is very small, that of the poor is very big. Therefore I demand fifty million acres of land. If there are five sons in your family, consider me the sixth. I claim one-sixth of the total cultivable land in the country for the poor. India is a country of god-intoxicated people. I believe that India can and should evolve a new type of revolution, based purely on love."

A landlord owning three hundred acres came and offered one acre of land. Vinoba said, "If I had been asking for a donation of land to erect a temple, I would have been satisfied with your one acre, but I ask for land as a right of the poor, and so I must ask you again to give one-sixth of your land to the poor." The man then offered fifty acres, and Vinoba accepted. Other landlords got up to give similar donations.

Eventually we arrived at Kalari. At the Sarvodaya conference, Vinoba spoke to the gathered mass of his followers. "Nineteen fifty-seven must be made the year of Total Revolution. The land must be distributed among the people. There is a feeling in the air that some change is imminent. This change cannot come about by mere charitable work. We must initiate an act of 'aggressive' love. I pledge that I will continue my walking pilgrimage until land redistribution is achieved, and the landless people throughout India have been given land.

"We have been trying to achieve a change of heart in the landlords by persuading them to see the problem in the villages as a land problem and to solve it by getting them to make voluntary donations of some of their land. But the land donated is only a small fraction of the land of the village; the major part of the land is still owned by a few rich landlords. The responsibility and problems of distributing the land are too vast for us. We must persuade the landlords that instead of merely donating a part of their land, they should transfer the ownership of all their land to the village community. Our new vision is to create villages with communal ownership of land, the gramdan.

"We are engaged in a People's Revolution. We must be supported by the people. It is not right for us to live off the interest of the Gandhi Memorial Fund. We must cut all ties with centralized financial aid and any bureaucratic organizational setup. We should express in our lives and work the ideas of nonviolent revolution. Let us go directly to the people and receive support from them. All the supporters of nonviolent revolution—those who made a gift of land, those who received land, and those who accepted nonviolence as a means of social change— should keep a pot in their house, a sarvodaya pot. A handful of grain should be taken by a child of the household and put into this pot once every day. The grain collected in this way will provide our livelihood. How else can we support our workers who are walking from village to village to establish village ownership of land?"

The conference proved to be a turning point for the Land Gift Movement. One reason was Vinoba's pledge that he would not stop walking until the land problem was solved. Second, the workers ceased to rely on centralized funds and made themselves dependent on support from the grass roots. Third, everybody reaffirmed a commitment to a total revolution to establish village ownership of land.

After three days of deliberations, people dispersed. I went to Mahadevi and asked her if I could walk with Vinoba for a while. She accepted me as a member of Vinoba's marching party.

As VINOBA MOVED from village to village, he inspired people, and thousands came to greet him. Then when he spoke, people took the first step toward revolution, signing papers donating land to the village. He spoke in the language of the common people, and this simplicity was one of his keys to success. It was miraculous that one man like Vinoba with his small army of volunteers could walk around the country and by his moral and spiritual authority be able to collect 4 million acres of land for distribution among the poor and thousands of villages pledged to gramdan.

While I was walking with Vinoba, I learned about Gandhi. Most of the people with Vinoba had either seen or lived with Gandhi. Vinoba's program for a new society, a communitarian society, was based on Gandhi's ideas.

I learned about nonviolence—that nonviolence is not silence, that nonviolence is not merely not hitting or hurting physically or abusing someone with words, but that it is a total relationship with the universe. This was a different concept of nonviolence from the one I had learned as a Jain monk. Then I had not learned to relate nonviolence to other people; it was much more a personal rule rather than a right way of living with others. Now I understood that any kind of exploitation is violence. This Gandhian tradition of nonviolence is referred to as walking with two legs. One leg is constructing the alternative society, the other leg is using noncooperation to resist the obstructions to change. Some of the more radical members of the gramdan movement thought that Vinoba was walking on only one leg, trying to create the alternative society without challenging the power structure that was protecting the old society. It seemed to them that Vinoba should launch a radical civil disobedience campaign to force the landlords to adopt the principle of community ownership of land and to force the government to change the laws of private ownership. Then the movement could get the momentum necessary for the Total Revolution which Vinoba was calling for. Talking about gramdan was preparing for revolution, creating consciousness, but it was not the revolution.

When I talked to Vinoba about it, he said, "Gandhi used civil disobedience successfully against the British only because the British government was not an elected government but an imposed authority. The situation is different now. We are living in a democratic setup. The people have elected the government. If we want a change in government, we should convince the voters, who, after all, are the masters. It is no good going to the government, which is a servant of the people. My task is to create revolutionary consciousness in the minds of the people." "But you should lead the people," I said. Vinoba did not believe in leadership. "If you look for a leader in me, you will be disappointed. The time for political leadership is over. Now the people should become their own leaders." His attitude was that to overcome landlordism, we should not resist the landlords but assist them to act rightly. "Revolutionary feelings cannot be developed in an atmosphere of opposition, because opposition is itself a form of violence. Opposition reduces the chances of a change of heart. Instead of creating an atmo-sphere of sympathetic understanding, it creates insecurity, through which a man is drawn to defend himself just at the point when he should be taking a new, impartial look at society."

He continued, "Take the example of a house. You want to enter this house, but it has high walls around it. You go to the wall and fight to get past it. You cannot. What happens? Your head is broken. But if you find a small door, you can get into the house and go wherever you want. But you have to find the door. Like that, when I meet a landlord, he has many faults and shortcomings, and his egotism is like a wall. But he has a little door. If you are prepared to find this door, it means you have risen above your own egotism and you can enter his heart. Don't worry about his faults, only try to find the door. I am in search of that little door in every capitalist landlord. If sometimes I can't find the door, it is my fault, my fault that I am banging my head against his shortcomings."

VINOBA HIMSELF had no ambitions. For him life was a search for knowl-edge of God. He saw the problem of India not as a political or economic problem but as a spiritual problem. He always said our *tantra* (technique) is gramdan and our mantra is *Jai Jagat* (the unity of the universe). So Vinoba went on walking. "If the landlords, the capitalists, and the ex-ploiters are not converted today, they will be converted tomorrow. I will not stop until the whole nation is converted."

Vinoba's call to be like a river, and his pledge that he would continue to walk the length and breadth of India asking for communal ownership of village land, stirred people throughout the country. Khadigram ash-ram in particular took his call to heart. As a result they decided to leave a minimum number of people to keep the ashram going, and the rest of the members started an "Ashram on the March," taking Vinoba's ideas to the countryside of Bihar.

When Vinoba heard about this plan, he said to me, "Why don't you join this walking ashram? Keep flowing like a river, don't get stuck with me." So after three months of being in Vinoba's "walking university," I traveled to Khadigram to join the walking ashram.

A group of sixty people from the ashram were ready to begin their new venture. They had a bullock cart loaded with literature, clothes and other luggage, and a microphone. On the first day a small group went to make advance publicity, followed by the main group, which arrived at the village at breakfast time. On the second day, people invited the marchers to their houses for breakfast. After eating, everyone went to join the working life of the village. In the evening an open meeting was held to encourage the villagers to unite to form gramdan. The response was good. The marchers stayed for two days more to get the whole village to sign a declaration of gramdan. A small part of the group remained for a longer period to consolidate the work while the main party moved on.

In the first few villages the reception was good. Then in one village, we were surprised to find that no one would give us a space to stay. We were told, "Keep your message to yourself, please don't come and stir up trouble." Nevertheless, we camped on the outskirts of the village. Not even the harijans would welcome us. They were afraid of their landlords. "You come today and you go tomorrow. We have to live with our masters, and we dare not annoy them," one passing young laborer told us. Such stiff resistance was unexpected. We all went hungry. Our leader, Ramamurti, accompanied by me and a few others, went to see one of the five village elders to discuss our concerns and ask for land. Ramamurti said to him, "Traditionally each caste selected one elder and the fifth was selected to represent the outcastes. The five elders were like the fingers of one hand working together in unity. In your village the fifth elder does not come from the harijan community; they are not represented. They have no land. Vinoba has sent us to seek justice for them." "I have heard much about Vinoba and about Bhoodan," said the elder. "I think that your movement will do more harm than good. By giving these alien ideas to our farm laborers, you are sowing the seeds of discontent. Harijans have no idea how to manage the land and how to plant the crops. Land will be wasted on them. It is better that we manage the land as we have always done."

As this village elder spoke, I recognized almost the same words as those of the agent of the temple land in Shekhwara. But I was truly amused to hear his elaboration of the role of the various castes. He continued, "Our society is like a human body. Brahmins are the head. They hold the knowledge and wisdom in their brains. We warriors are the arms and hands. We defend the land in times of war and manage the land in times of peace. Not you or Vinoba or anyone else can take away our rights. Merchants are the stomach, and the harijans are the legs. It is the duty of the harijans to obey our orders and work the land. I urge you not to disrupt this system."

Ramamurti came from the same caste as this village elder and found no difficulty in countering his half-baked ideas and self-serving interpretations. "The body is one," said Ramamurti. "Without healthy legs, the arms, head, and stomach are nearly useless. In this village, as indeed in most villages, the legs are weak and sick. When your legs are injured, will you not do everything possible to heal them? At the moment in our society, the caste system has broken down, the landless harijans are a world apart and disconnected from the rest of the body politic. In a healthy body all parts are equally important and command the same care and respect. If the harijans were indeed the legs of the village, we would not need to come and initiate the Bhoodan movement, but they are so feeble that the villagers are unable to stand on them and are using the crutches of false beliefs."

The dialogue went on intelligently, but the self-interest and prejudice were so firmly entrenched that hours passed and the village elder did not even offer us a glass of water. Such lack of hospitality in rural India is almost unheard of. We failed to find the door into the heart of this village and returned to our camp disenchanted. We slept under the open sky and beside the closed village. The stars and moon were shining above, but there was no light to be seen in the village.

As we marched on we found that people were warm to lukewarm at best, and hostile in many cases. I should not have been surprised. When Vinoba himself came to Bihar, he, together with his followers, was beaten in one of these villages. This area was a particularly hard nut to crack, whereas in other parts of Bihar, Bhoodan workers were receiving land in thousands of acres and gramdans were being declared.

ONE OF THE MARCHERS was Kranti, a young woman of twenty, with a round face, dark eyes, and long hair. I wanted to talk to her, but I was shy. On the march there was strict separation of men and women. When we arrived in a village, the women would go to one place and the men to another.

One day I went to Khadigram and came back bringing the mail for the marchers; one letter was for Kranti. I kept it in my pocket. But as soon as she saw me coming, she asked me if there was a letter for her, as she was expecting one from her father. I joked, "But you are a revolutionary; even your name, Kranti, means 'revolution.' You should not keep too close contact with your father!" She laughed. "Kranti or not, I have yet to find out whether you lot are revolutionaries."

It was the day of *Holi,* the spring festival of colors. People in the village were wildly throwing colored water at each other. In order to escape the color madness, we all went to a waterfall in the mountains, walking through a forest. The trees were tall, the mountains steep, and the footpath very narrow. I wanted to walk with Kranti, but she was with another girl. I was walking just in front of them, then stopped. To get past me, Kranti stepped off the path, and a large thorn got tangled in her sari. I bent down to remove the thorn, taking as long as I could about it, and the other girl went on. Kranti and I walked together, almost out of sight of the others. Kranti told me that her father's letter urged her to go home immediately: one of her relatives was very ill. She needed to leave that evening for Khadigram, and I agreed to accompany her.

When we returned from the mountains, the color carnival was still going on. We could no longer remain aloof. I made a bucketful of many colors and filled my squirter from it. I chased Kranti up and down and around, and she chased me. Every now and then I caught up with her and squirted colors on her beautiful cream and red sari and pasted her face with red powder, and she did the same to me.

In the evening we left the marchers. The bullock cart took us to the railway station. Although we were only about fifty miles away from Khadigram, there was no direct train, and we had to change twice and wait for connections. That morning of Holi I could never have imagined that by the evening I would be traveling with Kranti like this. We had some milk and toast and bananas at the railway restaurant. I asked her to tell me about her family. She said, "I have two sisters and a brother. My father is a professor at a college in a town in the foothills of the Himalayas. He grows herbs and eats natural, mostly raw, food. His passion in life is Nature Cure. When his students and friends are ill, he treats them with water, mud poultices, sunbathing, and fasting." "Are you planning to study at the college where you father is?" I asked her. She replied, "I don't want to go to college; it is a waste of time. I would like to look after young children and start a kindergarten. It is better to do something useful. I don't want to bury myself in books and exams."

In the train we were sitting close to each other. Kranti was tired, and she fell asleep. I asked her to lie down and put her head on my knees, which she did. I kept looking at her. Her face was serene and calm. We arrived at Khadigram in the early morning. The following day she left for her home, but although physically she was gone, my mind was full of her; every second I thought of her. Next day I sat down and wrote her a letter: "Dear Kranti, I hope you have arrived safely. You may be unaware that you have pierced someone's heart. Since you left I have not been able to do anything or think of anything but you. The images of the day of Holi festival keep flashing across my eyes like a film. When are you coming back? I can't bear to be without you. I have fallen in love with you. Yours, with love, Satish."

Kranti did not reply to my letter. I kept waiting for some word from her, like a child. After three weeks Kranti returned to Khadigram. I asked her, "Why didn't you answer my letter?" Kranti said, "I was not surprised to get your letter, but I didn't think that you should be encouraged. My father has been pressing me to get married. But I have no wish to marry. I don't want to marry, ever." "Why don't you want to marry?" She said, "For a woman, marriage means a life of domesticity, cooking, looking after husband, cleaning the house, caring for the children. I want to be free from all this. So if your falling in love means marriage, then forget it. My love for you is platonic. Love is like the ocean, you can't put it in a bucket of marriage."

Members of the ashram at Khadigram swapped places with people on the march from time to time. So Kranti and I were asked to stay in Khadigram so that other members could be released to go on the march.

Weeks passed. We worked together in the fields, and our friendship grew. Krishnaraj, one of the senior members of the ashram, called me to him. He said, "Satish, I want to talk to you about a serious matter. Your friendship with Kranti is causing concern in the ashram. If you and Kranti want, I will write to her father and see if it is possible to arrange a marriage between you, but it is not right in the discipline of the ashram that two young, unmarried people should be seen together so much." I said, "Kranti does not want to marry, and our relationship is platonic, a pure love untouched by physical sexuality." "I am sorry, Satish, but this must stop. This can't be allowed. If you both feel strongly for each other, I am afraid one of you will have to leave the ashram. We will not let the atmosphere of the ashram be filled with gossip and speculation. The life we have here must be disciplined."

I was taken aback by his words. I found myself in a crisis. I could not live in Khadigram and not meet Kranti. Even if I forced myself not to meet Kranti, I could not stop thinking of her. I found solace in Vinoba's dictum "Flow like a river, don't get bogged down." I decided that the best course was for me to leave Khadigram.

That evening I told Kranti what Krishnaraj had said. She was very upset. "Don't leave," she said. "Even if we do not meet and talk to each other, at least we can see each other here, but if you go, when will we ever meet again?" I said, "If I stay, we will both be miserable. If we are in the ashram, Krishnaraj has made it clear that we must accept the rules. I feel like I am back in the monastery, I cannot stay. I must move on. I have decided to go to Benares. You must come and see me there."

—∞∞∞—

CHAPTER 4

Benares

Benares was a mysterious city. The more I lived in it, the more I liked it. It was a city where nobody hurried. I lived in a house in a narrow alley where only pedestrians and cows were able to wander. In this old city I felt all around me a sense of timelessness; life seemed as it might have been a thousand years ago. In every street there were many things quietly happening. There were astrologers of great learning, teachers, musicians, and beggars, but behind the mask of a beggar might be a great *sadhu,* a spiritual seeker.

The city was full of dirt and filth, but the dirt was like compost for the growth of the spirit. Near the house where I lived was a Brahmin, a teacher of Sanskrit. I used to watch him every day through my window. He imparted his knowledge to his students in an intimate atmosphere. I watched him playing devotional ragas on his sitar and going to the Ganges every morning chanting Vedic verses. His students would come after bathing, with flowers in their hands. They worshiped a Shiva *lingam* (penis statue) together, offering flowers and burning incense. They sang aloud, Sanskrit songs and Upanishads, learned by heart.

One day I asked the Brahmin teacher how he earned his living. He looked at my face with surprise, and I felt ashamed of my question. He said, "I never thought about it. It just comes." He told me that he had been living in this street for fifty years and had never left Benares in his whole life.

From time to time I had been writing articles and reports of my work for the weekly newspaper of the Bhoodan movement, which was published from Benares. I discovered that there was a vacancy for a deputy editor, so I went to see Siddaraj Dhadda, the editor. He had liked my reports and was happy to employ me. This meant that I had an income and a place to live. The offices of the paper were on the ground floor of an old house, and the staff lived in rooms above, sharing the community kitchen. We observed some of the practices of the ashram—communal prayer early in the morning and one hour's spinning as our manual labor.

The life of a deputy editor was quite a different experience. The daily routine of a monk and an ashramite was turned on its head here. Every morning at 8:30 I had to open a large pile of mail, go through umpteen periodicals, newsletters, and magazines, read and write comments on reports, articles, and news stories coming from all over India, and discuss with Dhadda what should go into the paper. We produced a twelve-page tabloid every Friday, to be sent out to forty thousand addresses. Thank goodness the circulation department was not my responsibility! But meeting deadlines was something I had to learn.

I had an assistant who helped with editing and proofreading and who was experienced in the nitty-gritty of typefaces, type sizes, and print language. When it came to proofreading every Wednesday afternoon and evening, sometimes even late at night, we would work together. My assistant, Vasant, would hold the galleys, and I would read aloud the original manuscript to ensure that every word and every punctuation mark was correctly typeset. We had a small room at the printer's where we could work. I took great pleasure in designing the page, choosing type styles, and composing the headlines.

These were the days of metal type, the letters stacked in handmade wooden cases. Five compositors formed a great team, which worked together to produce our weekly paper.

Working with Dhadda, Vasant, the team of compositors, and the metal type was exciting and fun and proved to be one of the most enjoyable periods of my life.

. . .

KRANTI CAME TO BENARES and stayed in the community home. At dinner I asked her to come to my room afterwards. I kept waiting for her. When I heard any footsteps, I thought it was her. Hours passed, the night passed, and there was no sign of either sleep or Kranti. When we met at breakfast, I gave her a poem. At lunch she gave me a slip of paper: "If other people living in the building saw me walking to your room, it would create a misunderstanding, but I will meet you on the steps of Rajghat at eight o'clock tonight."

The afternoon became very long. I reached the appointed place almost an hour early. Kranti came exactly on time. It was a beautiful night. We hired a small boat and floated slowly to the other side of the river Ganges and sat on the shining sand under the moon. "You wanted to speak to me. Why are you so silent?" Kranti asked. "Perhaps I just wanted to be with you and say I love you," I answered. "Are you sure that you love me, because I see no connection between love and sex." "I don't think I could exclude sex from love," I said. Kranti replied, "True oneness is above physical sex." We lay all night on the sand. Kranti said, "I don't want you to suffer because of me. Why don't you get married? I would like to help you find a wife, and once you are married, all this gossip about our relationship will stop and our friendship can continue."

The next evening we met again and went for a drink of *bhang* (cannabis and milk). We walked through various bhang shops, watching the sellers preparing it. In one of the shops there were pictures of Shiva, the god of bhang. We went in. There was a pleasant smell of joss sticks. Two glasses of bhang with almonds, milk, and cream, were prepared and served. The taste was sweet, smooth, and cool. The bhang worked quickly on me. The whole shop disappeared, and the street came into it. One street came in, disappeared, then another came in. I saw a man enlarging his body to an enormous size so that the whole street was filled by him. His long hair was tied together on top of his head, his face was angry. He put on different bodies. He became my father dying. He became Monk Kundan lying dead, surrounded with flowers, incense, and peacock fans. In an instant he changed and became my guru. I was pursued by death. I started hitting my head to bring myself back to normal. Kranti called a rickshaw and helped me into it. I tried to jump out, but she held on to me. I cried out, "Let me go. There is no home, and no one is waiting for me there." She took me to the community house and lay me down on the bed. She sat by me and then brought me some lemon to drink, stroked my hair, and put a cool, wet cloth on my head. I fell asleep.

IN BENARES THERE WERE many Shiva temples. I used to go to the Nepalese temple overlooking the Ganges, where the walls were covered with erotic sculptures and carvings of gods and goddesses in various postures of union. At the center of the temple was a large Shiva lingam, erect, penetrating the *yoni* (vagina) of Parvati the goddess. Above the lingram hung a clay pot, from which drops of water fell and trickled down into the yoni.

There was a man sitting beside the lingam on a deerskin. He was old with glaring eyes, silver-white hair down to his hips, and a silver beard stained with the yellow of smoke. He was Babaji, the keeper of the temple. I placed fruit and flowers at the statue and sat beside Babaji in silence. I made the offering for many days.

One day Babaji asked me to fetch some water from the Ganges to fill up the clay pot above the lingam. The following day I found him cleaning the temple and asked if I could clean it. He put his hand gently on my head and gave me the broom.

Another day he said, "Look at all these people coming here to see the temple. They see the external forms, but they have no understanding of them." I asked what it was they did not understand. He said, "It is too late in the day. You must come earlier." "At six A.M.?" "Six o'clock is the devil's time. Four o'clock is the time of the Lord Shiva. What can you understand by coming to me? You see only this old beard, a toothless face, and a thin body! No need to come."

I got up at 3:30 the next morning and went to see Babaji. In the courtyard of the temple there was a little hut. Overshadowing it was a large old banyan tree, and underneath the tree was a blanket on which Babaji slept. I watched him do his yoga and meditation, first standing on his head, then standing upright and completely still. Babaji told me, "I practice Wam Marg (left path). I worship Shiva the three-eyed god and Shakti, his consort, the source of all energy and power." "What is the meaning of the third eye?" I asked. "The third eye is the eye of the imagination, the eye of vision, the eye with which you see meaning beyond form. Only the third eye is capable of seeing mystery, seeing the unknown, seeing in the dark." Babaji seemed as if he were in a trance. He stopped for a while and then continued. "The third eye is a symbol of all that we cannot know. It is like the third river of Allahabad, where the holy rivers of Ganga and Jamuna meet. Wise men and women have recognized the third river of Saraswati, and so the town is known by everyone as the confluence of three rivers, although with our two eyes we can see only two. The two represent negative and positive. The third represents both and beyond. Most of humanity fights over thesis or antithesis, the proposition or the opposition; with the third eye one can see and experience the whole, the totality."

I found Babaji's teachings illuminating and enlightening, but the teaching was only available at four o'clock in the morning. At six, he would sit in meditation in the temple, and the time for speech would be over.

Once he said, "Those who pursue things of matter act by day, but those who pursue things of spirit are alert at night. As man and woman unite together in love in the hours of night, the *atman* (soul) and the *paramatman* (universal soul), find union in the calm, cool, and quiet hours before dawn."

When Babaji talked about the love of man and woman, I seized the opportunity to ask him to speak about the worship of the Shiva lingam. "What is the connection between sexual union and spiritual experience?" "The way of tantra is the way of sacred sex. The spirit can blossom and flourish only when its home, the body, is totally relaxed and when you are absolutely happy. How can you be happy? Not by chasing your own happiness, but by loving someone else and by making someone else happy. This is the paradox. When you lose yourself, you find yourself. When a man and a woman are united in their bodies, they are free of all physical or mental tensions. There is no contradiction or dichotomy between sensuality, sexuality, and spirituality. This is the way of Shiva, of Rama, of Krishna, and of Vishnu. In all our temples you will find the statues of Rama in consort with Sita, Krishna in consort with Radha, and Vishnu with Lakshmi. But Shiva taught the ultimate path of *tantra,* and therefore it is not enough to see him with Parvati, we have to internalize him in sexual, physical bodily union."

Often I would go and sit by him without speaking a word. Conversation always came slowly. Often he would close his eyes and retreat into his inner world. If I asked ten questions, Babaji would answer half a question. He would say, "It is not possible for me to tell you in words.

I am seventy-seven. If you think I have achieved something, it has been by living and experiencing."

Once after I had been asking questions, he didn't reply but took a thin piece of loincloth four yards long, and chewed then swallowed it all except for a small piece, which he held in his hand. Then he slowly pulled it out, and on the cloth were stains of blood and food. It had gone down to his stomach. Another time he put a piece of string in one nostril and pulled it out through his mouth.

Babaji said, "The Serpent power in our bodies is like the cobra. When the cobra is provoked, it is one of the wildest snakes. It bites and you have no life. But it is hidden unless awakened. Through the *tantra* (technique) you can awaken the power centers of the body, the seven *chakras* (wheels) and the *kundalini* (serpent power). Sexual union is the basis of all. Orgasm without ejaculation by sucking the sperm back into the body up the spine, awakens the supreme energy of our consciousness. The center above the brain opens like a lotus. Then the body becomes the true temple of god."

One morning Babaji said, "I don't think you are ready for this path. If you want to do gramdan, do it. If you want to change the world, go away and change the world." I was frightened, I could feel his power challenging me. I sat down beside him and said, "Please teach me something more." He replied, "You need full commitment and total surrender, which I don't see in you. Either come in or go away."

We sat in silence. I put my head on his feet. He understood that I was leaving—he didn't ask me to stay.

VINOBA CAME TO BENARES on his way to Assam. He found our city very dirty. People had been using the banks of the Ganges as public toilets and then washing themselves in the river, believing Mother Ganges had the power to purify everything. At a public meeting, Vinoba urged people to build proper toilets. Then he said, "When I speak, only my beard moves, but if we all take brushes, we can move the filth away."

The next morning a group of us walked with Vinoba to the river holding brushes and wheeling dustcarts. By the time we had reached the riverbank, there were about a thousand people. The mayor of Benares was there, the leading members of the Brahmin community, the professors of Benares University—none of whom would ever think of touching a broom before now—were there carrying brooms. They were all photographed with Vinoba holding brooms; even if they did not help very much in the sweeping, they created a good impression, and the "Clean Benares" campaign got off to a good start. Together we cleaned the Dashashwamedh ghat, the holiest of the holy steps going down to the river.

Vinoba said, "We should not let this enthusiasm die down. We should organize a group of young people who will go from door to door persuading people to take their part in the 'Clean Benares' campaign." I joined a group of volunteers. Each day we walked through the city street by street. We cleaned and swept as we went. We visited homes. In the evening we held public meetings, and we were fed and looked after by the inhabitants of the streets.

While we were sweeping the streets and talking to people about the life and work of Gandhi and Vinoba, some of our listeners were not slow to point out that a new Gandhian complex of buildings, which included the offices of the paper of which I was deputy editor, was being completed on the outskirts of the city at the cost of half a million rupees. This could not be considered an example of simple living of the Gandhian kind. I agreed and wrote an article in a local newspaper, criticizing the building of such expensive offices for ourselves rather than using the donated money in the villages.

I also questioned the need to establish yet another organization, the Gandhian Institute of Studies, which was to employ university graduates at high salaries to do research and translate Gandhian ideas into the language of the social sciences, with an obsession for charts, facts, and statistics. This article bought me into direct conflict with the new institute. The deputy director said to me, "How can we trust you if you express your disagreement in public like this?" I said, "Whether I express myself in public or in private, the fact remains that we are wasting time and money in giving Gandhian philosophy an academic face. If our movement is a people's movement, it must speak the people's language, not the language of academics."

For me, this man, this institute, and this building represented that wing of the Gandhian establishment which was career-conscious, Western-suited, city-oriented, intellectual, salary-seeking—those who felt it necessary to do a public relations job on the movement to fit it to the urban, industrial twentieth century. They took the name of Gandhi but were diametrically opposed to the simplicity of Gandhi. My opposition to the institute and criticism of the smart new offices got me sacked from the Bhoodan paper, although against the wishes of the editor. In some ways it was a relief to me that I never moved into those buildings I despised.

WHILE I WAS WORKING with Siddaraj Dhadda, a friend of his was looking for a husband for his daughter Lata. Siddaraj wrote to his friend Suranaji proposing marriage between Lata and me. As was the custom, there was a lengthy exchange of letters giving life histories and photographs, and matching of horoscopes. From her photo Lata looked very attractive. Siddaraj told me, "Lata is nineteen years old, she has been to school for ten years, she is gentle and good mannered and able to cook and sew."

Dhadda and I traveled five hundred miles to Hinganghat to see Lata and her family. They had a large three-story house, the front of which was the family drapery shop. We sat in the shop on thick, large cushions on the floor. The whole family was there: the mother, the brother, the uncle and his son, and a few close friends. Lata's brother served us with tea and sherbet and a big tray of sweets and savories; pistachio and almond halva, gulab jamun, and samosas. Apart from Lata's mother, this was a male gathering. Women peeped through the curtained doorway at the back of the shop. After some time Lata came with a silver tray filled with betel leaf and nuts. She walked slowly but appeared full of energy; her eyes were cast down, her sari covering her head revealed just a little of her black hair, parted in the center. The sari was orange with a red border, and she wore a red blouse. Her bangles of silver and glass tinkled as she walked. Her face was round, her eyelashes edged her fish-shaped eyes. She offered the *pan* to me, after which she sat shyly near me. She was a fine-looking woman, but in a few minutes she was gone—there was no time for conversation.

Coming back in the train, Siddaraj said, "Marriage is a way of performing your social and communal responsibility. It is your dharma to accept the love of woman and unite with her. Love does not come by accident or chance, you don't fall in it, you cultivate it. In my view, Lata will be a good companion for you."

It was a long time before Lata's father wrote to us. Eventually the engagement ring was brought to me by Lata's brother, and I gave to him an engagement ring and saris for Lata. The date for the marriage was fixed.

About fifty friends of mine came with me to attend the marriage. Lata's family had arranged for a Brahmin to perform the ceremony. The house was decorated with young banana trees in clay pots, forming arches and pathways. Silvery stars in red, green, and blue hung from the windows. Coconuts entwined in ropes hung from the walls. Clay water pots painted in broad strokes stood on top of each other in corners. As we entered, young girls sprinkled jasmine, rose, and musk scent on the clothes of all the guests. Lata and I sat on silk cushions under a silk umbrella. The soles of her feet and the palms of her hands were intricately patterned with a red dye. Her face was powdered with glitter. Strings of jasmine flowers hung from her hair. She was wearing the traditional red sari with gold embroidery and jewelery on her body. Lata and I sat in the center of the courtyard as Agni, the goddess of fire, blazed in front of us. Agni was the sacred witness to our union. Lata's hand was placed in mine, and both our hands were bound together with a silk scarf. The Brahmin pronounced a mantra. A corner of Lata's sari was knotted to my shawl. The Brahmin pronounced another mantra. Thus tied together we walked seven times around the fire. Lata's uncle took her in his arms and carried her around me seven times. The Brahmin said, "Satish Kumar, take Lata as your companion in the living of your life. Look at her, never see enough of her, cherish her with the eyes of love. Lata, love him well forever, walk with him as his wife, and follow him like his own shadow forever. I marry you."

I put a garland of flowers around Lata's neck, and she put one around mine. Flute, *shahanai,* and drums played ceremonial music. Hundreds of people ate sweets and festive food and drank sherbets and milk shakes and rose-petal-flavored drinks; friends read poems giving us blessings.

The next morning Lata was sent to me wearing a yellow sari. Her mother was crying, and she was crying. Lata's brother accompanied us to Benares; when we arrived we were received at the station by many friends, and Lata was loaded with garlands.

In comparison with her family home, my flat was very small—no cupboards, and not much furniture. A friend of mine had decorated the flat with flowers and fruits. Lata's father had given us an eiderdown comforter, blankets, pillows, clothes, cooking pots, plates, and water jugs. In the evening, Lata's brother left, and we were alone for the first time. We unpacked, made the bed, arranged our new and shining possessions, laid the carpet, and sat eating sweets. Lata spoke very little. I longed to embrace her, but she was afraid: "Please don't come near me like this," she said. I kissed her. She said, "I am told it is very painful. I don't want it." She lay down on the mattress and covered her body and face. I lay beside her trying to think how to persuade her. It was dark. I drew back the cover slowly, opened the buttons of her blouse, and removed her sari and petticoat. I found my way inside her. She gasped, then turned aside to sleep. I lay awake, alone on my honeymoon night. It had just been a physical act without any love. It was an encounter between an unwilling wife and an impatient husband. I felt guilty and disappointed.

I had all kinds of ideas in my head about our life together. Babaji's teachings of tantra and visions of happiness with Lata were whirling around inside me. But for Lata it was a strange situation. In a conventional Indian marriage, Lata would have come and lived with my family. My mother would have looked after her, my sisters would have entertained her, my nephews and nieces would have teased her and amused her. It would have been a whole new world, and the passage into married life would have been smoothed and eased. She would have been not so much married to me as married to my whole family. I would have been the focus for only a small part of her attention. I would have met her in the evening to hear from her the events of the day, and if there were any little problems with my family, I would have been there to comfort her. But here was Lata, left all day in a two-room flat, thinking and worrying about our next encounter. For her it proved to be almost hate at first sight.

Her parents wrote saying it was their custom to take their daughter back soon after marriage so that she wouldn't feel homesick. So Lata's brother arrived to take her home. After a month I went to fetch her again. This time she was more relaxed and happy, but there was no sublime union, and the passion I was so eagerly anticipating never came into bloom.

SWAMIJI, A DISCIPLE OF VINOBA, was visiting Benares and looking for people to join his newly established ashram. I had just been sacked from my weekly paper and was looking for new work. Swamiji said, "Our new ashram is near Bangalore, situated in the Nilgiri hills with many sandalwood trees, mango groves, and beautiful lakes." It sounded enticing. Lata was also keen to move. Living in a community promised to be less lonely for her, so we jumped at the chance. We made the two-thousand-mile journey to the south and arrived in Vishwaneedam. There were a number of young women members living in the community, which made Lata's life more pleasant. They all worked together in the garden, and Lata and I learned to cook South Indian dishes. Swamiji was a celibate, yet he considered the whole community his family. All things were held in common. None of us was paid a salary, but all our needs were met from the common purse. Much of the food was grown on the community land. Bananas and papayas were in abundance. We sold some of our fruit and vegetables and also some grain. Our cows provided milk for the community.

Lata became pregnant. She told me it was the custom in her family for the daughter to return to her parents to have her first child.

———∞———

CHAPTER 5

Wanderer

ONE MORNING I was having coffee with Prabhakar Menon in a café in Bangalore. Prabhakar and I had become close friends since living in Vishwaneedam. He had with him the *Deccan Herald,* an English-language daily. He read out to me the news of Bertrand Russell's arrest at an antinuclear demonstration in London.

Russell had said, "Today a handful of people in a few countries are vested with power to preside over the destiny of humankind. It is the duty of every common man and woman to rise up and expose the intrigues of the big powers, which may lead to the destruction of humanity through nuclear war."

I said, "Here is a man of ninety committing civil disobedience and going to jail. What are we doing?"

Prabhakar had a brilliant thought. "Why don't we start a Peace March to Moscow, Paris, London, and Washington, the four nuclear capitals, and demonstrate physically our opposition to this nuclear nonsense?" It was a brainstorm, and I grasped hold of this amazing idea. "Let us do it," I shouted and thumped the table with my fist. Prabhakar said, "Do you think the two of us are enough for the job?" "It is the job that matters, not the numbers," I replied. We were carried away by our enthusiasm. We ordered more coffee. The decision had been made. I said, "Our journey will be a Peace Pilgrimage. By going to the nuclear capitals, we can attempt to exorcise them of nuclear terror."

I was reluctant to tell Lata of my scheme. As I wavered, a whole month passed. I was grappling with world problems, but the problem of leaving my pregnant wife seemed to defy all solutions and left me helpless. So I wrote her a letter, telling her of my plan to walk from Delhi to Washington, justifying it with some idealistic phrases such as "personal responsibility for the fate of the world," "not wanting to be a passive onlooker while the world is rushing headlong into a suicidal arms race," and "a voice crying in the wilderness."

I told her I would make my final decision only after she gave her wholehearted consent. The letter I received from her was a surprise. "Your undertaking is full of faith and courage. Had I not been pregnant, I myself would have liked to accompany you on your Peace Pilgrimage. Please don't make any decision before the birth of our child. As our first child, it takes precedence over us, doesn't it?"

I went to see her, and we talked about my plans. She suggested that, with her mother and brother, we should rent a house in Bangalore so that we could be together for the remainder of her pregnancy. We rented a small house in the suburbs of the city and made arrangements with the hospital. We all took care to give Lata an undisturbed pregnancy. During this time she and I had many discussions about the proposed walk, and she agreed to it fully. Her brother had found a job in Bangalore and wanted to stay. Her mother too was very happy in the city, so they both agreed to stay and look after Lata and the baby until my return. Vishwaneedam agreed to support the walk and pay me a grant, which was sent to Lata while I was away.

Swamiji said, "You are going to the world as emissaries of our Ashram."

On April 22, 1962, Lata gave birth to a baby girl in Bangalore Hospital. I was not allowed to be with her but waited outside the delivery room. An hour after the birth, I was allowed to see our infant girl. We called her Sadhana, which means "seeking." Lata's face was radiant; she had forgiven me for that harsh and unwanted act of love on our first night. With Lata's agreement, Prabhakar and I fixed the date—we would leave Bangalore on May 10 for our world journey.

My elation at now being free to go was tinged with sorrow and some reluctance to leave the newly born babe. Lata said, "Your baby will be in good care: I will look after her, and be father as well as mother to her. She will remind me of you but also keep me company in my lonely times. Don't let it be said that a woman held you back from your adventure."

Lata was there with our baby daughter on the railway platform to say good-bye. She had brought some flowers for me, but there were tears in her eyes. I was silent.

PRABHAKAR AND I WENT TO SEE VINOBA to seek his blessings. He was walking in Assam; when we arrived he greeted us with his familiar smile. He was already informed about our plans and started probing us about our journey, opening an atlas in front of him. He wanted to know which route we were taking, what preparations we had already made, and which countries we were going to visit.

Next morning we joined him in his "eternal" walk. He put his right arm on my shoulder, his left arm on Prabhakar's shoulder, and so we walked. He asked, "How much money are you taking with you?" We told him, "Some business friends have agreed to bear some of our expenses and will arrange for foreign currency to be available for us in some of the countries we journey through." Vinoba became silent. "Do we have your blessing, Vinoba?" I asked. He remained silent for some moments longer, then said quietly, "It is a long journey. You'll need some protection. I want to give you two 'weapons' to protect you." "How can nonviolent people carry weapons?" I asked. "Nonviolent people carry nonviolent weapons," Vinoba replied. "The first weapon is that you will remain vegetarian in all circumstances; the second is that you will carry no money, not a single penny." "Remaining a vegetarian I understand, but how can we live without money on such a long journey?" I asked. Vinoba said, "You were a begging monk for nine years. How did you live without money? Because your pot was empty, you could fill it. Money is an obstacle to real contact with people. If you are tired after walking, you will find a hotel to sleep in, you will find a restaurant to eat in, and you will never meet people. But if you have no money, you will be forced to speak to people and ask humbly for hospitality. Second, when you are offered hospitality you will say, 'I am sorry but I eat only vegetables.' People will ask you why. Then you can tell them about your principles of nonviolence and peace. This will open communication."

Prabhakar and I looked at each other. We were both convinced of the value of Vinoba's "weapons" and promised him that we would do as he suggested. Vinoba said, "I am very happy. Go with courage. Have faith in God and trust in people. The world will meet you with open arms, you will fulfill yourselves in this journey. I bless you. God bless you."

The sky was overcast. Again and again we had to quicken our steps to keep up with Vinoba, who was walking briskly along the zigzag path leading through the mountains. We felt as if he was teaching us how to walk. He asked again about our route. We told him that we intended to travel through the Khyber Pass, enter Afghanistan, cross over the Hindu Kush mountains, and take the direct route to Tashkent and thence to Moscow. Vinoba said, "Although that route is the most direct, it may not be the best for your purpose. In the Hindu Kush there are few passes open through the year and very few people live there. Also after Tashkent there will be long stretches of desert between villages and nowhere for you to stop for the night. Why not take the more populated route through northern Persia? The cultural links between India and Iran have been strengthened by many travelers over the centuries."

Once again he put his hands on our shoulders and silently looked at us with great love.

We left Vinoba and went by train to Delhi.

EARLIER WE HAD APPLIED for our passports in Madras. The authorities there interpreted our walk as "political" and forwarded our applications to the Foreign Affairs Ministry in Delhi. They told us we had to furnish a guarantee of twenty thousand rupees as security in the event of our needing repatriation. Who was going to bear this responsibility for us? My friend Kishor from Calcutta presented the security. But in spite of completing all the necessary formalities, we were still without our passports. In the scorching heat of summer, we made the rounds of the various departments of the Foreign Affairs Ministry. In the bewildering desert of government bureaucracy, a passport was like a mirage, always beyond our reach. Finally we decided to abandon the wild-goose chase for the passports and start our walk without them.

The clouds we had seen in Assam soon caught up with us. On June 1 they suddenly burst, letting loose torrential rains. That day we went to Gandhi's grave. As we stood there in silence, a cool breeze started blowing, awakening in us a new sense of life. It was under hanging clouds that Vinoba had given us his blessings; and now standing before the grave we were once again enveloped by rain and clouds. I seemed to hear Gandhi's soft, almost caressing voice in the falling rain. "Don't forget that the people are as generous as the clouds and their hearts can be as tender as the raindrops." Gandhi and Vinoba. Vinoba and Gandhi. Somehow their separate blessings mingled into a single sound—soothing our anxieties, filling our hearts with courage. We made the pledge: let people alone be the source of our sustenance, and let us never carry money during the course of our walk.

A newspaper published the news that two peace marchers were going on foot from Delhi to America to promote the cause of world peace, but the government had failed to provide them with passports. There were questions in Parliament as to why the government had failed to give us passports. Nehru, then prime minister, promised he would look into the matter himself, and just as we were nearing the Pakistan border on July 2, two state officials came searching for us and delivered the passports into our hands. We had walked nearly 370 miles in thirty-two days in the burning heat of June. Each day we had set off in the cool hours of dawn, usually after a breakfast of mangoes and milk. But for the first few days we suffered from bleeding blisters and aching muscles.

Thirty-five men and women came to bid us farewell at the border town of Baga. We knew no one in Pakistan, and everyone seemed anxious about what would happen to us when we entered. One woman friend came with parcels of food and urged us to carry some food with us in case we didn't get anything to eat. She thought we were going to an enemy country. After all, India and Pakistan were in a state of war. We said that taking food with us would mean that we distrusted the Pakistani people. "These parcels of food are parcels of mistrust. You are very kind, but we cannot take food with us." The woman was in tears. She hugged us and said, "You are crazy, but you are my sons. Do your best for the world . . ."

This was my first day, ever, out of India. Waving good-bye to our friends, we made our first steps into a foreign land. We went through the passport check. The huge numbers of policemen and heavily armed soldiers seemed to watch us keenly but asked us no questions. Anxiously we came out of the customs control.

A young man was waiting for us. "Are you the two Indians who are on a Pilgrimage for Peace?" We could not believe our eyes or ears. We said, "Yes, but how do you know about us?" "I read in my local newspaper that two travelers are coming with a message of peace, with no money in their pockets. I decided to meet you and take you to my house, sixteen miles from here in Lahore. I have been waiting for you for hours. Please come with me in my car and be my guests."

We said, "How kind you are. We would love to come to your house, but not in your car. Give us your address, and we should reach you by evening." The young man seemed unconvinced. He said, "You may meet someone else on the way who will persuade you to be his guest, and I might never get the chance of being your host. So please come with me now, and make an exception." We said, "We promise to come and stay with you." He thought for a moment and said, "I accept your promise on one condition. You are walking, you need to travel light, you don't need your rucksacks on your backs. Give me your rucksacks as a guarantee that you will at least come to collect your baggage." We laughed and gave him our rucksacks. A short while before, my Indian woman friend had been in tears, worried that no one would feed us in Pakistan. Now there were tears of joy in our eyes, at meeting such determined hospitality.

A few hours later another man rushed out into the road and stopped us. He said, "Your host for tonight has told me all about you. I have prepared your lunch. Please come and rest and eat lunch with me." We were moved. Hungry and thirsty, we went into the cool of his house. He had prepared rice and salad and lentil soup, but the main dish, cooked specially for us as a treat for his guests, was fish freshly caught from his pond. We were hesitant to say to him that we could not eat fish. However, when we explained that we were vegetarians, he understood.

As we entered Lahore, by the Shalamar Gardens, we saw our host approaching. He said, "It is better that I walk with you so that you don't get lost in this huge and congested city." And indeed Lahore was huge and congested. The rickshaws, the buggies, the cars, the buses, and the pedestrians filled the narrow streets. We walked through Anar Kali Bazaar, where life was in full swing. Men walked along wearing freshly starched muslin shirts (kurta) and trousers, and white, embroidered muslin caps. Hundreds of men clad in white packed the pavements. Against this white background stood out the black burkas in silk or cotton of the women. The women were covered from head to toe, with only a small area of gauze as their contact point with the outside world. The unmarried young girls were the only ones to add color to this black and white world. They wore skintight trousers and shirts in gaudy colors of red, yellow, blue, purple, and pink, all gleaming in silk and satin. A thin nylon or chiffon scarf was thrown over their hair as a token of feminine modesty on their provocatively clad, youthful bodies.

Our host guided us through this sea of humanity. He lived in an old house in a small lane. He begged us to stay for more than one night. We met his friends, walked around the city, ate our fill of Lahore delicacies. And on the third day we bade him farewell.

It took twenty-six days to walk the distance of 327 miles across Pakistan. Whether it was a rickshaw driver, vegetable seller, or farmer, whoever saw us on the road with placards on our front and rucksacks on our backs would stop for a moment to have a word with us. Everywhere people would ask to which community or religion we belonged. To all such questions we replied, "We are human beings, first and last. Our religion is our faith in humanity—and there can be no religion greater than that. If we come as Indians, we will meet Pakistanis. If we come as Hindus, we will meet Christians or Muslims. If we come as socialists, we will meet capitalists. If we come as human beings, we meet human beings everywhere."

At last we found ourselves at the frontier post, the Khyber Pass. The local authorities warned us that to walk from Delhi was all right, but to go on foot through the tribal pass wasn't safe. We assured them that we came to "observe, listen, and love." After some difficulty, the government authorities in Peshawar agreed to let us go, on the condition that we were accompanied by four armed guards. We walked the winding roads of this mysterious land alongside the small, snaking river which constantly provided us with refreshing and cool, thirst-quenching water. To the left and right of us mountains rose steeply, piercing the sky. Every now and then we met an army post guarding the frontier—the frontier through which so many invaders had come. Walking through this land of battles, we murmured our mantra of peace in the presence of our armed guards, who stayed with us for the twenty-four hours it took us to get through the pass. On our way we had frequent talks with the tribal people (Pathans) whom we met. "Much malicious propaganda is made against us," some of them told us. "Consequently, we feel ignored and isolated. We believe that if a guest comes, God comes in him. We carry arms to protect our guests, even at the cost of our own lives."

Near the Afghanistan border, suddenly a car stopped and started reversing toward us. "Do you want a lift?" the man asked. From his accent we realized he must be American. "No thank you, we are walking," we said. "Where are you walking?" the man asked. "To America." There were four men in the car, and they all burst into laughter. "Do you know where America is?" "We have seen it on the map," we replied. The man sitting beside the driver got out of the car and said, "I don't believe you fellows can make it to America on foot, but if you do, here is my card. I live in Philadelphia. If you ever reach America, call me and be my guests." We took his card and packed it away carefully. Collecting addresses was one of our most important activities; because we had no money, addresses became our greatest treasure.

After the Khyber Pass, we walked through the barren plains and high mountains of Afghanistan. When we were hungry, we walked into gardens by the road and picked huge egg-shaped melons with yellow and green stripes. The taste, texture, and flavor were such that we called them fruits of paradise. Both melons and grapes were abundant—even the donkeys were given them to eat. We feasted on almonds, pistachio nuts, and many kinds of dried fruit, which people gave us as we passed through mountain villages and nomad camps. In the evenings we went to the *kahva* (green tea) houses, where there were handwoven, earthy-colored carpets and people sitting cross-legged, relaxing with round cushions behind their backs. When we asked if we could stay the night, the response was always positive, and we would be given cup after cup of tea with fresh, home-baked bread.

IN KABUL WE STAYED with an Indian businessman. He was very happy to see two of his countrymen on a journey of adventure. He equipped us with warm clothing, soap, toothpaste, and shoes, and provided us with enough stamps to write to everybody back home and to some contacts en route. We rested and wrote our travel stories.

Kabul appeared to us as the capital of glorious donkeys. They brought fruit, vegetables, and nuts from the surrounding countryside and took back the consumer items of the city. They added their charm to the Kabul streets. A week's stay in the cool breezes of Kabul refreshed us, and we moved on.

There were three roads to Herat: the northern road built by the Russians, the southern road built by the Americans, and the traditional track, which cut through the mountainous center of the country straight to Herat. We took the last of the three—the caravan route, used by donkeys and camels, which proved to be as difficult as predicted by the locals. We had to climb peak after peak, meeting occasional camel caravans or shepherds with their flocks of sheep when we were near a village. After climbing a peak, we would sit down on some rocks completely out of breath and gain strength to climb the next one. We carried old army water bottles, but sometimes water was scarce. We saw mirages in the dry desert between the peaks. Blisters became my constant companions, and every evening Prabhakar would perform a minor operation on my feet with scissors, plaster, and hot water. One day in the mountains my feet became so swollen that the pain was unbearable. I walked ten steps, then had to sit down. We were being guided by a local horseman, and he insisted that I should sit on his horse. I said, "From Delhi to here I have walked every inch, and I don't want to give up." He laughed, saying that I shouldn't be so dogmatic since the body was the most important thing to carry out the walk.

Our average speed on mountain paths was two miles an hour. One day we left at five o'clock in the morning. We met peak after peak, and not a single village. When we started to climb a peak, we hoped and expected to see a village from the top, but when we arrived at the top of the peak, we saw another peak and no sign of any habitation. So it went on, peak after peak and hour after hour. We must have crossed at least fifteen peaks. By three or four in the afternoon, we had finished all our water. Sometimes we did see a village in the valley, but when we arrived there we discovered only ruins. By sunset we were really worried. Now we had to continue walking in the dark—and if we were to get lost in these mountains, who would ever find us? We had seen nobody all day, but we kept on walking. We were hungry, thirsty, and exhausted.

At about nine in the evening we heard a few dogs barking. Our faces lit up. "There must be a village." We followed the sound of barking. At the outskirts of a village, three or four dogs barked at us loudly. We heard a man calling off the dogs. We approached the voice. He was standing in front of a large black tent: a Pathan who had come from the town of Kandhar in the plains to the south. He was a merchant traveling by camel, trading in cloths, brass pots, salt, and green tea. Fortunately in his journeys to Pakistan he had learned Urdu, a language very similar to our own. We had very little energy left for talking, but he understood instantly our need for shelter for the night. He made us hot tea, and gave us some flat bread with cubes of white sugar and goat cheese. We slept in his tent.

Next morning the clear yellow rays of the sun woke us. Our Pathan host was up and ready for his journey. His white turban was tightly bound around his head. He wore a black waistcoat on a loose, big, long shirt, and underneath it lavishly pleated, baggy trousers gathered at the ankle above his handmade Afghan shoes with upturned points at the toes and tops of painted leather. We sat drinking tea and eating flat bread, cubes of sugar, and goat cheese. "How is your great leader Gandhi?" the Pathan asked. He was shocked to hear that Gandhi had been assassinated fourteen years before. "What a crazy world. The Prophet of Peace was killed by a bullet. The world will never understand the value of such great people. Our beloved leader Abdul Gaffar Khan is rotting in a prison of the Pakistani dictators. Gaffar Khan is our Gandhi. He is the Lord of Love."

We knew well of the Frontier Gandhi, as he is known throughout India. Like Mahatma Gandhi, he had struggled for the independence of India with complete adherence to nonviolent means—a concept almost unknown among the Pathans, who are warriors. Mahatma Gandhi had always said, "Gaffar Khan's achievement is greater than that of any of us. We are teaching nonviolence to a people who have no weapons and have a tradition of nonviolence behind them. Gaffar Khan is the Badshah—Lord of the Lords—he teaches nonviolence to a people who carry guns." Our host said, "I have traveled back and forth so many times that if it were added together it would be more than a journey around the world, but I have done it only for my bread, and you are doing it for the peace of the world." "I am surprised to see that you are an admirer of Gandhi and Gaffar Khan and still carry a gun on your shoulder," I said. "This gun on my shoulder is like my turban on my head, but I pray to Allah that there will be no need for me to use it, as Allah has enabled me to live so far without ever using it."

We came out of the tent and saw the glorious sun making the mud huts of the village shine like gold. The village was in front of us on the slope of a hill. It lay in heavenly peace. No sign of modern civilization, no cars, no radio, no road, no electricity, no telephone, no machinery whatsoever. Men and women were healthy, handsome, and strong. A young woman passed us by, going to the river. She carried a huge basket on her back, which hung from a strap around her forehead and reached from her shoulders down past her hips. In it she collected cattle dung and firewood. Her face was fair, gentle, and innocent. This woman, I thought, will never go to school, will never travel. She will blossom and wither in this valley, oblivious of political intrigues and nuclear explosions. Our Pathan host is the only connection between this village and the outside world.

WE REACHED HERAT, the last town of our Afghan journey. No house was higher than one story. The whole town appeared to be under one roof, with the dome of the mosque over it. The people were tall, brown, and handsome, wearing large white turbans and black embroidered clothes. We walked around and met many Western travelers in search of inner peace and hoping to find it through the fresh smoke of hashish, which was openly available. These were the beatniks and the first hippies, singing and playing their guitars, absorbed in the sounds. Many were on their way to India, and when they saw us they surrounded us, full of curiosity and questions about the ghats of Benares, sadhus, yogis, and meditation. Herat was at the crossroads. We, the Eastern travelers, were going to the West to shake off dogmas and sectarianism. They were going to India to break out of intellectual and technological strait-jackets, hoping to find wisdom in the simple life of the ashrams.

The story of two Americans lost in the stormy desert was going around Herat, and when the local police commissioner heard about us he approached us and tried to persuade us not to walk but to take a bus. He informed us that at that time there was a particularly bad sandstorm raging in the border area of Afghanistan and Iran. We waited a few days in Herat in the hope that the storm might subside, but when it showed no signs of doing so and we were told that it might take weeks for it to pass, we decided to leave. Since we insisted on walking, the police commissioner found a villager who knew the desert tracks to act as our guide. If we hadn't had that friendly villager with us, we would have been unable to find our way out of Afghanistan. There were only seventy-five miles from Herat to the border, but it was the most difficult part of our walk so far. For days we were completely enveloped in the whirling sandstorm. We wrapped layers of cloth around our heads, especially covering our noses and mouths, just keeping a little space through which to see—even then the sand found its way to every inch of our bodies. The sun was defeated by the sand; it was so dark that we had to walk holding the hands of our village guide. With the help of the guide, we stayed with various local farmers and village chiefs in their mud houses. We ended the journey staying in a government guesthouse on the border and next morning crossed into Iran.

WE PASSED THROUGH many small villages and usually became the guests of the dehdar—the village chief—but occasionally there were problems. In Khurmabad we went straight to the dehdar and found him in his shop. In our broken Persian, we explained to him that we needed some shelter for the night. He asked many questions. Soon a small crowd of villagers gathered around. The dehdar told us that his house was too small and there was no room for us. We said that we could sleep in the courtyard, but this wasn't acceptable. We waited there for almost half an hour, but no one in the crowd offered to give us shelter. It was the first time we had been refused hospitality. Apparently they suspected that we were spies. We asked some villagers where we could find a place to sleep for the night. Again we were refused hospitality. We walked on to seek refuge in the next village, where we were more fortunate.

The Caspian Sea lay on our right, green cotton fields and rows of pomegranate trees on our left, and ahead of us the long track which disappeared into the Demavand mountains, through which tunnel after tunnel was being bored as part of a new road to Tehran. One time we had to crawl a few hundred yards through a narrow hole only three feet high, and while we were in the hole we heard shouts of "Danger, danger." We crouched to the side with some workers. A dynamite blast shook the mountain, bringing rocks and dust down around us. We crossed the mountains, came down into the plains, and arrived in the capital of Persia, the city of Tehran.

We went straight to the offices of the *Kheyhan International,* one of the daily newspapers in English, and told them our story. Next morning there were banner headlines with our pictures and a long article. This made us celebrities. The Indian Embassy and the Indian community in particular received us with enthusiasm.

We had written to the shah requesting an audience. We were now informed through the Indian Embassy that the shah would be pleased to receive us. Naturally there were one or two formalities with which we should comply—the customs of the court. The court minister told us that we should present ourselves in black suits with matching ties. Neither of us had worn a suit in his life. The Indian ambassador was very eager that we should not miss this opportunity and offered to provide us with suits. We felt that this was against the spirit of our whole venture and we should go as we were, in our Indian shirts and trousers. We wrote to the minister expressing our sentiments. After an exchange of letters and telephone calls, apparently the shah granted us an exception, and we went to see him in our ordinary clothes.

The meeting was cordial. He recalled his own journey to Moscow by plane and warned us that we would have to cross the high, snow-covered peaks and passes of the Caucasus, where any walking would be most difficult since it would be winter when we got there. He avoided talking about the problems of peace, armaments, and military pacts, and whenever we tried to bring up the point he either blamed the big powers or cited the vulnerability of the small nations, but he showed great interest in our human endeavor of walking around the world. He wanted to give us money to help us in our journey, but when we explained that not only did we not accept transport but also we could not accept money, he laughed and said, "We are the same. I also never carry any money! The shah and the *fakir* (a begging muslim monk) meet on the same ground."

He listened carefully to our route through the rest of Iran, and afterwards we discovered that the shah had informed his people along the way, and we were given sumptuous royal hospitality.

While we were in Tehran we went to the Soviet embassy to arrange our visas. As it turned out it had been much easier for us to walk through the mountains of Afghanistan and the deserts of Iran than to get Soviet visas from these officials. The first time we went, we were told that it would be too cold to walk through Russia between January and April. The second time, the same official repeated his arguments about the cold and the snow and added that our political propaganda against nuclear weapons wasn't necessary in the Soviet Union. The third time he said we would be far more usefully employed if we went to Western Europe and America, for they were causing the nuclear arms race. The fourth time the official went with us to the Indian Embassy to ask their advice. The first secretary for the Indian Embassy said that the Indian government wasn't responsible for our beliefs in disarmament, and it was up to the Russians whether they gave us a visa or not, but the Indian Embassy in Moscow would give us, as Indian citizens, any help that might be necessary in Russia.

We returned to the Soviet embassy. The Russian official then offered us tourist visas for twenty days, provided we went only to big cities and provided that we deposited enough money to cover all our expenses in the USSR with the Intourist agency. We told him we were traveling without money and that we must walk, adding "Till now, people have been sympathetic and generous to us everywhere, and we have no reason to believe that the Soviet people will be different. The visa is for your satisfaction. If we have no visa, we will cross the border without it, and if your police arrest us and put us in prison, that will be their responsibility. At least we will be in the Soviet Union."

When we went again we saw the consul. He told us that he had phoned Moscow and talked to the Soviet Peace Committee. They had taken responsibility to be our hosts. He would treat our case as an exception. We were given four-month visas.

We happily left Tehran heading northwest toward the Soviet border. Our Tehran host, a Sikh businessman, had kindly reequipped us with warm coats, sleeping bags, and tough military boots to face the Russian winter.

ONE COLD EVENING the sky was clouded over. All around us the earth was covered by green, dewy grass. Fully wrapped in our warm clothes, we were walking all alone on a deserted road. Nobody seemed to be in a hurry to come out of his home. All was quiet except for the wind, which was blowing hard. Suddenly a Volkswagen Beetle stopped. A man got out. "Would you like a lift?" he asked, to which we replied, "No thank you, we are walking." "Where are you walking to?" "Our final destination is Washington," we replied, "but for tonight, the nearest village where we can stay." He looked aghast and said, "Where have you come from?" "From India." "And you have walked all the way?" "Yes, we have walked all the way." "Never mind," he said, "it is such a cold evening and getting dark. If you break your vow of walking for one day, nobody will know about it. I won't tell anyone, and you can stay with me in my home." "It is not a question of anyone knowing. We want to walk." His wife intervened. "The nearest town is Qazvin, fifteen miles away, and before that there is no decent place to stop." The man said to her, "I know, they are followers of Gandhi, who fasted for forty days. These Indians seem to have strong willpower." Turning to us he said, "I will give you our address. Come and stay with us tomorrow."

When, the next afternoon, we arrived at his home, we saw him on his knees on the veranda offering *Namaz* (prayers), his head bowed to the ground. We waited at one side, but when he looked up and saw us, he leaped up and seemed to completely forget his Namaz. He came to embrace us. "Don't let us disturb you in your prayers," we said. He replied, "Receiving a guest is Namaz in practice. Please come in and let me welcome you as Allah has commanded." He called his friends and family around, and we all sat down to the national dish of Persia— chilo kebab (kebabs with rice). We didn't take the kebab, but there was for us a sumptuous meal of fruit and nuts and buttered rice.

The next morning he took us to the *hamam* (the public bath) and arranged for a barber to cut our hair. He packed our rucksacks with dried fruit, nuts, and biscuits. A few hours later on the road, he gave us another surprise by appearing with his wife and two daughters with a picnic lunch for us all.

We had experienced a hundred days of such wonderful Muslim hospitality in Persia by the time we reached the border.

WE SAW THE FRONTIER GUARDS standing alert, equipped with guns and binoculars. The Iranian guards waved a signal, in response to which a Soviet military guard advanced to the border and opened the gates.

The next moment we were in a different country. It was January 1, 1963, seven months after we had set out from Delhi. The commander of the Soviet frontier guards made a sweet little speech to receive us: "Your arrival reminds me of Afnasi Nikiten, who went to India on foot a few centuries ago. Now you two travelers have come to our country with a message of peace. I hope that soon the boundaries dividing humankind will disappear and we shall be able to realize the ideal of world unity. We will no longer need armies or bombs."

A message from the central office of the Peace Council in Moscow was waiting for us: "It will be extremely difficult for you to travel on foot during the winter months. You shouldn't worry about your expenses; the Peace Council is willing to bear responsibility for you. Please come to Moscow directly by plane." But we stuck to our decision to walk.

We walked for forty days through the villages and towns of Azerbaijan, Armenia, and Georgia, through the Caucasus mountains and along the Black Sea. By radio and newspaper, people had learned of our walk—many of them had never seen a foreigner.

One day we met two young women and started talking. They read our leaflet, which we had prepared in Russian. They said, "We heard you on the radio." A few minutes later one of them said, "This is the tea factory where we work. Will you come and have a cup of tea and meet our fellow workers?" We said, "Yes, any time is teatime!" We went with them. We were served tea and a meal. Workers gathered around us, and we made a brief speech: "All over the world it is the people who bear the burden of the bomb. It is they who pay for it in rubles, and dollars, francs and pounds. Millions and millions of them, and it is they who will be killed when the bombs are used. Therefore it is the people who should raise their voices against the bomb. Peoples of the world, unite to stop the arms race. You have nothing to lose but bombs."

One of the women who had invited us into the factory stood up and rushed out of the room. Moments later she came back with four packets of tea. She said to us, "What you are saying, I fully agree with—every word. Here are four packets of tea made in our factory. I know you are walking and you want to travel light, but these packets are very important. Please carry them with you. They are not for you. Please give one to our premier in Moscow, one to the president of France, one to the prime minister of England, and one to the president of the United States of America. Tell them that if they get mad in their minds and think of pushing the button to drop nuclear bombs, they should stop for a moment and have a fresh cup of tea from these packets. That will give them a chance to remember that the simple people of the world want bread not bombs, want life not death." Everyone applauded her words. We gladly accepted the packets of peace tea and became the messengers of an Armenian mother.

A few days later we came to Idzewan. As we approached the town, hundreds of people came to greet us, bringing food, sweets, and chocolate. They took us to the town center, where we spoke to several thousand people.

Later we stayed with the head of a collective farm. On our arrival his youngest daughter brought a towel, soap, and a bowl of hot water to wash our feet. I was embarrassed. She insisted. "It is our custom to make our guests feel at home." She took off my shoes and socks and bathed my aching feet in warm water, with ceremonial delicacy.

Then her father took us out into the garden. He wanted us to inaugurate the wine season and to be the guests of honor. Prabhakar and I dug up a large barrel of wine, buried in the ground, and then filled the glasses of the thirty people who had been invited for dinner. I was asked to propose a toast for peace and to empty the glass in one gulp. It was a difficult moment. I said, "No, I don't drink." My host replied, "You don't drink! What do you do? Here wine is the only drink—water is for washing." Everyone was quiet, holding glasses ready, looking at us expectantly. After a few moments of panic and confusion, I seized the glass and emptied it down my throat. There was a roar of applause. Dinner that night lasted for six hours. Toast after toast was proposed.

One of the daughters asked me to dance. I had never danced with a woman before, but she took my hand. The whole atmosphere grew madder and madder. I sang songs of Tagore.

One of the young women who was in the party came next morning and said, "I could not sleep all night and kept thinking of your walk for peace. Can I join in your journey? I will come with you all the way to Washington." We were stunned. This Armenian in her early twenties was firmly convinced that it was right for her to leave everything behind and come with us. Friends and neighbors listening became alarmed and told us that it would be impossible for her to get a passport. We suggested that she should come with us for a few days before committing herself. She had come prepared with her rucksack.

She walked with us that day. When we stopped in the next town, her mother came to us and begged us not to take her daughter with us, as she was the only daughter and her only support. The members of the local peace committee and party officials also discouraged both her and us. So the next day she was not there.

· · ·

IN GEORGIA WE ARRIVED at Gori, the birthplace of Stalin. We were put
up in a small guesthouse and soon fell deeply asleep. In the middle of
the night we heard someone knocking at our door. Prabhakar went to
the door. "I am a taxi driver. I saw you walking with your banners. I
read your leaflets. You are good boys." He got twenty rubles out of his
pocket. "This is my day's earnings. I want to give it to you to support
your cause." "Thank you, but we are sorry, we do not carry money,
we cannot accept money. Please don't feel that we are rejecting your
help and support," we said in our primitive Russian. "Why not?" he
protested. "I too am against the bombs. It is no good Khrushchev talking
about peace and blaming the West for the arms race. If there has to be
war, let us fight a conventional war. At least in it we can show some
courage, some ingenuity, but there is no skill in dropping nuclear bombs
on sleeping people, so let me give you these rubles as a contribution of
an insignificant taxi driver." "We are delighted to hear your words, and
your words are worth more than a hundred rubles. Please don't insist
on giving us money. We have taken a vow not to handle it on our
journey." "All right then; please don't walk tomorrow. I will take you
to wherever you are going in my taxi." "Oh dear," I said to Prabhakar,
"how can we make him understand that this is also against our vow?"
The man was disappointed to know that he could be of no practical
help to us. He left, wishing us luck.

By the time we reached Sochi on February 12, the Soviet Peace
Committee in Moscow seemed worried. They flew a special messenger,
Mr. Paladin, who tried to convince us that it was impossible to cross
the high ranges of the Ural mountains in mid-February because all the
roads were blocked with snow. He argued that we should fly direct to
Moscow. We said, "If the roads are blocked, we will stay somewhere
in a village until they are cleared." But Mr. Paladin replied, "You know
nothing of the Russian winter, and you'll be stuck there for months."
"So be it," I said. "We are not in a hurry. It is already mid-February.
Let us spend two months by the Black Sea meeting and talking to people, and then we can head towards Moscow." This idea did not please
him at all. This Peace Committee official somehow felt uncomfortable
about our peace message. After four days of argument, we found ourselves in a stalemate. He explained, "The roads are blocked with snow.
The Peace Committee cannot take responsibility for you in such cli-
matic conditions, nor can the Soviet government allow you to proceed

on foot. You are in our country, and you must accept our advice." His "advice" came as an order.

Under duress and having no alternative, we agreed to fly over the mountains and land on the other side at Voronezh. But as we were crossing the mountains in the plane, an announcement was made: "Due to bad weather conditions, the plane cannot land at Voronezh and has to fly straight to Moscow." None of the other passengers seemed at all affected. We suspected that the Peace Committee representative had deliberately misled us and were in despair when we landed in Moscow. A car awaited us; we were driven to the center of the city and put up at Hotel Budapest.

Not knowing what to do, we telephoned the first secretary of the Indian Embassy and walked immediately to his house, although it was ten o'clock at night. We told him how our walk had been frustrated and asked him if he would help us to go to Voronezh by train, so that we could walk back to Moscow. But he made a helpless gesture with his hands and said, "It is Russia, you can do nothing."

Although deeply upset, we had to live with this fait accompli. To soften the blow, the Peace Committee went out of their way to organize visits to the Bolshoi, museums, and a journey to Yasnaya Polyana, the birthplace of Leo Tolstoy. No effort was spared in their attempts to reconcile us to our forcible abduction from Sochi. They organized meetings, interviews with newspapers and radio, and dialogue with politicians.

Our most important task in Moscow was to meet Mr. Khrushchev and deliver one packet of tea to him. We wrote to him for an audience. It was good to receive his reply, signed by him personally, but we were disappointed to learn that his diary was too full for him to see us. However, he arranged for us to be received by Mr. Tikhonov, the president of the Supreme Soviet in the Kremlin. I could see from the expression on his face that Mr. Tikhonov was very touched by the gesture of the Armenian woman. I said, "This peace tea has given us added courage and a new reason to keep walking. We have become the messengers of the Armenian woman and her fellow workers. Only by your unilateral action can you set an example which will force other nuclear powers to abandon the bomb." Mr. Tikhonov's reply was diplomatic and evasive: "After losing twenty million people in the last war, we cannot risk the security of our nation, but there is no greater champion of peace than our premier Mr. Khrushchev. He has personally asked me to receive you and assure you that the Soviet Union will never be the first to use nuclear weapons. I will gladly give him this symbolic packet of peace tea on your behalf."

Mr. Tikhonov very kindly gave us a guided tour of the Kremlin, which was as impressive and imposing as the Soviet empire. The czars may have been eliminated, but their pomp and paraphernalia were still being maintained. The splendor of the Kremlin was a far cry from the life of the proletariat, although when Mr. Tikhonov brought us to the flat where Lenin lived, we were impressed with its simplicity.

It soon became clear that in spite of the Peace Committee's lavish hospitality in Moscow, they had never accepted our plan to walk freely through the villages of Russia. The visas we had obtained from the Soviet Embassy in Tehran were valid until April 1963, but one day the authorities took our passports from our hotel without informing us, canceled the previous visas, and instead gave us visas due to expire on March 14.

The officials of the Peace Committee tried to persuade us that we had spent long enough in their country. They said they had arranged for us a free flight from Moscow to Warsaw so that we could make more profitable use of our time elsewhere. Next day a Peace Committee interpreter arrived with two plane tickets. We refused to accept them and made it quite clear that we had no desire to resort to any transport for our journey—except our legs. Any more discussion with the Peace Committee was pointless. We went directly to the visa officials. They told us they had received a letter from the Peace Committee that we were going to Warsaw by plane, and accordingly they had made the necessary changes in our visas. If we wanted to have our visas in their original form, we would have to get a letter from the Peace Committee to that effect; only then could they make alterations. We wrote a letter to the Peace Committee saying that we intended to set out on our march according to our original plan.

It was March 13, 1963, and darkness had fallen. We put our rucksacks on our backs and came out of our hotel. Moscow was covered by a white sheet of snow. With heavy steps we trudged along the streets, groping our way in the dim pools of light from the lampposts. The white masses of snow shimmered in the dark night. We walked out of the city area and found ourselves in the greenbelt area, which was pitch black and uninhabited. We went to the trolleybus terminus to try and sleep there, but at midnight a woman came to lock it up and asked us to leave. We suggested that she lock it from outside and leave us inside for the night, then in the morning we would go on. She couldn't understand why we didn't have anywhere to sleep. She remembered reading about us in *Pravda,* so she took us to the Hotel Ukraina, a huge skyscraper hotel, where she knew somebody. She explained the situation to him, and he gave us a room for the night.

The next morning we set out on our journey, ignoring the fact that our visas expired that day. Every time we saw a police car or a policeman, we feared arrest. But, mysteriously, nothing happened. We felt liberated, having come out of the maze of Moscow's skyscrapers, to roam once again through the Russian countryside, to be among the warm and hospitable villagers and farmers. The country surrounding Moscow had witnessed many a bloody battle. The wounds of the last war were still fresh and would start bleeding at the slightest pressure. "Both my father and brother fell in the war. Now I am completely alone," someone said. "I lost my eyes and one hand in the war—and though I go on living, my life is of no use to anyone." We often heard such sad remarks. Once we were staying in a house where only two women lived. All the male members of the family had been killed in the war. In another village an old couple had lost all their sons and were now living alone with their memories.

Another time, in a small village, we met a farmer. His eyes rested on us for some time before he decided to speak. "They say you are the messengers of peace. You are coming from India and will go to America. Is it true? Will you convey my message to the American people? Will you tell them that though they fought in the war, the actual war was never fought in their country? The very thought of war seems nightmarish to us . . ." He spoke for a long time with great passion. After he finished, he took us in his arms and kissed us.

The temperature was thirty degrees centigrade below freezing point, but we were convinced that if the Russian people could perform their daily work in winter, we could at least manage to walk. Sometimes the freezing wind blowing from Siberia made our bodies numb and every step forward a torture. We had never experienced such biting cold in our lives, nor had we ever seen such masses of snow, which enveloped the entire world around us. We would walk for ten minutes until our bodies felt like stone, as if our blood had stopped moving, then we would desperately look for someplace to stop and warm ourselves. I had icicles on my nose; my mustache and beard were frozen solid. Although we had been given fur coats and caps by the kind Russian people, no clothes could be made that would keep out the Russian cold.

ONCE A PEASANT INVITED US to spend the night at his house. His wife had gone out on some errand, so our host cooked food and made up beds for us. When his wife returned, our host whispered to her in the kitchen that we were going to stay the night with them. There was a long, heated argument between husband and wife, and the wife burst into tears. "This is a home not a guesthouse. You keep bringing strange people here. I can't bear it. If you want them to stay, then I will go. They might be spies," she said. The husband stalked out of the kitchen, saying over his shoulder, "Do what you like, I won't stop you." Before we could intervene, the wife took their baby in her arms and rushed out into the cold. We, the "messengers of peace," had caused trouble in a family. We got ready to find shelter elsewhere. "Where can you go at this hour?" the peasant said in despair. "It is pitch dark outside, and the streets are full of mud and sleet." He thought awhile, then went out. A little later he reappeared and told us a friend of his had agreed to put us up. Holding each other's hands, we stumbled through the mud along the dark lanes. The man kept apologizing to us and cursing his wife. We said, "Don't worry; we have had such marvelous hospitality from the Russian people that a little walk now to find a bed is no trouble to us."

At his friend's house everyone had gone to sleep, but the farmer there woke up his two children and made them sleep in one bed. Prabhakar and I took the other one. Next morning they made a large, warm breakfast for us. The wife said, "Why don't you stay here longer? After walking for so long, won't it be better to take some rest?" But we went on.

FORTY-FIVE DAYS FROM MOSCOW, after four months in the Soviet Union, we reached the border. The police officer examined our passports. "You have been in this country illegally. Your visas expired long ago," he said to us. "Where have you been all this time?"

We told him the whole story, but he wasn't satisfied and telephoned someone in Moscow. Now the time had come to face the consequences of ignoring the authorities. We anticipated being arrested. All along, our way of traveling had puzzled the Russian authorities. They didn't know quite how to deal with us. The police officer turned to us and shrugged his shoulders. "You have done some strange things, but you are going anyway. It is too late, no point in keeping you here any longer. *Daswi-daniya* (Good-bye)."

On May 1 we arrived in Poland. Through Warsaw, Posnan, and many other towns we enjoyed the friendship and generosity of the Polish people. The winter was left behind, and it was now sunny spring. Once, to rest from the heat of midday, we went into a school and found a few teachers to chat to during their lunch break. This was not acceptable to the disciplinarian headmaster, who came and said, "The school is not a chatting house," and asked us to leave. Shocked and embarrassed, we stumbled out and found some shade under a tree. A child, watching the incident and seeing the headmaster disappear, came and asked us where we came from. When he found out that we came from India, he looked in one of his books and found a picture of the Taj Mahal. "Is this where you come from, the country of the Taj Mahal?" "Yes," we said. "Oh, what a shame. I always wanted to go to India, but now I can't." "Why not?" we asked. "When you came to my country, my village, my school, you were treated so badly by the headmaster, how can I possibly dare to come to your country?" We said, "It is not your fault. You can still come." "Not unless I see that you receive hospitality here. Can you come to my home for tea?" "Where is your home?" "This way." He pointed eastward, back along the road we had traveled. "We must head westwards, your home is not in our direction." "If you can walk from India to Poland, a couple of miles extra is nothing to you." He was almost in tears. He could not have been older than twelve or thirteen, but he was so persistent that we followed him. "Mummy, Mummy, look who I have brought—the people from India, the country of the Taj Mahal, where I will go one day." His mother was as pleased as he. With such rich experiences, we passed through Poland and arrived in East Germany.

A thorough check of documents and rucksacks was made when we arrived at the East Berlin border. The faces of the Russian and German soldiers were tense. They seemed to be performing their duties so mechanically and without heart that we started talking to them. In the beginning, they were skeptical of our peace talk, but suddenly one of them burst out, "You are right. We have no peace of mind here, at home or at the front. We are longing for the day when we can throw away all these arms and join you in the fight for peace." He was an East German soldier in uniform, guarding the border of a tensely divided city at a crisis point in the Cold War—it was just before President Kennedy was due to visit West Berlin. The other four soldiers looked at him as though he were mad to talk in such a way to strangers.

Passing through West Berlin and East Germany, we arrived in West Germany. One evening, looking for shelter, we saw a very impressive church and beside it the minister's house. We knocked at the door of the house. In the door there was a little spy hole, and we could see that someone was looking through it. A moment later the minister opened the door a few inches. We saw the edge of his gown, the Bible in his hand, and his frowning face. We offered our leaflet, which was in German and which explained who we were and what we were doing. He didn't accept it. "What do you want?" he asked nervously. "Some shelter for the night." "No place here. Go away." He banged the door shut. We thought there must be some mistake and knocked again, hoping to explain ourselves properly. He opened the door and shouted firmly, "Don't knock at my door. There is no place here, go away immediately." He gave us no chance to explain anything. We felt sorry at distressing him and left.

A few hundred yards away we found the police station. Not knowing what to do, we went in. A young policeman smiled at us. "What can I do for you?" "May we sit down for a few moments, and we will explain to you?" He shook our hands and offered us comfortable chairs. We gave him our leaflet, which he read carefully and asked in a curious voice, "Is this really true? How long did it take you to walk from India to here?" We quickly came to the point that our most urgent need at the moment was to find shelter for the night and asked if he could suggest anywhere. He thought for a moment, then lifted the telephone and rang somewhere. Receiving an affirmative answer, he said, "All right, come with me." We went back past the church and arrived at a large house. It was a hospital. "You don't mind spending the night in a hospital, do you?" he said, and handed us over to the nurse in charge. We were taken aback—this was the first time we had stayed in a hospital. The nurses were very kind. We had a sumptuous meal of fruit, vegetables, milk, cheese, and bread, and next morning were given not only a large breakfast but also some sandwiches to take away with us. We passed once again the church and the police station and waved good-bye to the good-hearted policeman.

After walking through Hannover, Dusseldorf, and Cologne, we arrived in Bonn. We had written a letter to Chancellor Adenauer, asking for an appointment. We had talked about German problems with the minister of foreign affairs in East Germany, and we wanted to have similar talks with West German officials. When we arrived in Bonn, we went to the chancellor's office. After we had waited there for a long time, we were asked to come again the next day. Finally, on the third day we were told that neither the chancellor nor any other official would be able to meet us "for political reasons." Since no government official was willing to see us, we decided to stage a demonstration in front of the chancellor's office. We arrived there at nine o'clock in the morning. Just after our arrival the police also appeared and snatched everything—placards, books, and leaflets—away, and we had no alternative but to squat there empty-handed. We sat protesting until evening.

FROM GERMANY WE WALKED through Belgium, then northern France, and arrived in Paris on August 5. While we were walking through Belgium, Russia, America, and Great Britain signed a nuclear test ban treaty, but President de Gaulle refused to sign it. We wrote a letter to President de Gaulle explaining that we were carrying a packet of peace tea for him from Armenia and asked him to give us an audience, but we received no answer. We wrote two more letters with no better results.

We were welcomed in Paris by a number of peace groups: War Resisters International, Amis de l'Arche, and the French Campaign for Nuclear Disarmament were among them. We were given hospitality and wholehearted support for our mission. Having still received no response from President de Gaulle, we announced to the press and the peace groups our decision to demonstrate in a nonviolent and peaceful manner in front of the Elysee Palace. Hearing the news of our plan, two young men from Germany and Denmark, Wolfgang and Ole, came to join us.

A Paris peace group had advised us not to go on foot to the president's house since the police might arrest us on the way, so the four of us went by car. Many journalists and photographers had gathered, and the police were everywhere. We got out of the car just in front of the palace and started to open our banner, BAN THE BOMBS AND STOP THE TESTS, but as we were unfolding it, the banner was snatched from our hands by the police who had surrounded us. The chief of the Elysee Palace security came down the steps and invited us inside. The atmosphere was tense—the police pushed us into the palace and barred the way to the press. We were taken to a palatial room. "You are creating a disturbance in Paris," the security chief said. We replied, "Please inform the president of our request to see him. We wish to deliver a packet of peace tea. We must see him personally to explain the purpose of our walk from India and to give the message from the Armenian tea workers." "The president has received your letters and even knows where you are at present, but he is unable to meet you." "Then the only choice left to us is to go on demonstrating," we replied. "You cannot change the government's policy." "Nor can the government change ours," we said.

A few minutes later we were pushed into a heavily guarded police van and driven out of the palace through the back gate to a police station. We were put in an underground, semicircular cell. After two hours of interrogation, the police officer said, "I'll let you go if you promise not to demonstrate in front of the president's house again." "Unless we get an assurance from the government that France will not conduct nuclear tests, we cannot leave Paris or the Elysee Palace." Next we were taken to the police headquarters, where we had to wait for another two hours. It was 9:30 P.M. when we were taken to a police lockup. We didn't know what was going to happen. Late that night we were put in cells. The cells were dirty, freezing cold, and the air heavy with strange smells. There were two damp mattresses on the floor, stained and sticky, and no blankets or sheets. All our possession had been taken away, and we were left with the barest minimum of clothes, minus the cords which held up our loose Indian trousers. The only other thing in the cell, right beside the mattresses, was an open toilet, which stank.

It was the first time in my life that I had been in such a place. Everything we had worked and walked against was institutionalized in this place—fear and mistrust alive everywhere, in the walls, the locks, the sounds. The deterioration of the human situation was terrible— an old man shaking and stuttering on the stairs, a drunkard shouting and the police kicking and beating him, ill and disturbed people screaming out all night. I had thought of Paris as one of the most civilized and rich cities in the world, and was now seeing humanity on the most degraded level—it was a shock, like being thrown from the top of a mountain. I had not expected that in the land of Liberty, Equality, and Fraternity we would be thrown into a stinking cell. We had been free like the wind, and suddenly we were locked into an eight-foot-square cell. All night there was the glare of a naked lightbulb. We were unable to sleep, minds spinning round and round. Was this the final point of our journey? How long would we be here? Was Delhi to Paris one long road ending in prison? All the colors—green forests, brown mountains, white snow, yellow fruit, and blue lakes and seas—flashed through my mind in the dark, stinking atmosphere of the lockup.

The next morning while in the washroom, we managed to have a few words with Wolfgang and Ole and decided to make a hunger strike as a protest against our treatment and the conditions of the place. For two days we refused to eat the food that was pushed into our cell—porridge, bread, meat, and potatoes. I could fast, wait, and meditate. I had learned that during my monkhood. On the second day we felt the bite of hunger; our tongues, teeth, and throats were dry and sour. Prabhakar was very distressed and lay on a mattress unable to do anything. I massaged his back, chest, and head, helping him to relax. I felt very close to him. He was a dignified, determined, and dedicated man. During our walk together from Delhi to Paris, we had never been separated, not even for a day, and we hardly had any arguments or disagreements. It was extraordinary to reflect that we had survived so many ups and downs, comforts and hardships without exchanging one angry word. Mostly it was due to his patience and generosity, but also because we were so engrossed in our task that all minor egotism had evaporated. Now being in the police cell brought us even closer together, and we talked about our personal plans if we ever got out.

On the third day we were taken to the police headquarters. Two officials of the Indian Embassy were there. The police officer said, "You are a problem for us. Inside you will die, and outside you will sit in front of the palace, and we are inundated with phone calls from your supporters." He handed us our passports, a deportation order, and two air tickets, saying, "Tomorrow morning you leave Paris by Air France for Delhi."

It had taken sixteen months to get to France, and we were going to be flown back in sixteen hours. We tried to change the police officer's decision to send us to Delhi, but it was no use. So we spoke to the Indian officials, asking them to do something. They talked to the police officer, saying that it would create a "serious misunderstanding" between France and India and bad publicity for France. They asked that we be handed over to them and guaranteed that they would get us out of France within twenty-four hours. The police officer agreed. The choice for us was whether to be deported to India by plane or leave France by train for England. In the circumstances we decided to compromise and accept the latter.

As we came out of the room, we saw Madame Petit, one of those who had demonstrated with us. She had been arrested on September 16 for distributing our leaflets but was later released. When she saw how weak and worn out we looked, she asked permission to bring some fruit, biscuits, potato chips, and coffee for us. Then we were taken back to the cell.

Next day we were taken to the police headquarters again. The Indian ambassador himself was there to greet us and to make arrangements for our "deportation" to England. Afterwards he drove us to his home, gave us a sumptuous supper, and saw us on to the train to Dover, handing over two tickets. Wolfgang and Ole were deported to their respective countries by plane.

FROM DOVER WE WERE GLAD to set off on our feet again, passing through Canterbury, Maidstone, and other towns. In all these places we received particular welcome from the Quakers. Ever since we had been in Western Europe, people involved in antiwar movements had provided hospitality and organized publicity in many places. The nature of our walk had changed—the almost daily adventures in the East of finding food and shelter and the unexpected offers of hospitality were replaced by the less eventful demands for publicity and lectures.

When we arrived in London, we felt as if we were in the Mecca of the Peace Movement, and we received wholehearted support and cooperation from many peace organizations and activists. Campaign for Nuclear Disarmament (CND), the Committee of One Hundred, War Resisters International—all identified with our walk. *Peace News* had been covering our journey ever since we started from India, and people were waiting for us to arrive. We were surrounded by friends, supporters, and admirers, and finding hospitality was no longer a problem. *The Guardian* wrote a feature article about us, and the BBC and ITV put us on their screens.

The response to our request for a meeting with the prime minister, Harold Wilson, was lukewarm. We were informed by the PM's office that it was not possible for him to receive all the visitors who desired an audience. However Lord Attlee would receive us, and accept the packet of peace tea on the PM's behalf. We were mollified to know that at least we would be talking with the man who, during his premiership, brought an end to colonial rule by granting independence to India.

Prabhakar and I were received with courtesy and warmth at the House of Commons in a room overlooking the Thames. The English politeness, and the tea served in Spode china, could not hide the fact that all politicians seemed to have predictable answers. "We are doing everything possible to achieve nuclear disarmament. It is the Soviets who are blocking progress. You yourselves have been to Russia—surely you know what a threat they pose? We cannot risk our national security." Our counterarguments prolonged the discussions but brought no satisfactory solution. The packet of peace tea was accepted with a chuckle.

The most important person for us to meet in England was Bertrand Russell. It was he who had given us our original inspiration and impetus to undertake our mammoth task, but unfortunately he was not in London. In response to our letter, he sent his secretary to meet us and give us the message that he would be extremely disappointed if we did not go to see him. I said to Russell's secretary, "We cannot dream of departing from England without making a pilgrimage to the prophet of peace." His secretary drove us by car all the way to Penrendendraeth in North Wales, where Russell had retired to a cottage set in the Snowdonian mountains.

What an honor it was to sit beside this man, small in body yet giant in stature, old in age and young in courage, weak in limbs and strong in action; a man who was as dedicated to peace as to philosophy and mathematics. While he poured tea and served cake to us, he said, "I am flattered to know that my small action of civil disobedience inspired you to make a great walk across continents." After talking about his efforts to bring peace between India and China, he said, "In order to avoid the death of humanity and the destruction of our planet, it is urgent and essential that we discard the bomb." I said, "At one level I agree with you, but I also feel that peace should be promoted for positive reasons. Fear of the end of the world cannot be sufficient motivation for me to work for peace." We sensed an area of disagreement here; but Russell bypassed this, asking, "You desire to reach Washington, but you cannot walk the Atlantic. How can we help you?" Prabhakar and I explained that we could not accept money, but we would gladly accept two tickets to New York. Russell turned to his secretary and said, "Let us start an Atlantic Fund for our peace walkers to raise money for their passage to America, and please arrange two tickets on the *Queen Mary* for them."

Prabhakar and I were thrilled and grateful. That afternoon with Russell was the pinnacle of our travels. We left Russell delighted and happy. His secretary drove us back to London.

Obtaining an American visa was no easier than it had been to get one for the USSR, and it was made even more difficult by the fact that we had been in Communist countries for nearly six months. Another obstacle was erected by the American Embassy: the fear that we might wish to settle down in America. None of the embassy officials of any of the countries we had visited had been able to understand how we were going to survive without money—least of all the Americans. Familiar questions were raised, such as "How are you going to eat? Where are you going to sleep?" In the end, the official said, "The only way I can grant you a visa is that you find a reputable American citizen to sponsor you."

We had been inspired by the writings of a great pacifist thinker, A. J. Muste, so we wrote to him explaining our difficulties, seeking his help and sponsorship. A. J. proved to be a man of compassion and trust. Without delay he undertook "complete responsibility" for our stay in the United States. It took twenty-two days to obtain our American visas.

Strong legs and plenty of time were our assets in exploring and discovering London. We stayed with the pacifist Peggy Smith in Earls Court, and from Richmond to Hampstead, from Greenwich to Southall, we measured the length and breadth of London with our stride.

We walked to Southampton, and on the morning of November 22, 1963, we boarded the *Queen Mary* bound for New York. Here we were, two travelers without any money, on one of the most luxurious liners in the world, with a separate cabin to ourselves, and a bell to call a steward at any time to bring us specially cooked vegetarian meals. Thanks to Vinoba's weapons, we were traveling in style.

As we sailed the stormy Atlantic, Prabhakar and I had plenty of time for talking and reflection. Going into the unknown world and confronting it without a penny in our pockets had meant that differences between rich and poor, educated and illiterate, all vanished; and beneath all these divisions, a common humanity emerged. Whether we slept in comfortable beds or on the floor of a barn or under a tree, it was all a gift. As wanderers we were free of shadows from the past. The experience of a beautiful emptiness within myself, with neither material nor spiritual possessions, unlocked my soul. It was a journey without destination; journey and destination became one, thought and action became one. I felt myself moving like a river. A river and its flow are not separate things; I and my movement were not separate. The journey was me. It was as much an inner journey as an outward one. It was a journey into detachment. The contradiction between movement and stillness ceased. I was on the move in stillness. I was a wanderer, wandering through life. Living from day to day, from inspiration to inspiration.

In wandering I felt a sense of union with the whole sky, the infinite earth and sea. I felt myself a part of the cosmic existence. It was as if by walking I was making love to the earth itself. Wandering was my path, my true self, my true being. It released my soul-force; it brought me in relation to everything else. I stood like I stand in front of the mirror. People, nature, everything became like a mirror, and I could see myself in them, what I was. I was born in a dream of wandering, a seed conceived in my mother. My dreams are of wandering. From birth I was wandering—as a monk, with Vinoba, and on the walk—whatever I learned came through wandering.

My two legs were the most creative parts of my body and the most creative expression of my energy. Without these two legs I would have been nothing. But with my two legs there was no place in the world that I could not go. I felt like the god Wamanavatar (Vishnu reincarnated as a dwarf), who was outraged to see that an evil king was terrorizing people and the world with his armies and weapons. The god came to the king as a dwarf Brahmin beggar and asked for a small gift. "What do you want?" said the king. "I have nothing. Will you grant me a small piece of land?" said the dwarf. No Hindu king can turn away a Brahmin empty-handed, so the king asked, "How much land do you want?" The dwarf replied, "Let me walk three steps, and whatever space of land I cover, give me that land." The king laughed. "I have the whole earth under my rule, so walk three steps, little man, wherever you want, and take that land." The dwarf grew into a giant. He took his first step to heaven, and his second step covered the entire earth. Then he said, "Where can I have my third step?" And he put his foot on the head of the evil king.

We were taking our four steps to Moscow, Paris, London, and Washington. In all the countries, politicians, soldiers, and people in responsible jobs argued, "We're all right, we are peaceful. The other party is the troublemaker." The Russians said, "Go to the West"; the Westerners said, "Go to the Communists"; the Pakistanis said, "Go and sort out your own country." Always the other, the other . . .

We met no one on the walk who didn't want peace, but no one seemed to know how to achieve it. Politicians were as powerless as the common people. We couldn't convince people to accept our arguments. Argument merely breeds argument, and all people have their own answers. But walking as we were, going from country to country, to different cultures and religions, going in jungles, forests, and mountains, we were perhaps able to communicate a sense of the inner power of the individual and the loss of fear of "the other."

Many times during our walk people had pressed us to accept money. At Jalalabad in Afghanistan, the editor of a daily paper told us that he would like to help us in the name of peace and tried to give us some Afghan money. At Kabul we were talking with a shopkeeper who was so impressed that he took a handful of banknotes out of his cashbox and put them in front of us. When we refused to take the money, he presented us with two writing pens.

Because we weren't carrying any money, people were more concerned to look after our basic needs. When we reached Kabul, two friends from India sent us some warm clothes to carry us through the cold weather of Afghanistan, and our host in Kabul presented each of us with a fur cap and a pair of warm shoes. In Behshahr, in Iran, someone saw us walking in worn-out, tattered shoes. He asked us to wait, and after some time he came back with two pairs of brand-new shoes. In Tehran an Indian merchant bought us sleeping bags, pullovers, winter shoes, and coats, saying, "Take whatever you need. I am only the trustee of the wealth I possess."

For two and a half months, between Kabul and Tehran, we were completely cut off from friends in India and from any news of what was happening in the world. Occasionally our hosts in different countries helped us to mail letters; at other times we would carry letters with us, and whenever any car stopped to ask if we wanted a lift, we would ask them to stamp our letters and mail them instead. This happened a lot in Russia, especially with truck drivers. At Tabriz in Iran, the postmaster general presented us with a large pile of Aerograms. And when we stayed in some house, our host invariably gave us a cake of soap, razor blades, stamps, and other things we needed for our daily use. In one village in Russia our host didn't have any safety blades, only a cut-throat razor, so he himself shaved off our beards.

NOW WE WERE on the *Queen Mary,* by courtesy of Bertrand Russell and other peace campaigners. It felt like a welcome break from walking and a holiday from giving lectures and trying to convince people. The comforts of the swimming pool, ballrooms and dance floors, bars and cinemas, were something we had neither planned nor dreamed of. The vast Atlantic Ocean below and the vast blue sky above gave me a sense of eternity, which was so different from the ephemeral worlds of politics and commerce.

After seven days of sailing, we suddenly saw the Statue of Liberty, the Empire State Building and umpteen other skyscrapers. What a contrast it was to all the European cities we had visited! As our ship sailed into the harbor, we stood on the deck and gazed at one of the wonders of human civilization.

We were met by A. J. Muste and a group of antiwar campaigners. As soon as we arrived we started walking again through the streets of Manhattan to Brooklyn, where we stayed. There was something magical about our walk that captured the imagination of so many individuals and groups who were working for peace. Every evening that we were in New York we were invited to tell our story to a gathered audience, varying in size from fifty people to two hundred, and we were invited by different families to wine and dine with them; it was an atmosphere of partying and celebration.

We spent ten days in New York preparing for our last leg to Washington. A. J. Muste personally worked out the route for us and made arrangements so that every night bed, food and meetings were planned, and he wrote to the White House informing the president of our achievements and our desire to meet him.

Unfortunately, quite a lot of walking had to be done on tarmac roads, as noisy and smelly cars speeded past. We were unable to find secluded footpaths or little country lanes. "Such things do not exist in America," we were told. We were delighted to find that our path went through Philadelphia. We were longing to say hello to Dr. Scarf, who had offered us a lift in the Khyber Pass and who had invited us to his home if we ever got to America. The night before we were due in Philadelphia, we phoned him. "Do you remember two Indians you met in the Khyber Pass?" "Yes, I do. Where are they?" "We are about ten miles away and planning to come to Philadelphia tomorrow. We hope to see you then," we said. "I can't wait till tomorrow. I want to see you tonight," said Dr. Scarf, and so he did. His first words were "So your dream came true."

We spent some time narrating our story to him. Then Dr. Scarf gave us directions to his house, where the next day a party of twenty, including the other three occupants of the car in the Khyber Pass, gathered to celebrate our arrival. Dr. Scarf proposed a toast: "We thought that our guests were totally mad to think that anyone could walk from India to America, but here we are; eighteen months later these two men have made it. So let's drink to the successful conclusion of their journey."

IN WASHINGTON we had wanted to make an appeal to President Kennedy. However, when we eventually reached there on January 9, 1964, after walking eight thousand miles, President Kennedy had been killed, the victim of an assassin's bullet. It was to the cemetery and not to the White House that we went to look for him. And it was at his tomb, where the young president had ended his journey, that our walk also came to an end—a long walk, from Gandhi's grave to Kennedy's grave.

Never during the walk did I feel such a sense of desolation and weariness as when I faced the tomb of the dead Kennedy. As we stood in silence, soft drops of rain fell on the flame burning there. The hair on my body stood on end as I shivered. It had been raining when we had started from Gandhi's grave. We had walked from the other side of the world for peace, and had come to America, the biggest symbol of military power. At Kennedy's grave there was neither peace nor war but something beyond—a moment of complete stillness. Gandhi and Kennedy. Kennedy and Gandhi. The grave, the bullet, the rain. The rain and the flame become one. The moment of beginning and ending became one.

The only remaining task now was to deliver the last packet of peace tea to the White House. As with the other heads of state, President Johnson was unable to find time to receive us personally, so he deputed his special adviser on disarmament matters to give us a cordial welcome.

As we entered the gates of the White House, we could not help but remember our encounter with Soviet officials in the Kremlin. The two biggest world powers, entrenched in their prejudices and fear, made us feel small and powerless. The response at the White House was not too dissimilar to the response at the Kremlin. "We are constantly proposing sensible measures to reduce armaments, but we are always forced back by obstructions from the Soviets," said the president's representative. However, behind this formal answer, he appeared to be touched by the story of the Armenian woman and her packet of tea, which came wrapped in a plea for peace. "Of course we know that the ordinary people of the Soviet Union desire disarmament as much as people in any other country, so that resources can be diverted from military hardware to better living conditions. But how do we guarantee our national security if we are faced by evil dictators like Hitler and Ho Chi Minh, who ignore the wishes of the people and impose their will by military means?"

To me this was the same tired old argument about evil men in the enemy camp. For me there is no such thing as evil. There is only fear and ignorance. Wars and weapons are born from fear and ignorance. I found fear in Moscow and fear in Washington, fear in Paris and fear in London. The enemy is neither Russia nor America. It is fear, which is the enemy of twentieth-century civilization.

Visiting the White House did not give us any solace or comfort: it was an anticlimax. I felt a sense of disappointment—eight thousand miles and eighteen months of walk ended in the bureaucratic defense of fear. I was depressed. What now? What next? We could not leave America at such a low point.

The uplift came in the form of an invitation from Martin Luther King to visit him. He had just delivered one of his greatest speeches in Washington: "I have a dream that black and white, rich and poor, strong and weak, will be united in common humanity. I have a dream." Martin Luther King had become the symbol of the new America, an America of hope and trust. A civil rights campaigner from Washington, a staunch supporter of King, drove us south.

As we arrived at the home of Coretta and Martin Luther King, we felt an immediate sense of uplift. Seeing a large picture of Mahatma Gandhi hanging on the wall of their room made us feel at home. I had seen so many phony warriors hiding behind the shield of fear in the Red Army headquarters and in the Pentagon, but here was a true warrior out to destroy discrimination and division. He said, "My nonviolence is a revolutionary nonviolence, touching the deepest corners of human consciousness. I am convinced that we will win. We will bring an end to all discrimination and division." His words flowed from his mouth like water from a fountain. Silently listening to him, I felt renewed and refreshed—all that walk was worthwhile just to come and see Martin Luther King.

After seeing King we went to Albany to see the civil rights movement in action. It was here that I came face to face with fear and experienced what thousands of black people experience every day. I went to a cafe with John Papworth, an English friend who was with me at the time. It was elegantly decorated and comfortable. We found a quiet corner and sat down. A waitress in a white apron came to take our order. "Tea and cheese sandwiches for two, please," John announced. The waitress went. We became immersed in our conversation. The waitress came again and said, "Sorry, we have no tea and cheese sandwiches." "Can we have coffee then?" John asked. "No, we have nothing, sir." The waitress disappeared quickly. We went to the manager, who was standing at the cash register. "Can't we have a cup of tea?" I asked. "No, you can't. Please leave immediately," he replied. "Isn't this a cafe to serve the public?" I asked. "It is my cafe, and I serve whom I like," he replied. "We won't leave here without a cup of tea," I said. His face became red and his lips swollen, and his breath was short, fast, and loud. He pulled open a drawer and took out a pistol. Pointing it at my chest he said, "Are you getting out, or should I teach you a lesson?" "There is no need for your gun, nor for your anger. I just want a cup of tea," I said anxiously. John stepped in between us and put his body in front of mine. The waiters and waitresses and various customers gathered around and pushed John and me out of the cafe. I was shaking—I had been at the point of death. Never before had I focused on the fact that the color of my skin had any significance. My interest in the civil rights movement had been rather academic until then; I then realized what black people in America were going through, what a great battle Martin Luther King was fighting, and how much courage it takes to fight with nonviolent means.

WE RECEIVED A LETTER from the War Resisters of Japan asking, "How can you complete your Peace Pilgrimage without visiting the only victims of the Bomb against which you have been walking?" They were right, and we agreed to return to India via Japan.

We arrived in the country of the Rising Sun to find Buddhist monks, Christian pacifists, and students at the airport to greet us. We were taken to a hall near the airport to tell our story. A married couple and two young female students who were at the meeting spontaneously offered to walk with us, to act as our interpreters and guides. An American pacifist woman, Mary Harvey, flew from America to join us in our pilgrimage to Hiroshima.

Under the glare of television cameras, we started walking from the center of Tokyo. Tokyo to Yokohama was one unending city. We stayed in a guesthouse where we were received by the mayor. After ceremonial speeches, he presented us discreetly with an envelope tied with a red ribbon, which contain a few thousand yen—a support for peace. Nearly everyone who came to meet us brought some present—calligraphy, wall hangings, door hangings, drawings, paintings, and dolls.

We had our first experience of a Japanese public bath, which later became an essential part of our daily routine. I had never seen so many naked bodies together and was shy to take off my pants. In India we would never be naked in public and would always wear pants when taking a shower. But here in Japan nobody would dream of bathing in pants. First we would wash our bodies sitting on a low wooden stool beside a warm tap, soaping ourselves and rinsing with bowls of water. Then we soaked our bodies in a small swimming pool filled with very hot water. There was a thin bamboo wall which separated the men's from the women's areas, and one woman sitting in the doorway was in charge of both. When we had completed our bath, we put on cotton kimonos provided by the guesthouse. On a summer evening the majority of people would be walking around after their baths in these comfortable kimonos.

The Japanese dinner was always a delight. Bowl after bowl of soup, rice, vegetables, and pickles with plenty of seaweed, soy sauce, and tofu.

My Japanese hosts would break into laughter seeing me fail to use their beautifully decorated chopsticks. One dish I much enjoyed was tempura, a variety of vegetables enveloped in batter and fried, but I was happiest when sukiyaki was prepared. Then I could choose exactly what I wanted to eat and hear no grumbles about my vegetarianism and the Japanese love of fish and fish eggs.

At all times we were given tea to drink. Tea before dinner, tea after dinner, tea during dinner. Sometimes it is green tea, other times black tea. If it is summer you drink ice-cold barley tea; in springtime, cherry blossom tea. I wish the Coca-Cola culture would keep away and leave Japan to tea.

Much of our time during the walk was spent with the peace groups who, although they were very active to bring peace to the world, had no peace within themselves. Broadly speaking, the peace groups were either communist or independent. The communists insisted that America and the capitalist countries were responsible for the lack of peace in the world. They derived their strength from the trade unions and therefore were very powerful. The independents comprised the anarchists, Christians, and Buddhists. Fortunately both groups supported our walk. Always we urged them not to put so much emphasis on their ideological divides and instead unite for some common program. But we were no more successful in bringing peace to them than we had been elsewhere. Only when there is peace within can the peace without be established. Although the peace movement in Japan was stronger than in many other countries, it was no more successful, partly because of its internal disagreements.

Our route took us to Nagoya, Kyoto, Osaka, Kobe, Okayama, Fuku-yama, and then to Hiroshima. In forty-five days we walked an average of fifteen miles a day. Often Buddhist monks accompanied us with their chant of "Namu-myo-ho-renge-kyo" and their drumming to evoke harmony and peace in the world. The presence of these monks on our walk transformed us into pilgrims. I experienced an inner calm while walking in Japan, possibly because my Buddhist companions brought with them a strong sense of dharma.

After walking seven hundred miles, we arrived at the Peace Garden of Hiroshima. Here I was reminded of the fact that it takes a calamity of Himalayan proportions to make us realize that power and prosperity need not go through the gates of war. Japan is now on the road to enormous economic strength because it spends almost no money on armaments. It is able to devote all its human ingenuity and resources not on wasteful military research but on the fulfillment of human needs—although I still doubted that Japan would know where and when to stop its economic growth and how to maintain a balance between the needs of its people and the needs of its environment.

AFTER TRAVELING BY BOAT from Japan to Bombay, once again we stood in front of Gandhi's grave in Delhi. It was October 2, 1964, the anniversary of his birthday, and people were saying prayers, chanting mantras, and turning spinning wheels. There was an autumn sun and a strong wind. As I laid yellow marigolds on the black stone of Gandhi's grave, I felt again the power that graves have on me.

From Delhi we went to see Vinoba at his ashram in Pawnar. The ashram is situated on a hill beside a river. We climbed the stone steps; at the top there was a temple, and beyond it, under the shadow of a large tree, Vinoba was sitting on a wooden platform surrounded by members of the ashram. There was the quiet voice of Vinoba, teaching from the Upanishads. When he saw us, Vinoba smiled and beckoned us to sit by him. He put his hand on my shoulder and said, "How are your feet? I have heard stories of your blisters!" He laughed. "They are the ornaments of walking," I said. "With your blessings and the armor of no money, we have completed our walk. Thank you for insisting that we go without money. Having no money totally freed us."

Vinoba reflected, "You have done well. It is brave and courageous, but ultimately you need to go nowhere to find peace, it is within you." He looked around and continued, "The center of the earth is here. Do you remember the story of Ganesh? One day the supreme god Vishnu called all the gods and devils together and said he would give his blessings to the one who went around the earth and was the first to come back. All of them left immediately on their various transports—riding on a lion, a peacock, a swan, a bullock, et cetera—each one wanting to be the first to return. But the little elephant-faced deity Ganesh, the son of Lord Shiva, was puzzled and thought, 'I will take ages to travel around the earth on my transport of a mouse, and I am bound to come last.' So he drew a circle on the ground, wrote inside it 'Om Vishnu,' and rode around it on his mouse. He returned to Vishnu, who was sitting on his lotus throne, and put his head on Vishnu's feet saying, 'I am the first to return. Give me your blessings.' One by one, the gods and devils started gathering and eagerly awaited Vishnu's verdict. When everyone had returned, Vishnu gave his blessing to Ganesh. None of the gods could understand how Ganesh on his mouse could have come first, and they begged for an explanation. Ganesh said, 'What you see in space and time is only an illusion. The real essence of the universe is Vishnu himself. So you don't need to go anywhere to circle the world, the world is here.' "

We had walked around the world, but Vinoba told us it wasn't necessary to go anywhere!

WE WENT ON BY TRAIN to Bangalore. Lata came to the same place where I had left her almost two and a half years before. As the train drew slowly into the platform, I opened the door of the carriage and stood on the step, my eyes searching for her among the people milling around. Suddenly I saw her dark hair bound in a bunch on top of her head, with a white jasmine flower ring around it. She was standing with our daughter in her arms and a garland of red roses in one hand. I waved, and she came running toward me. We embraced and stood there holding each other. I tried to lift my daughter into my arms to kiss her, but she hid her face in Lata's sari. Lata said, "Darling, this is your papa." I was the papa she had never known.

Prabhakar and I stood awkwardly at the taxi stand, our paths about to separate. He got into a three-wheeled scooter taxi, and I saw him disappear into the traffic, waving his arms.

—⊰∞⊱—

CHAPTER 6

Escape

I HAD TRAVELED AROUND THE WORLD, I had talked about peace, I had received publicity in India and abroad, I had been welcomed by the people for my "adventurous journey," and I relished being in the lime-light. I returned with great enthusiasm and impatience to act, but the question was—what to do? Going on a walk into an unknown world with a known action proved easier than finding the right action in the known world. During the month in Bangalore with Lata's family, I received many letters, particularly from gramdan workers inviting me to speak about the walk. Lata and I set off with our child on a tour of India. As soon as I stopped walking and started talking, I was caught up in the illusion of self-importance. After two months Lata became un-happy with the traveling and talking. It seemed best to sit down and write a book, so we went to Benares.

We rented a flat in a beautiful house owned by the queen of Benares, with a balcony overlooking the Ganges. From here I wrote my first Hindi book, *Journey Around the World Without a Penny*. The publisher wanted the book as soon as possible, so he gave me a typist, to whom I dictated the whole book straight onto the typewriter. The pages were sent to the press as soon as they were typed. The whole book was written in a month and printed in another month. The publisher said he had never had an author who worked so fast, nor had he published a book so quickly. A hardback edition of five thousand copies sold out in six months, and then a paperback edition of twenty thousand copies was published. I received many more letters, especially from young people, who were inspired and who wanted to undertake a similar trip.

Martin Luther King had given me his book *Stride Towards Freedom*. Only by translating it into Hindi could I express my deep admiration for him and release the emotion I felt toward him. But Lata started to feel anxious about my writing and my view of life. She said, "Whatever you do, the world is not going to change. Wars and exploitation will continue. There have been hundreds of great saints—from Buddha to Gandhi, they have all come and gone. Do you think that you, Saint Kumar, can change the world? You will not change the world, you will only ruin our lives. Stop trying to solve other people's problems and solve your own."

One day we were sitting on the balcony, watching the trains go over the bridge across the Ganges. Lata said, "Your revolution is all very well, but now you are married, we have a child, and I am expecting another one. Children need security and a safe life. I don't want to have children with unfulfilled needs." I argued with her, and she became angry, saying, "If you are such an idealist, why did you marry?" I said, "You are right, I should not have married." Lata said, "I have written to my mother and brother asking them to come, and they will be arriving tomorrow." That was news to me. I asked her why they were coming. She said, "Life with you is not going very well. I would like my mother and brother to talk with you." "They can't solve any problems which we ourselves can't solve," I told her. "I don't think it is a very good idea to bring your mother and brother into our problems. We should sort them out ourselves." She said, "You are so stubborn that I don't think I can get anywhere with you."

This left me taken aback, wondering what was happening. As a result of my being away for two and a half years, Lata and I had grown apart from each other. Our ideas and interests had developed in opposite directions, and the separation had made us strangers. Lata's mother and brother came, and we discussed the situation. Lata's mother said, "You will never make a good living by writing books. You and Lata's brother should start a drapery shop that will give you a regular income. We will loan you the money."

Although all the male members of my family were successful businessmen, I couldn't see myself sitting in a shop with a yardstick, measuring cloth to sell, and I said so. Lata's mother replied, "You've led the life of a vagabond, traveling around the world, and now it is time you settled down. I am suggesting this shop because you have no degree or qualifications, so it is the best solution for you." The three of them were very serious. Lata said, "You must decide by tomorrow morning what you are going to do. If you don't decide anything positive, I cannot stay any longer, and I shall go back with my mother to Bangalore." What an ultimatum!

The next morning I said, "No, I cannot sit in a shop all day. I would be a failure, I cannot keep accounts." Lata's mother said, "Don't worry, my son will take care of the shop. You just have to work with him." But I said no, and the discussion ended in argument. That evening, Lata, her mother and brother, and my daughter all left abruptly.

A NOVELIST FRIEND from Delhi, Rajendra, came to see me. He understood precisely the reasons for the breakdown of my marriage. He was witty and amusing and a good support for me at that moment. One evening Rajendra and I took a boat on the Ganges. Rajendra said, "What are you doing after all these fantastic adventures, sitting around moping over your wife and marriage? Get out of this mess. The problem is not how to make your marriage work but to see it as it is and understand it. You have to calm down and get into something challenging and creative."

We were walking on the other side of the Ganges. The moonlight over the city gave it an eerie, silvery glow. Rajendra said, "Make yourself tough and find your own way. People are going to criticize you whatever you do."

We crossed back over the river and, after walking along the ghats, came to the Nepalese temple of Shiva: Shiva the terrible, Shiva the peaceful, Shiva the creator and destroyer, Shiva the symbol of unity, unity in opposites, unity in multiplicity. Shiva who drank all the poison of the world, which turned his body blue. Shiva who opened a third eye in the center of his forehead and burned all the lust and greed of the world with the fire from his eye. In Shiva's presence the breaking of the marriage meant the making of a new life. I turned to Rajendra and said, "I will come to Delhi, and we will publish a magazine." We sat on the steps of the ghat looking at the river flowing by—the Ganges, which has been a shelter like a mother for me, a silent witness of everything, but never interfering. A body wrapped in yellow cloth was being burned by the river. I thought of it as myself, the flames burning my marriage. I wanted to find Babaji, but he wasn't there.

I arrived in Delhi. Rajendra met me at the station. I found a flat in Connaught Circus in the center of New Delhi and started working on the magazine, *Vigraha* (Dialectics).

Lata wrote to me that she had given birth to a son but that she was happier without me and would not come back. "I don't think we can be happy together." I felt rejected and lonely. Everything around me seemed bleak and meaningless. Life without Lata was empty, and my restlessness grew by the minute. I had found the world but lost Lata. I was enveloped in a black blanket of pain and frustration. What should I do? India seemed more alien to me now than any other country I had been to. Coming to India was in no way a homecoming.

After nine issues of *Vigraha,* it became obvious that the magazine wasn't going to be a success. There was too much competition, and the capital I had started with was nearly used up.

One hot evening in October, a friend of mine from Benares, Anant, whom I had known for many years, came to visit me. We went out to eat and talked for a long time. It was midnight, and as Connaught Circus was empty, we went for a walk around. I showed Anant a letter from Danilo Dolci of Italy. "You walked around the world for peace. We are walking from Naples to Rome for peace. Will you come and join our walk? You have been such an inspiration to us— please come." This letter had come to me like a raft to a drowning man. "I want to go to Italy," I said to Anant. "You have never been out of India. Why don't you come with me?" Anant went back to Benares, consulted with his family, and sent me a telegram to say that he had decided to come.

This was a sudden decision. No one knew I was going. I just walked out, leaving everything—magazine, office, papers, flat, furniture—to die without me.

It was midnight when our plane was due to depart. There were a few moments of panic when the officials took away my papers to check them. But they were returned when everything was found to be in order. It was a cold November night, and the journey reminded me of my escape from monkhood. I breathed a sigh of relief.

—⊗⊗⊗—

CHAPTER 7

Floating

Dolci's march from naples to rome had already started. We were given a lift to the town where the marchers were staying the night. There were students and young workers, militants of the new left, pacifists, and conscientious objectors. Anant and I carried placards and spoke at meetings. We marched to Rome in ten days. There we were joined by a large crowd, to demonstrate in front of the American Embassy.

This was 1968. Europe was in turmoil. The Vietnam War had sparked a deep sense of protest against the culture of violence. It was clear to me that European civilization is built on the foundation of violence toward people and violence toward nature. Now, even the opposition and protests against violence were violent. Danilo Dolci was an exception and was facing great difficulties in containing violence in the young people.

Many people call Dolci the Gandhi of Italy because he carried a candle of compassion in the dark tunnel of violent Europe. "Our struggle is more difficult than Gandhi's. He was standing on the foundation laid by men like the Buddha. Heroes of Europe are war heroes. We are challenging our deep-rooted notion of domination. It is very hard indeed," he said.

While in Italy we met people from many parts of Europe; we made a plan to travel, to witness the revolutionary fervor of the students' movement, hippie culture, and peace actions. On our trail through the continent, we came to Brussels.

One morning in Brussels my host read in the paper about an art exhibition. I was still in bed upstairs, but he shouted up to me because it sounded so exciting. We went to the exhibition. I became enthusiastic and intrigued by the bold paintings with such strong primary colors, and I didn't want to leave without seeing the artist. The paintings communicated to me something fresh and raw. I asked the woman in charge of the gallery if she would give me the artist's address. Instead she promised to pass on my address to the artist, Marie Clay.

The next day the artist telephoned, and we made an appointment to meet in a coffee bar. The bar was crowded, but the moment I entered I saw only one person, and that was her. When she talked, her eyes went across my whole body and her hands went in the air, on the table, under it, all over the place—there was no shyness or inhibition in her at all. Instead of talking about her paintings, the first thing she said was "You are so handsome." That made me shiver. I had never seen a woman as beautiful as Marie. I started asking questions, but I didn't know what I was asking nor did I hear what she was answering. We spent three hours in the coffee bar just looking at each other and talking. I said, "You are not a painter, you are a painting!" She laughed and said, "It is good to meet somebody with emotions."

She took me to her house. It was full of paintings and sculptures; and everywhere there were colors, brushes, stains of spilled paint. Painting for her was not a job but a way of life. The colors were part of her being. Her husband was screen-printing in the basement. Marie gave me one of her paintings as a present. It was of a penis, the top of which was very red. On one side was fire, and on the other a calm atmosphere of abstract design in blue, which I associated with water; the penis seemed like the bridge between the opposites. The painting reminded me of the Shiva lingam in the Nepalese temple of Benares.

She kept pouring more wine in my glass. I said, "I am not used to drinking so much wine." She said, "A man coming from the land of the Kama Sutra, tantra, and erotic sculptures must drink wine!" Later she drove me back, and in the car she kissed me passionately.

When she arrived home, she immediately telephoned to say that I had left the painting in the back of her car and asked when I was leaving. Since we were due to fly to London the next day, she said she would come with the painting in the morning and then drive us to the air terminal.

At the terminal we kissed and kissed, and she said, "I need more time with you."

While I was in London, Marie Clay sent me another present of a painting, together with a letter saying, "My Traveler Friend, You are beautiful, you brought a beautiful moment and a beautiful experience, but still unexpressed and longing to be expressed. I dreamt your hair was in my hands and I was holding it and moving my fingers through it. After the dream I got up in the night and could not stop myself from taking a brush and colors, red and black, which you liked most, and I painted a picture. I am sending it to you with this letter. For a traveler, no destination is far, and something tells me you will soon be in Brussels."

This was a letter beyond my wildest expectations. I was thirty-two years of age, and never had I experienced a gesture of such friendship from a woman. Marie Clay's letter created an unfamiliar longing in my heart, and I could not wait to return to Brussels.

Not long after receiving Marie's letter, I also received an invitation to attend a conference in Brussels. When I arrived, I telephoned Marie, and she came to the house where I was staying. It was evening, and we had dinner with my host. After dinner she whispered in my ear, "Can I stay here tonight?" "But you are married," I said. She whispered, "I want you."

She went to the telephone and rang her husband, saying straightaway, "I am going to spend the night with Satish." There was an exchange of heated dialogue on the telephone. Her husband sounded upset and angry. She said, "I want to have an Indian experience." Her husband was shouting so loud we could all hear, "Do you think I will lie down in our bed, knowing that my wife is in somebody else's arms?" She said, "I don't want to be dishonest with you. We have been married for ten years, and I have never gone with anybody else. But tonight, I can't stop myself. Whatever you want to do, you can do, but I am not coming home tonight, because I can't come. My body and soul are unable to leave. I can't explain why, but it is so." She slammed the receiver down. I was amazed at the passion of her decision.

In the bedroom I kissed her eyes, and she kissed my ears, gently licking them with her tongue. She brought her lips onto my nose and gently bit it, then pressed my head to her breasts, kissing my hair. I opened her shirt and started sucking her nipples, stroking and kissing her warm breasts and belly. She put her hand on my forehead and said, "Relax, let your body rest and feel the touch of me without thinking." There was complete trust and communication between our two bodies. I lost contact with the outside world totally. I was in a dreamlike state. My body completely and joyously let go of itself. Marie Clay was like a serpent.

It was the first time I had really experienced the ecstasy of love in a woman and the intensity of sex. Marie gave me full acceptance and feeling. I never thought that I would meet someone like this, who was ready to experience two bodies meeting in complete sexual union. I felt that the kind of meditation that my guru had taught me was happening in the complete melting of two egos and two bodies. Through many different postures and positions, I felt my whole body going to a deeper level of joy, where there was total presence of body and soul in the act of making love. Marie Clay released in me a hidden fire—I was on the peak of Everest, my head in the clouds.

The night passed like a moment, and the morning sun made unfriendly intrusions, which we ignored. Our bodies were unwilling to part, our lips were refusing to separate, our arms had forgotten how to release each other's bodies. We were in love; in love with each other, in love with the universe, in love. Period. I knew what happiness meant, I knew what my body was capable of, I knew what it means to be searching and what it means to be arriving. Just for once, I knew my destination. It was Marie Clay.

The next day she telephoned to ask me to have supper with her and her husband. I was shocked and said, "Do you want your husband to shoot me?" She explained that she had been completely open and honest with her husband, adding, "This is the best part of love. Love knows no guilt. There is nothing to hide."

Marie Clay was a generous friend. I could phone up and say, "I am here," and she would come. She was an ideal combination of everything

I was looking for: an artist whose life was part of the counterculture. She was both challenging the taboos and deep-rooted conformism of the old system and living and constructing an alternative lifestyle. Being with her recharged me. She was like a nest to which I could fly back. I felt a deep communion with her. She wore no mask, nor had any pseudoambitions. Her body became my home, a source of bliss, of love and longing.

I forgot all the problems that had troubled me in India. I was floating with the wind, and wherever the wind took me I went. I was meeting people, eating and dancing with them, seeing rivers, coming across new cities and countries.

In Belgrade, Anant and I were staying in a youth hostel. We met someone who was driving from Belgrade to Stockholm and then back to Istanbul. He offered us a lift. I did not want to drive so fast through Europe, but Anant decided to take the lift to see Scandinavia before returning to India. After traveling together for five months, we parted. Then I traveled to Budapest, Prague, Berlin, and London.

THE SOVIET GOVERNMENT had given me an award for my book *Around the World Without a Penny* and a certificate for "outstanding work for peace and freedom." I went to the Soviet Embassy in London and was received by the cultural attache. I asked him what the point was in giving awards to foreign writers when Soviet writers were still being imprisoned for their own work. I wanted to return my award, but he refused to take it. I came out of the Embassy, tore it up in the street, and threw it in a dustbin.

I went again to Belgium and spent two weeks in the seaside town of Knokke. Late one night I received a phone call from Michael Randle of War Resisters International in London. Czechoslovakia had been invaded by the members of the Warsaw Pact, and Michael asked me if I would go to Budapest to join a small group to protest the invasion. Similar groups were to be sent to Moscow, Warsaw, and Berlin.

I went to Brussels and applied for a visa but was told that because I had "journalist" written in my passport, my application had to be approved by the foreign ministry in Budapest. I waited for a week; nothing happened, and so I left for Vienna. There I got the same answer. In the embassy I saw an advertisement for Malev, the Hungarian airline, together with a note on an arrangement for getting visas at the airport in

Budapest. I bought an air ticket and arrived at the Budapest airport. When the authorities saw my passport, they said, "You are a journalist, you can't come in like this." "I'm here now," I answered.

It was Sunday. They said I had to report to the foreign ministry the following day and gave me a visa for twenty-four hours. The next day I got a four-day visa from the foreign ministry. I met the other members of the protest group in a cafe. One of them was Wolfgang, who had been in jail with me in Paris in 1963. They had passed through customs with leaflets in German and Hungarian strapped to their bodies. We planned the demonstration.

On September 24, 1968, in Liberation Square, we put up a large banner—END THE OCCUPATION OF CZECHOSLOVAKIA. A nearby policeman paid no attention until we started handing out leaflets to the large crowd which soon gathered. Ten minutes later the banner was torn down by plainclothes policemen. The crowd was broken up, and the five of us were arrested and taken to a barbershop until a police van arrived. We were told that giving out subversive leaflets in a socialist country meant from six months to three years in prison. That night we were driven to the political police headquarters and then to a large fortress, which was a prison. They put us in separate cells and gave us prisoners' uniforms.

In the interrogations which followed, the authorities wanted to know why we had chosen Budapest, what was behind our demonstration, who financed it, and who was our leader. After three days of hard interrogation, we were all expelled and driven to the Austrian border.

IT WAS IN BUDAPEST that I met a Hungarian painter, Hinsz Gyula, who gave me a painting on the theme of African liberation. It was a large painting, and a rucksack wanderer of my kind would have been unable to carry it and keep it safely. Nevertheless, it was so beautiful and precious that I took it with me to Prague. In the hotel where I was staying I met Canon John Collins, a champion of African liberation, who was attending a peace conference. What a surprise it was to meet him in a Prague hotel! I had met him in London during my walk around the world, and we had liked each other instantly. I realized that John Collins was the *supatra* (right pot) for the gift, so I gave him the painting.

We spent the next three days talking about the surge of revolutionary violence in Europe. John said, "It is good to see the young raising their voices against war and injustice, but throwing stones at the police is not going to take them very far. They need to learn the Gandhian way of civil disobedience" "Yes, I agree. They need training in nonviolence." "Nineteen sixty-nine will be the centenary of the birth of Mahatma Gandhi. It would be a real tribute to the great man if we established a school of nonviolence in London." He paused for a moment and then continued, "Will you come and help me do it?"

What a question! What a challenge! What an offer! My imagination took off in leaps and bounds. I flew with John to London. We made our plans on the plane. We decided to call it simply the London School of Nonviolence, and my book *Nonviolence or Nonexistence* was published to coincide with the opening of the school.

John introduced me to Colin Hodgetts, director of Christian Action, at the church of St. Martin-in-the-Fields in Trafalgar Square, where we established the school. Three evenings a week and during most weekends we held classes where I and others lectured on the theory of *satyagraha* (nonviolent resistance) and organized practical training in the methods of confronting the police without anger, protesting without hatred, and demonstrating for peace as well as being at peace.

But I was restless again, I missed my friends in India, and I grew tired of London. The pressures of city living, traveling in the underground, living in the crowds, shopping centers, fumes, and the whole consumer world were getting in my head and up my nose. I got the feeling that some part of me was dying, some part of me was suppressed. My legs were itching to be on the road and my eyes itching to see the blue sky over trees and mountains, rivers and deserts.

Canon Collins had promised to pay my plane fare back to India, but I persuaded him to buy me a secondhand car instead. It was Gandhi's centenary year. I painted a map of my overland route to India on the car together with several quotations from Gandhi and wrote to various people and groups on the way. Canon Collins's son Mark had just finished at Eton and was taking a year off before going to Oxford. "What better way to spend this year than to travel with you? And then I can see India. May I come with you?" asked Mark. "Of course. Traveling is always better with two." So we took off in our Ford Cortina. On the road again.

. . .

AFTER DRIVING for eighty days, we arrived in Delhi on October 2, 1969—the centenary of Gandhi's birth. Posters lined the streets, and near Gandhi's grave a gigantic 20-million-rupee exhibition had been set up, showing his life and message.

On my return to India, I heard the news that my old friend Dhani was on the run and that the police were searching for him because of his involvement in the armed struggle on behalf of the landless. My heart went out to my old friend. I was told that he was in Benares, so I went there and searched for him.

Since I had been away, the Naxalite movement had become strong in Bihar and Bengal, especially in Calcutta, where Naxalite activity had created such panic that it was virtually a police state. Every day there were bombings and killings of landlords and police.

After telephoning friends who might know of Dhani's whereabouts, I was given an address. I went to the house, only to be told that he had left a few days before, but they gave me another address. Dhani had also left that place; at every address I went to, it was the same story. He was in hiding, changing his address to prevent anyone from finding him. I left messages at the various addresses, asking him to contact me.

Late one night, when everyone else was asleep and it was totally quiet, I was woken by a knock at the door. It was Dhani. "All those who want a real revolution should join the Naxalite movement," he said. His eyes penetrated into me. The power of his argument was less strong than the power of his eyes and his physical presence, especially late at night in the small, dark room with only a lantern burning. Dhani said, "The landlords will never give up unless there is an armed struggle. The enemy today is subtle and difficult to pin down. We cannot use the same tactics and strategy as Gandhi used during the independence movement." I said, "The state is too powerful for armed resistance. We have to find another way. Unless the oppressed are aware of their oppression, they will never get rid of it." "So our task is to fight on their behalf," said Dhani.

When it started to grow light, he said he couldn't stay any longer—it was dangerous for him to be in the streets in daylight. He left, and I lay down but couldn't sleep. My mind was spinning round and round. I was thinking about the culture of violence in Europe. I was thinking about the London School of Nonviolence, and I was asking myself, Is India any better? I was shocked, saddened, and challenged.

.   .   .

VINOBA HAD DESIGNATED one of his closest disciples, Krishna Raj Bhai, together with about a hundred gramdan workers, to turn the principle of gramdan into reality in Saharsa district. Saharsa is one of the poorest parts of Bihar, where 70 percent of the people were landless laborers. Krishna Raj Bhai was a close friend of mine. He wrote to me: "If gramdan succeeds in Saharsa, the movement succeeds for the whole of India. The Naxalite movement is spreading into Saharsa and has made people believe that unless there is an armed struggle, nothing is going to change. This is the testing point, the last battle for victory. I would like you to come here and see what we are doing." So I went to Saharsa.

The town of Saharsa was neither a village nor a city. It was a newly created government settlement with badly-built houses and shacks, crowded with the landless from the villages and the jobless from the city. There were over five hundred villages in Saharsa district, which was divided into twenty-two blocks, each having its headquarters town, under which there were a number of villages. One hundred gramdan workers were divided up among the twenty-two blocks, with Krishna Raj Bhai acting as coordinator. I was assigned to a group whose task it was to organize land distribution in the village of Chatrapur.

As I was walking to Chatrapur along a track, a man suddenly stepped out of a bamboo thicket onto the path. He was dressed in laborer's clothes and carried a long, oiled bamboo staff. "Where are you going?" he demanded aggressively. "What is it to you where I am going?" I replied. "What are you here for, then?" "I am with the gramdan workers," I replied. "Keep off this area, and don't interfere and delay our revolution. You might distribute some land, which is probably barren, since the landlord didn't want it, and you will make a big noise about it. What is a little bit of land? Hardly enough for a dozen families. Let the dissatisfaction get deeper into the hearts of the people, and let the landless, who are in the majority, unite to fight the landlords. Only then will this problem be solved." I asked him how he thought the revolution would take place. "Revolution will come when every peasant rises up and seizes all the land, every inch of it." His voice was strong and full of conviction. "Vinoba is a saint perhaps, but a state-appointed saint. He never says anything against the government." "Are you a Naxalite?" I asked. "There is no such thing as Naxalism," he replied impatiently. "That is just a name given by the press. We are Marxist-Leninists." After that he remained silent and at the next village, turned to go.

Chatrapur was a large village. The rich lived in the wide, square bazaar in large brick houses, replacing their thatched roofs with modern corrugated iron. In the front courtyards stood large granaries, the symbols of wealth. The laborers lived in ghettos in the surrounding neighborhood, so overcrowded that the little bamboo huts stood back to back, each family sprawling into the next. I was invited to stay at the local school. That evening I went to an area where the landless laborers lived. Men sat around the glow of a straw fire. I greeted them, but their reply was silence and suspicious glances. I edged my way into the circle and introduced myself. "Chatrapur is a gramdan village, isn't it?" I asked. They replied, "The Vinoba people came a long time ago and took signatures—they promised us land. Then some communists came and promised to give land. And the government officials have been promising for the last year. But it seems as if we won't get anything until after we are dead. At the moment we are not even sure if our huts are safe, and our masters have given notice to stop us sharecropping their land."

A young voice spoke out of the darkness. "A few days ago a strange man came here. He said he was a new kind of communist and that the old communists who came before had made a pact with the landlords and won't help us anymore. He said that voting is no more use now, that we will have to fight the landlords ourselves, and that in some districts the fighting has already begun. We might have to kill our masters, he said, because unless we do something and are ready to act ourselves, we will never get land. Is that true?" "Was he from Chatrapur?" I asked. "He came from outside. He didn't tell us his name—he just arrived one evening, bringing his food. He stayed for two or three hours and left the same night. He belonged to our caste, though."

How could I hope to win their support and gain their confidence by giving more words, then deserting them again? What right had I to try to create suspicion in their minds in regard to a man who came from the same caste, brought his food, and experienced the exploitation not merely intellectually but physically? After all, who was I? Someone who wore clothes worth enough to feed a whole family for a month. What a vast gulf separated them from me! Why should they believe me? Dozens of politicians and gramdan workers had come before, and what could I tell them that was new? I said, "When the times comes for revolution, we will see. But at the moment, why don't we try to get the land some other way first? If you are all ready, we can ask the landlord straightaway. If it works, why resort to violence?"

Heads nodded slowly in agreement, but not confidently. They could only see the landlords in their normal role as oppressors who goaded them to work harder and harder. I was seized by a feeling of frustration as I gazed into the leaping flames, watching the straw consumed to make white-hot ashes.

After seeing the despair and hopelessness of the landless and the cynical resistance of the landlords in Chatrapur, I was filled with grief and compassion. I was grateful to Krishna Raj for bringing me literally down to earth and allowing me to participate in the herculean task of land reform in India.

ONE DAY IN BENARES, my friend Anant said to me, "My father has a farm in the forest, where very few people live. I would like to leave Benares—and I could persuade my father to give us some land." I said, "Can we go to see the place tomorrow?"

The next morning at dawn we drove out of Benares, then headed south through the Vindhaya mountains. We arrived at Jumudi village, where Anant's father had his farm. We got out of the car and sat under a mango tree by a well. People from the village brought us pomegranates, papayas, and other fruit. The village consisted of tribal mud huts, with colored clay painted on the walls. Around the huts were the animals— goats, cows, and buffalo. There was a large monsoon pond with buffalo in it.

We walked into the forest to see the land. The forest itself was silent, full of herbs and wild fruit trees, and there was a river. We felt this was the right place for us. Anant and I built our own little hut and started living in the forest among the tribal people. We worked on the land, grew vegetables, and cooked food. Anant's father gave him twenty-five acres of land, but there was no water on it, so we asked a dowser from the village to help us locate water. He walked around, looking at the color of the leaves and vegetation, then told us to begin digging near some anthills.

For three months we dug the well, our bodies covered with earth from lifting it and carrying it in buckets on our heads. We went on digging, trying to finish it by the beginning of the monsoon. When we had dug down thirty feet, we hit rock. We went on digging, and then one day, the earth started bubbling. We had hit water!

The monsoon was over, and everyone was busy harvesting. Every day was spent out in the fields with other people, cutting the golden brown rice with a sickle and stacking it in rows. The whole village cooperated. It was so different from Saharsa—one day people gathered to harvest one farmer's land, then they moved on to harvest another's. When all the grain was gathered in, the farmers distributed it to the craftsmen of the villages—the shoemaker, carpenter, potter, washerman, cowherd, blacksmith, and the Brahmin priest, to settle accounts until the next harvest came. Then there was a big festival to mark the completion of the harvest—*diwali,* the festival of lights. The people ate, drank, dressed up and danced, and went from village to village, visiting each other. What a delight it was for me to see old India surviving intact in this tribal land.

Every morning I got up with the sunrise. After doing yoga and working in the fields, I lay down under the sun and was massaged by Anant, feeling the slow touch and quiet movement of hands on the body, feeling the muscles and nerves and bones and flesh relaxing. Then, using mustard oil, I massaged each toe of my foot, each part of my ankles and heels and instep. Afterwards, I bathed at the well.

Gardening became a real joy—looking at each plant growing every day, seeing the leaves coming, then the flowers, and after a few days the fruit, which then became bigger and bigger; and every day weeding, putting water and manure down, and tying plants with string if they were blown over.

Often I walked by myself in the riverbed, which had many bends. There were trees with roots exposed by the river, and flowers and leaves and butterflies all around. Other days I went with the village people to get wild honey from the forest trees. We made a fire under a tree and waited until the bees flew away and the honey dripped into a pot under the combs.

Every night the tribal people lit a bonfire. A lot of people gathered around it. Someone started playing the flute and drums, and all the people joined in, singing and dancing and chanting, going deeper into the night, deeper into the music, deeper into the flames of the fire. In their chanting, dancing, and music, they forgot everything and became absolutely absorbed, in union with themselves and their whole existence.

.   .   .

ONE MORNING I GOT UP EARLY and walked into the forest. It was dawn. There was dew on the grass and leaves. I came to a tall tree with large overhanging branches, sat down cross-legged under the tree, and closed my eyes. I looked into my body and saw a dark tunnel, a deep hollow inside. I went into it, drawn inwards.

Instead of smelling outside, my nose was smelling the inner happenings and my ears were hearing the sounds inside. I could hear the sounds and voices of the ego pushing me in different directions. But I sat quietly. Slowly the battle calmed down, it slowly faded away. Gradually peace came.

I saw the events of my life as one thread, the same thread which united the whole universe and which was each person. I saw a struggle without conflict, a pain without misery. I saw a love so great that it had to remain hidden. I felt myself part of my mother and father, and in all the people through whom I had been expressed. I was being reborn. I felt like a child, like an innocent person, just living and growing, engaged in the journey from action to nonaction, from struggle without to struggle within. Life was an eternal journey, a journey to the center, the source, searching for the soul.

Everything became meditation. I felt a sense of divinity. This newness brought a surrender, a surrender where nothing mattered, where everything was accepted. It was beyond happiness, beyond pleasure. I experienced the zero level of existence, the void, the beauty of the void and the beauty of nothingness: *shunyata.*

I opened my eyes. I saw a snake about three yards long curled around the trunk of the tree beside me. I sat still. The snake disappeared into a hole among the roots. I must have sat there for six hours, for when I returned it was after ten o'clock.

—⊗⊗⊗—

CHAPTER 8

Mukti

AFTER I HAD BEEN LIVING IN THE FOREST for a year, I walked with Anant one morning to the town of Anuppur, five miles away, to buy some food in the market that was held there every Wednesday. There was an astrologer in the marketplace who predicted the future by calculating how the stars and planets affected a person at a particular moment. He was a coarse-faced sadhu, skinny, short, and dark, with a shaven head and light brown robe, sitting on the floor cross-legged with a young disciple and several townspeople around him. When I arrived he asked me why I had come so late. The way he spoke, it was as if he had been waiting for me. I didn't answer.

He said, "I speak only between nine and twelve o'clock, and after twelve I keep silent. Now it is coming close to twelve." He went on, "You have a very good friend. He trusts you, you trust him. He supports you in everything. You are happy with his support, but his wife thinks you are an enemy. She wants to change her husband's mind. She quarrels with him and with you." That was my relationship with Anant and his wife. Then he said, "Very soon you are going on a long journey over the ocean . . ." I interrupted him, saying that I had just returned from Europe and had no desire to go away again. "What I see, I tell you," he said. "Once you are in the far land, you are going to meet someone in that land who will completely change your life." He paused and said, "Now it is twelve o'clock. It is time for my silence, and I cannot speak anymore." He then closed his eyes and withdrew into himself. I gave him a gift of five rupees and left.

It was an astonishing prediction. Within days of this meeting, the war began in Bangladesh and millions of refugees started pouring into India. Canon Collins wrote asking me to give him a firsthand account of what was happening, then suggested I come to England with information and photographs to put on an exhibition about Bangladesh which Christian Action would sponsor. The words of the sadhu came true. I collected photographs of the refugees and flew to London.

The exhibition was in the crypt of St. Martin-in-the-Fields in London in July 1971. I asked Operation Omega (formed to get peace workers across the borders into Bangladesh) if they could send someone to talk about their work at the exhibition. They sent June.

I stood in the crypt watching the guests arrive. It was a Saturday afternoon. From the dark crypt of the church, I saw the sun shining outside. There was a lull for a few minutes when no one came in. And then I saw someone coming, a young woman of extraordinary radiance. The light was on her back as she came down the steps of the crypt. Her silhouetted figure was captivating: my whole attention was held like magic. I had never seen anyone like her before. "I am June, from Operation Omega," she said. "I was in Bangladesh just before the war broke out. Now I am helping the movement for the freedom of Bangladesh."

After the meeting I said to her, "I am planning to take this exhibition around Europe. Would you like to come with me to speak about your experiences of Bangladesh?"

She said, "No." The answer was very firm. The only thought in my mind was if I would ever see her again.

After my tour of Europe, I went back to London, where I received the news of my mother's death:

At the age of eighty your mother felt that she had served the family and fulfilled all her duties and that now it was time for her to meet death. She decided to separate herself from her worn-out body by fasting. She had no fear of death. She believed that only death could bring new life and that she must die to live again. She went around the town, to family and friends, saying good-bye and asking forgiveness for any wrong she may have done. From the next day's sunrise she took no more food or drink except a little boiled water. The news of your mother's fast unto death spread by word of mouth. Monks came to bless her and be blessed, since it is considered brave and holy to die in this way—to embrace death rather than let it capture you unaware. Hundreds of people came to have her last darshan and to ask for forgiveness. She didn't talk much but by her look acknowledged the receiving and giving of forgiveness. People sat outside singing songs and praying. After thirty-five days of fasting, your mother died.

I received this news with a mixture of sadness and celebration. Even though I was a rejected son, I always felt a benevolent protection coming from her to me. The thought that I no longer had a mother sent a shiver down my spine. But what a brave and wise mother she was! I have met many people—gurus, teachers, poets, philosophers, and celebrities—but none could compare with my mother in her simple wisdom. She was illiterate, she could not even sign her name, but she was pure and truthful. She brought us up, all eight of her children, to be true to ourselves. "Human relationships are the greatest wealth you have, do not abuse it," she would say. "When God made time he made plenty of it, so what is the rush?" she would say. "Friends first, business later," she would say. Her words always ring in my head. Physically she is no more, but her wisdom is eternal.

MY ONLY REASON for coming to London again was to find June and see her once more. I phoned the office of Operation Omega, but I was told that she was not there. I kept phoning. In the end I was told she was ill. I went to see her at her home. I knocked on the front door. For a few minutes nothing happened, then she opened it. She was in her dressing gown.

I stepped back and said, "How are you? I hear you're not well." She smiled and said, "Come in."

June was alone in the house and had not eaten all day. I went to the kitchen and found half a cabbage. I put the cabbage soup on to boil, then took some oil from the kitchen and massaged June's stomach, head, legs, and feet. Later I gave her the soup to drink. I read to her, and she fell asleep. As she was sleeping, I looked closely at her face, wondering if this was the person the astrologer in India had said would change my life. That night I slept downstairs on a couch, and next morning I got up early to make her some tea. June got well soon, and her home became my home. Spring came, and we sat in the garden. Memories and contacts with India, family, and friends seemed like a thousand years ago. My beard and hair grew long with love.

June told me of a dream she often used to have in her childhood. A vast desert stretched out before her, and in the distance was a figure. It was a man walking across the desert toward her. She was terrified. She always woke up before the man could reach her, while he was still walking, never reaching his destination.

In the summer we traveled from London to Stockholm to attend the first UN conference on the environment, and stayed there for two weeks, in a peaceful flat. There, in the complete acceptance of each other, feeling a sense of warmth, touch, and belonging, we conceived a child.

In the autumn we went to live in a commune of European peace workers in a small village in Germany. There, June and I worked in the garden, cooked together, practiced yoga and meditation, and every afternoon for an hour went walking together—sometimes to the forest near the house, sometimes along a river called "the inner stream," sometimes to the town three miles away. We enjoyed the trees, air, and fields and told each other stories. Then every evening I massaged June with oil and felt the child move as I was doing so. We thought that as we were feeling a sense of freedom at that time, this feeling should be part of our child's name. So we decided on the name Mukti, which means "freedom" in Sanskrit.

At the beginning of March 1973, just before Mukti was due to be born, we returned to London by train. I had a dream. In this dream I said to June, "I know where my soul is. Hurry, let's go." We started walking and came to a thick forest. June held on to my shirt. Then we climbed mountains so high that we passed through the clouds. Coming down the other side, we were stopped by soldiers, who allowed us to cross their country only if we did it in one day and didn't stay the night. They escorted us.

We came to a river. June and I walked on opposite banks. I became a woman in a pink and orange dress. A man rode toward us on an elephant, peered closely at us, then rode on. June walked over the water to me, and we shouted to the man on the elephant. He told us he was searching for Satish to tell him not to worry, that his soul was safe. I said I was Satish. He was surprised I was a woman. He turned his elephant around and rode in front of us. I saw mountains in the distance. Night fell, and there was a long line of people coming down the mountainside with flaming torches, disappearing and appearing again as they came down a winding path. We walked on. The procession came toward me; one of the people was carrying a golden box on his head. I opened it. Inside was a bundle of silk cloth, which I unwrapped. Inside the silk was a lotus, and wrapped in the petals of the lotus I found the word *Atman*. I had found my soul.

A few days later Mukti was born. I sat on the bed beside June, helping her to push. At the moment of birth I was holding June's body in my arms, June was pushing—and Mukti was revealed.

I CAN'T IMAGINE what life would have been for me without the canal leading from Camden to Regent's Park. From spring to summer I would rise early, take a walk along the canal, and run barefoot on the cool grass of the park. Squeaking squirrels, tall trees, and the quacking ducks swimming in the lakes—the park was an oasis of peace, surrounded by the traffic jams and their poisonous fumes. Like a tunnel, the canal leads to this oasis, hardly noticing the monstrosity of industrial London.

When I missed my morning yoga of taking this walk, I would go with June and Mukti in the afternoon. One such afternoon, returning to Kentish Town, I saw a man busy planting flowers in a window box. He resembled John Papworth, but it couldn't be, since he was in Zambia working as an adviser to President Kaunda; and if he were in London, he would surely be in his own comfortable house in St. John's Wood. As I was coming to this conclusion, he turned, and I saw that it truly was John Papworth. We fell into each other's arms, filled with the pleasure of meeting. He invited us in. Almost the first thing he said was that *Resurgence* magazine, which he had founded, was about to be closed down for the want of an editor, an editor who would work for love rather than money. "So, Satish, God sent me to find you here, and I daresay that you will be the editor, and let us speak no more of it."

I was taken aback. "I have never learned proper English, had no schooling, and I can't spell a word. True, I can speak it, but with this little knowledge of English, how can I edit a magazine with the reputation of *Resurgence?*" "You can and you will, especially with the help of your companion, June. You will have no trouble." Thus *Resurgence* fell into my lap. It was summer 1973. I decided to put my energies into the magazine for a year or so and get it off the ground once again. I didn't like to deny the request of an old friend or to refuse something which was coming to me by fate. I decided to put off thoughts of returning to India with June and Mukti until the end of 1975.

I should have known that life does not operate on the basis of plans, no matter how rational. My nature is to let things happen rather than make them happen, and I felt that I should stick to it. So the plan to go to India was interrupted by the onset of dictatorial rule there in June 1975. The prime minister of India, Mrs. Indira Gandhi, had declared a state of emergency, and a large number of my friends and colleagues were put behind bars. A total censorship of the press and curtailment of normal civil liberties was enforced. The greatest shock of all was the arrest of J. P. Narayan, with whom I had worked closely.

I canceled the scheduled meeting of the London School of Nonviolence and instead held an emergency meeting on India. Nearly one hundred people gathered at the school in the crypt of St. Martin-in-the-Fields. From there we launched the Free J.P. Campaign and invited Philip Noel-Baker, who in the British Parliament had moved the bill for the independence of India, to preside over it. I edited and produced a fortnightly news sheet *Swaraj,* a digest of news and comment about India published in the European and American papers. This circulated clandestinely in India from hand to hand and was even smuggled into prisons. This voice of solidarity strengthened the courage and the struggle of the resistance movement. My own return to India was postponed indefinitely, since there was no point in walking into a jail, which—my friends in India wrote—would be my fate. I could perhaps help the resistance movement more from the outside. Sarur Hoda and others had their passports impounded, and my name was certainly on the government's list.

I organized the first European Sarvodaya conference in the Conway Hall, to introduce the true nature of J.P.'s movement, as well as to show the relevance of Gandhi's ideas to Western industrial societies. Lanza del Vasto, E. F. Schumacher, John Seymour, Leopold Kohr, Edward

Goldsmith, and Thich Nhat Hanh were among the speakers. Five hundred people turned up.

The political situation in India was such that I could not return, so I began to look for somewhere to live in a rural area, where I could combine the intellectual work of editing *Resurgence* with the manual work of growing food.

CHAPTER 9

E. F. Schumacher

I MET E. F. SCHUMACHER in 1968 after reading his essay on Buddhist economics. Nothing before and nothing since have I read by a Western economist which moved me so much. Here was a voice of wisdom and reason united. The moment I read his essay, I phoned him. "Come to my office at the National Coal Board," he said, "and we will have lunch together." He took me to an Italian restaurant, and we lunched and talked for two hours. It was instantly a meeting of minds, and the beginning of a relationship which was to last beyond his death.

When I took over the editorship of *Resurgence* in 1973, again I went to see Schumacher at his home in Caterham, Surrey. Although he had written occasional articles for *Resurgence* while John Papworth was editor, I wanted to persuade him to write for every issue. When we had finished our business discussions, he gave me a guided tour of his garden and home. He was very pleased with his motorized wheelbarrow as an example of appropriate technology. He said, "When you get old like me, you need some power-assisted tools, but technology should not replace human input—rather, the role of technology is to aid human hands." He had just planted forty trees in his garden and was very proud of them. "Silviculture and forest farming are the only way to safeguard our future and the health of the planet," he said.

When we returned to the house, he showed me his hand-operated flour mill, which had two millstones for grinding flour for domestic use. "This is my pride and joy," he announced. "I grind wheat which I buy directly from the organic farm of Sam Mayall and bake bread for my family for the week. Bread made from freshly ground flour is vastly superior to other breads. So those who want the most nutritious bread must grind their own flour. Many people eat bread which has little more nutritional value than a paper napkin."

He believed that the decisions he made which affected everyday life were as important as his advice on policy matters to the National Coal Board, where he was head of the Statistics Department.

As Schumacher talked, I felt that I was in the presence of a great man, someone who could see the truth beyond received opinions. "Any fool can make things complicated, but it requires a genius to make things simple." He expressed his exasperation with our high-technology society, which makes life unnecessarily complicated.

He was sent by the British government to advise the government of Burma. Recalling his time there, he said, "Within a few weeks of my arrival in Rangoon and after visiting a few villages and towns, I realized that the Burmese needed little advice from a Western economist like me. In fact we Western economists could learn a thing or two from the Burmese. They have a perfectly good economic system, which has supported a highly developed religion and culture and produced not only enough rice for their own people but also a surplus for the markets of India.

"When I published my findings in Burma under the title of *Buddhist Economics,* a number of my economist colleagues said, 'Mr. Schumacher, what does economics have to do with Buddhism?' My answer was simply that economics without Buddhism is like sex without love. Economics without spirituality can give you temporary and physical gratification, but it cannot provide an internal fulfillment. Spiritual economics brings service, compassion, and relationships into equal play with profit and efficiency. We need both, and we need them simultaneously."

Schumacher was one of the first Western economists who dared to put those two words—*Buddhist* and *economics*—together. This was an act of courage. When his fellow economists called him a crank, Schumacher took it with a sense of humor. He said, "What is wrong with being a crank? The crank is the part of the machine which creates revolution, and it is very small. I am a small revolutionary! It is a compliment."

It was in Burma that he got the idea of intermediate technology. "The Buddha taught the value of the Middle Path. For instance, in agriculture many Third World countries still use sickle technology to harvest their crops. This could be called stage one. Whereas in the West we have the automated and highly sophisticated combine harvester, which has nearly eliminated the human element in farming altogether. This could be called stage ten. So I thought: what has happened to all the stages in between? This is my theory of the disappearing middle. As a consequence, I launched the Intermediate Technology Development Group to research and reintroduce some of those middle technologies which are human-friendly, environment-friendly, and which render considerable help to farmers around the world without the depletion of resources and loss of employment that high technology involves."

At that time he had just published his first book, *Small is Beautiful;* he gave me a copy, eagerly explaining why he attached so much value to the question of smallness. "Industrial and technological advancement is obsessed with the economics of scale. As a result, huge bureaucracies, giant companies, and enormous factories have come to be seen as the symbols of success. But the reality is that things are done according to the rules, and human relationships have become secondary. As giant technologies are antihuman, so are giant organizations. In big schools, pupils are reduced to numbers; in big hospitals, patients are reduced to numbers; in big factories, workers are reduced to numbers. Economics should serve the values of humanity and even the spiritual growth of human beings. In my view that cannot happen if our organizations are beyond a certain size. That is why I called my book *Small is Beautiful.*" I had not heard this kind of philosophy in the West— and from an economist who had been through Oxford, *The Times,* and a national- ized industry.

From November 1973 to August 1977 he contributed twenty-three articles to *Resurgence.* When I phoned to discuss them, he listened care- fully and was prepared to alter or shorten his pieces to fit the magazine. He was one of the easiest authors to work with, but he preferred a clean, clear layout for his articles. Once our adventurous *Resurgence* designer put a faint illustration as a background to the whole page. He didn't like that and said so. "The purpose of design is to make reading easier, not more difficult," he said.

My association with E. F. Schumacher was a deep learning experience. His courageous and eccentric idealism stood before me as a beacon of inspiration. Therefore, when his daughter-in-law, Diana Schumacher, phoned me to say, "During a train journey from Zurich to Berne in Switzerland, Fritz met with a heart attack and died," I was profoundly shocked. It was not only the loss of a personal friend, it was also the loss of a close colleague whose energy, enthusiasm and activism had been fueling the movement for social and spiritual transformation. Upon receiving the sad news, I called my friends John Seymour, Leopold Kohr, Maurice Ash, and Elaine Morgan to discuss what we should do. Within weeks we established the Schumacher Society and announced that we would hold a series of annual lectures in his honor so that the vision and worldview for which E. F. Schumacher was working could be further developed and moved forward.

The Schumacher Lectures became an outstanding success. Year after year people from all over Britain gathered in Bristol to proclaim and strengthen the onward march of the green movement. Ivan Illich, Amory Lovins, R. D. Laing, Fritjof Capra, Hazel Henderson, Lester Brown, Wendell Berry, Gary Snyder, Vandana Shiva, Wangari Maathai, Maneka Gandhi, and dozens of others who formed the backbone of the ecological worldview presented their groundbreaking ideas on these occasions. These lectures proved to be an appropriate tribute to this remarkable thinker and I am delighted to have played a pivotal role in establishing them.

ENCOURAGED BY THE SUCCESS of the British Schumacher Society, I went to the United States, where I found a receptive group of friends. I was able to persuade Bob Swann, the founder of the Land Trust Movement, and his partner, Susan Witt, a tireless campaigner for local economy, to take the lead and establish an autonomous E. F. Schumacher Society in the United States. Kirkpatrick Sale, the author of *Human Scale,* and David Ehrenfeld, author of *The Arrogance of Humanism* and a biology professor at Rutgers, were among the early supporters. In the United States, too, annual lectures were established as in Britain and with similar success.

Because of these societies and lectures Schumacher's name has become synonymous with a decentralist, biocentric, low-tech, nonconsumerist, egalitarian outlook. Schumacher's name also unites ecologists around the world who are otherwise unable to find a common intellectual view.

Out of the Schumacher Societies and Schumacher Lectures grew Schumacher College, which I describe in a later chapter.

—⦿—

CHAPTER 10

Maya

Editing and publishing *Resurgence,* a magazine advocating decentralization, from the metropolitan center of London was not in keeping with our aims; so when the opportunity of moving to Wales presented itself, I welcomed it. Wales is a small nation; it has not lost its cultural identity, and I felt so much at home. The hills of the Prescelis and the gentler slopes of Carn Ingli moved me deeply. When I went to live in Wales, I made a vow that I would not travel out of the country for one year, and that I would allow myself to put my roots down there and learn the Welsh language.

At the Sarvodaya conference I had met an old friend, Peggy Hemming, an Oxford economist who was deeply interested in the ideas of Gandhi and rural regeneration. I said to her, "If we want to be part of a sustainable future, people need to return to the land, and we ourselves must set an example."

Peggy totally agreed with me and said, "This is music to my ears. I have inherited some money; the best use of my resources would be to invest in the land, and in people who could live in a community working that land."

Ever since the Sarvodaya conference, John Seymour had been encouraging us to move from the city and return to the land. He said to us, "Ninety-five percent of British people are living in cities, working in the industrial economy, and the five percent who are left in rural England have turned agriculture into industry and business. This type of lifestyle is unsustainable and is bound to bring an ecological catastrophe—the only way to save the Earth is for people to learn the practical skills of self-sufficiency." John's message touched our hearts. We went to see him and his wife, Sally, on their farm, Fachongle Isaf, in Wales. It was truly a moving experience. Our lunch consisted of homegrown vegetables, homemade cheese and butter, with bread baked that morning from the wheat grown on his farm, together with home-brewed beer. There were young people plowing the land, tending the vegetable garden, churning the butter, mending fences, taking care of the cows, chickens, ducks, and bees. Sally was a supreme example of self-sufficiency in action. There was almost nothing that she could not do. She was a magnificent illustrator and potter, drawing cats, chickens, cows, and owls on tiles, bowls, and plates which she made. She was also spinning, knitting, and weaving wool from her Jacob sheep which she had sheared herself.

John and Sally's three daughters and son were also engaged in the activities of organic farming and crafts. This example of culture and agriculture embodied in their lives made us feel envious, and we wanted to lose no time in beginning a lifestyle which would incorporate some of the features that we had just seen.

Peggy, June, and I were of one mind in our desire to come and live near John and Sally. Peggy was ready with her checkbook if there was any small farm we could acquire. And we were lucky. Within walking distance from John and Sally was Pentre Ifan, which was for sale. We went to see it and instantly fell in love with it. A modest old house with a considerable number of outbuildings, woodland, running stream, spring water for drinking, fertile soil, and a view from the kitchen window of the cromlech—a sacred site of standing stones some thousands of years old. It seemed an ideal place, and we bought it with Peggy's money. Tony, Vivian, and Ian, three young people also inspired by the ideals of ecological farming and community life, joined us.

WE STARTED WITH FOUR GOATS, digging the land for a vegetable garden. It was July 1976. By December we had purchased a cow. These

were a most exhilarating six months, working on the land in the mornings and editing *Resurgence* in the afternoons. However, these six months
also proved to be months of discussion, debate, and disagreement among
ourselves. Ninety-six acres of farmland seemed to be too big for us inex-
perienced communards to manage. My inclination was to work with
ten acres and leave the rest fallow for a while until we got our plans
worked out, but Tony and Peggy felt that this way we would be wasting
the land. They felt it would be better to purchase a tractor, have more
animals on the land, and make as much hay as possible, either to feed
our own animals or to sell. To me that seemed rather like conventional
farming, not the kind of ecological, organic, and sustainable principles
which had drawn me to the land. I would have liked increased wilderness and more people working the land with hand tools, rather than
mechanization and meat production.

The debate became intense, and disagreements disturbed the fragile
basis upon which all of us had come together. Tony and Vivian left;
that shook Peggy's confidence—she felt that my approach was impractical. Peggy went to see her family for Christmas and never returned.
June, Ian, Mukti, and I were left on the farm. As a compromise measure
we rented most of the land to a neighboring farmer and kept a ten-acre
field for our cow and goats.

I had not imagined that things would turn sour so soon and that
dreams would be shattered so quickly. Early in 1977 I received a letter
from Peggy saying that in her view our experiment had no future and
therefore she would like to offer the farm to Urdd Gobaith Cymru, the
Welsh youth organization. I could not believe my eyes when I read the
letter: this was totally and utterly unexpected.

I wrote back to Peggy saying that it was still possible to rescue our
project. We had given up everything to come to Wales, and now we
had nowhere to go; but that did not move her, so I proposed a compromise. Let the Urdd have eighty-six acres with the extensive outbuildings, and let ten acres and the house be put into a trust dedicated to
an experimental project for self-sufficiency, organic farming, and the
publication of *Resurgence*. But something had happened: factors and
events unknown to me had totally changed Peggy's mind. Either she
became disillusioned or disappointed—she wanted us to leave Pentre
Ifan. I talked to John Seymour and Leopold Kohr (a friend of Peggy's
and mine), as well as Gwynfor Evans, who was a Welsh nationalist, a

supporter of Urdd, and our friend. The three of them said that it was unfair of Peggy, and they supported the compromise we were proposing.

For the first time in our lives we had to consult a solicitor and a barrister and decided to take the matter to court. During this time June became pregnant with Maya, and therefore the threat of being made homeless caused even greater anguish. Never in my life could I remember a time when I had endured such a failure of friendship.

An astrologer friend looked at my birth chart and concluded that Saturn was overshadowing the entire year of 1977. As a result, things were bound to be difficult, and therefore I should just keep going. That gave me some consolation, but nothing could really soften the blow of a failed experiment, a failed friendship, and the possibility of being forced out of our home.

As we carried on, our solicitor advised that the best course for us was to sit tight and let Peggy go to court and get an eviction order. I wrote to Peggy, urging her to wait until our child was born, as it would be too traumatic to find a new home in the present circumstances. That slowed down the proceedings and gave us a few months of respite. In the meantime, we looked forward to the birth. Mukti had been born in the hospital, and June was determined to avoid a repetition of the experience. She wanted to have a home birth, but very few doctors seemed to like the idea. The conventional wisdom was that pregnancy should be treated as if it was an illness. If the mother was at home rather than in the hospital for the birth, it would cause too much inconvenience to doctors and midwives if there was any complication or emergency. So never mind freedom of choice and the wishes of the mother—everyone was insisting on a hospital birth.

But as it happened, a new doctor arrived in Newport whose wife was a nurse and who believed in giving mothers the choice between hospital delivery and home birth. Through a common friend, June met Judy and Roger, and to our great delight they agreed to assist in the birth of the baby at home. Once Roger committed himself, the district midwife also expressed her enthusiasm and preparedness to be on call.

IT WAS OCTOBER 29. Mary Tasker and Jane Thomas from Bath, and Sue Blennerhesset from London were staying with us for a few days. Sian Roberts was working for *Resurgence* and living with us, so there was a soft and supportive feminine atmosphere in the house. June was relaxed, happy, and at ease—what a contrast to the pressures which we had gone through at the time of Mukti's birth! This time she was in command of her own body and her situation.

At about six o'clock in the evening, June thought labor had started and wondered whether she should go and lie down. I said, "Don't go and lie down, better to stay, engage in talk with our guests, and in this way be distracted from your pains." At about eight o'clock she decided to go and lie upstairs as the pains were stronger and she needed to concentrate on her breathing. At about nine o'clock she was convinced that the birth was imminent yet still felt strong enough to come downstairs and phone the midwife and the doctor. At 9:45 the midwife arrived, and at 10:00 we saw the head of the baby. Mary, Jane, Sue, and Sian were all present in the room. As I saw the head, I rushed to Mukti, who was fast asleep. "Mukti, Mukti, wake up, the baby is being born." He rushed out of his bed and came to watch the new baby being born. June hung on to me as she breathed and pushed. None of our four female friends had had the experience of giving birth, so for them this was an electrifying occasion. There was a sigh of relief when the midwife held the baby in her hands and said, "It's a girl."

We called her Maya. Mukti represented our longing for liberation, and she came to us in the midst of worldly engagement. Maya was the mother of the Buddha; Maya was the ancient culture in South America; Mair is the Welsh name for the mother of Jesus; Maya is the world we see; Maya is the wealth and beauty of life; Maya is our daughter. Her birth proved to be a turning point. When Maya came, Saturn was becoming weak and his influence was waning. I felt a new sense of optimism. Gwynfor Evans communicated with Peggy that her support of the Welsh Youth would be of no help if that meant making Satish and his young family homeless. She must find a solution by which Urdd would be helped and Satish would be happy. This was strong advice from an elderly Welsh statesman. Even if Peggy was not moved by this advice, Urdd was. They communicated with me stating that they would like to maintain the farm as an undivided unit, but they would be prepared to make me some financial compensation which would enable me to purchase a house for my family. This was a gesture of goodwill, and I wanted to go with the flow rather than fight. Nevertheless, all the negotiations went at a snail's pace, and it was not until the end of 1978 that a written agreement was reached. I accepted the sum of £9,000 and a year in which to find a new home.

Meanwhile, we continued to edit, manage, and publish *Resurgence* from our home. This was a big change in my working pattern. In London, the *Resurgence* office and my work with Christian Action had been based in the East End, but we lived in Radlett. I used to leave home at 8:00 A.M. by train, changing at Kings Cross for the underground, and arriving at my office at 9:30. Again in the evening I had to commute back and arrived home at seven o'clock in the evening. Physically and psychologically, I used to become totally drained. The only thing I did for our son, Mukti, was to read him bedtime stories, and the only satisfactory time I spent with June was during the weekends. It was a time when I felt emotionally and spiritually starved. That pattern of life was alien to me, but large numbers of people in the modern world consider it normal. No wonder family relationships in industrialized societies are at such a low ebb.

Even though our life in Wales had the constant strain of uncertainty and tension, June and I shared our lives much more intimately. I milked the cow, June made the butter and cheese, I cooked the evening meal, June prepared the lunch, and we both worked in the vegetable garden. We read together every article which came for publication in *Resurgence* and all the letters from our readers and contributors. With a group of voluntary helpers, June and I dispatched the magazine. In every sense of the word it was a true partnership. We shared the joys and pains of life as companions. There was no division between living and earning a livelihood, there was no division between intellectual work and practical work, there was no division between man's work and woman's work, and there was no division between home and office. I felt particularly happy that June and I were bringing up the children together.

Growing up in this kind of shared experience, Maya was an extremely happy baby. Bringing her up was not a burden for us. By now Mukti was big enough to come with me to bring the cow in from the field and stay with me while I was milking. He was also big enough to entertain and amuse Maya. Unaware of any shadows over their existence, they grew up among trees, animals, and fields. I always encouraged them to climb trees, which is the best way to stretch children's bodies, to be adventurous and fearless, and to learn to value the significance of trees in nature. Even an occasional fall from a tree was a good experience for

Mukti and Maya. Their bodies seemed to be relaxed, and they fell like ripe fruit!

Our children helped to bring us in contact with our neighbors. The Welsh and English neighbors alike took interest in our children, particularly when Mukti started to go to a school where all subjects were taught in Welsh. Our Welsh neighbors, as well as the schoolteachers, willingly and eagerly helped him along.

SINCE MUKTI WAS BEGINNING to learn Welsh, June and I also decided to learn. Dyfed and Robina were enthusiastic supporters of the Welsh language. Robina was from Sussex, and since she married Dyfed she had become a fluent Welsh speaker. They kindly and generously agreed to come to our home and give us a weekly Welsh lesson without charge. This was a wonderful offer; a number of our friends took this chance of getting together, not only to learn Welsh but also to celebrate Welsh culture.

Dyfed and Robina were not only enthusiastic but also extremely skilled teachers. They combined words with stories, with songs, and with practical examples. When they wanted to teach us words about gardening, we would go to the garden and identify plants and vegetables with direct learning methods and without the use of English; similarly we would go in the kitchen and learn from everything there directly. We made very little use of books.

Sally and John Seymour with their son, Dai, came regularly, and so did a number of others. Brian and Inger Johns, who had given up a comfortable and secure university life to live a simpler one of partial self-sufficiency, combining manual labor with intellectual pursuits, also came. Through learning Welsh together, we developed a close friendship with them. Although Brian and Inger had given up many of the modern conveniences which they had possessed in Durham, they still had their washing machine, so we bartered milk from our cow for the washing of clothes. This is only one of many examples of the benefits of our Welsh language class.

Dyfed and Robina were also involved with the adult education program run by the local county council, so they asked me to teach a yoga class, for which I was paid £8 an hour. This was another circle of friends, who were interested in Indian philosophy, religion, and culture. There was some overlap between the two classes, and it was exciting to discover some similarities between Celtic Wales and Sanskrit India. Many people like us had moved away from the cities, the attraction being not only the idyllic rural life but also the deeper values that are found in traditional Indian and Celtic cultures: for example, a belief that all life, not only human life, is sacred. Land and mountains are sacred; therefore our relationship with nature should be that of reverence and not of exploitation. One of the principal Upanishads states that every tree, every river, every mountain, every blade of grass, what you see and what you don't see, all and everything is the abode of the gods. You are a guest in the home of the gods. They have provided you with abundance. You are invited to make yourself at home, and to take what you really need, but not to waste or squander anything; to consume with consideration for the other guests of this great house and also remember the generations of guests who will come after you.

This Indian philosophy and way of thinking compares well with the concepts of the Celts. The Celtic saints communicated with the fishes of the sea and the creatures of the land and considered them members of the mysterious divine family.

The group which came together to learn Welsh and yoga also shared this worldview. This community of kindred spirits gave us a tremendous sense of belonging, and therefore when we started to look for a new home our hearts were torn between staying in this area and finding a home elsewhere.

THE £9,000 WE RECEIVED as compensation money was not enough to buy a house to accommodate ourselves and *Resurgence*. June's mother, who was living on a very small pension, came forward and offered her entire savings of £4,000. Also a touching gesture came from Brian and Inger Johns, who promised to invest £5,000 in our new property. A similar gesture of generosity and support came from Jon Wynne-Tyson, an author and reader of *Resurgence* who made £2,000 available as an investment. Still all this amounted to only £20,000: not enough to obtain a house which would meet all our needs.

We started to look for a house near the Center for Alternative Technology, Machynlleth in North Wales. Gerard Morgan-Grenville, the founder and then chairman of the center was very keen for us to join forces with the work of the center. He thought that *Resurgence* could act as an informal organ of the alternative technology and ecology movement, emanating from the Quarry. So we went to meet the people involved and discuss the possibilities of our cooperation.

I was impressed by this visit. Gerard and his team of mostly young people were working on an adventurous, idealistic, and pioneering project. In this age of fossil-fuel dependency, here were a group of visionaries who were researching and developing renewable energy resources. Their windmills were pumping water, their solar panels were heating water, their house insulation methods made space heating almost unnecessary. Thousands of visitors were pouring in to see the energy of the future in the making.

We went around looking for a house which we could acquire, but everything was expensive and nothing was suitable. Also, even though I was greatly interested in the activities of the center, I was reluctant to make any arrangements by which *Resurgence* might lose its total editorial independence.

When we returned from our visit to Machynlleth, I received an invitation from Maurice Ash, chairman of Dartington Hall Trust, to visit him in south Devon. In fact, Maurice had invited me earlier, but I could not accept his invitation as I had taken a vow that I would not leave Wales for a year. Now I was delighted to receive a second invitation. I had always been fascinated by what I had heard of Dartington and its connection with Rabindranath Tagore.

Maurice Ash and John Lane, a Dartington trustee, gave me a warm welcome and spent a large part of their day showing me around this eight-hundred-acre estate with magnificent medieval buildings and a variety of thriving businesses, which had been established by Dorothy and Leonard Elmhirst in the twenties. Leonard, a young Yorkshireman, married Dorothy, an American heiress. Both were inspired by the ideals of the great poet, artist, and educator Rabindranath Tagore. The Elmhirsts wanted to establish a center for rural regeneration, artistic excellence, and progressive education. So they acquired dilapidated buildings and a run-down estate and with great imagination and dedication restored it to its present glory.

However, after the death of the founders it seemed to me that the trust had lost some of its vision. It was difficult to find the soul of Dartington beyond the splendid gardens, amazing art collection, and successful businesses. Maurice himself was fully aware of this loss of spirit and was trying to bring about a renewal of its former idealism and make the trust activities responsive to the crisis of modern times.

He said that, for him, *Resurgence* represented that kind of inspiration which he felt Dartington needed. "*Resurgence* embodies the free spirit; it does not have dogmas, it does not claim to have found all the answers; the sense of uncertainty and inquiry is its strength. In this age which is bewitched by language, *Resurgence* represents the search for meaning. This is refreshing, and I would like to see *Resurgence* go from strength to strength." This was music to my ears, especially coming from Maurice, who uses words sparingly and is perhaps one of the most profound philosophers of the environmental movement.

Soon our discussion moved to practical matters. When I told him about our predicament and the need to find a home for *Resurgence* as well as ourselves, Maurice said, "Dartington Hall Trust is largely limited to activities in Devon. Therefore if you were to find a suitable house in Devon, the trust could help you." This offer was made in the spirit of friendship, with no strings attached.

John Lane immediately said, "Why don't you come with me to north Devon, stay in my house in Beaford, and see whether you can find a suitable property there? North Devon is quite similar to where you are in Wales." I happily agreed. John drove me, passing through Ashburton, over the Dart River, and then we were on Dartmoor: wild, rugged, and stunning. Looking around the changing landscape, I suddenly thought it seemed ideal to come and live in the neighborhood of this moor. The hills and streams and ancient woodlands of Dartmoor struck me, and released me from my attachment to Wales.

John and Truda Lane are artists in every sense of the word. John paints, Truda sketches, draws, and illustrates, but more than this formal pursuit of the arts, art is a way of life for them. Every activity, every movement, every chore is done with grace and elegance. Their kitchen, their dining table, their food, are all a work of art. Moreover, for them, human relationships themselves are an art.

I liked Dartington, I liked Dartmoor, I liked Devon, and I found in Maurice and John a great source of strength and friendship. Now the only thing that remained was to find a suitable house. John and I went to all the major real estate agents and looked at a score of properties, but nothing took my fancy. After two or three days of searching, we gave up momentarily as I had to return to Wales, but I asked John to keep looking for me and to let me know if a suitable house came on the market. I returned to Wales.

John Moat also lived in north Devon. He had been writing a regular humorous column in *Resurgence,* so when he heard from John Lane that I was contemplating moving to north Devon and looking for a house, he joined in the search. Within a few days he wrote to me, "What good news that you and June might come to live in our neighborhood! There are two unspoiled cozy cottages, with outbuildings and nine acres of paddock, in Woolsery. If you would like to come and see them, you will be most welcome to stay with us in our house." John also enclosed the real estate agent's description and a photo of the cottages. It was May 1979. I said to June, "It is your birthday month and therefore a time of high energy for you. I have seen north Devon and I like it. This time you go and see what you think."

June had not had the experience of meeting Maurice, traveling over Dartmoor, and staying with the Lanes. She was reluctant to leave Wales, but at the same time my enthusiasm for Devon was sufficient to persuade her to make at least one trip.

June went with Maya, now eighteen months old. The Woolsery cottages did not impress her. John and Antoinette had collected information about a number of other houses, Ford House in Hartland among them. But John considered this house unsuitable as it was very close to the village. Hartland is a conservative, traditional Devon village with a strong sense of its own identity and an unwillingness to have this diluted by outsiders. It does not find it easy to welcome strangers from other parts of England, never mind someone from as far away as India.

However, the next morning John said to June, "We will leave a little early, and on our way to the station I will show you Ford House." When June saw the house she said to John, "I think this house is worth considering. Satish would like it."

June and Maya returned to Wales and described the house to me. It sounded good. June had also warmed to north Devon. I phoned John Moat and John Lane, and they encouraged me to come and see the house myself as soon as possible since it was to be auctioned the following week.

I lost no time. I was on the train to Barnstaple, where I was met by John Lane. John Moat was waiting for us at the Anchor Inn, Hartland.

The three of us walked down to see the house. Tarmac courtyard, an eighteenth-century stone-built Devon longhouse, slightly run-down, no central heating, not modernized, a one-and-a-half-acre field with a running stream—everything as I wanted it! Mrs. Willoughby, the owner of the house, was expecting us. She had lit the fire, which was in an old inglenook with a traditional oven. It is becoming rare these days to find such an open fireplace. We exchanged information while sitting by the fire. Not only my body but my heart was warmed too. After showing us various rooms of the house, she took us into the kitchen, where there was a solid-fuel-fired Aga, exactly like the one we were using in Wales. This fully insulated and efficient cast-iron stove, designed by a blind Swedish engineer, is perfect for cooking, baking, heating water, and keeping the kitchen warm. June always calls it mother Aga, the living fire smoldering continuously in the heart of the house. The open fire and the Aga convinced me fully that this was the house where I would like to live.

As we came out, John Moat greeted the next-door neighbor, Henry Conibear, a blacksmith-smallholder who shoes horses, fashions and repairs farm tools, keeps a cow and a horse, and makes hay by hand. What a good neighbor to have! We walked back to the Anchor Inn. "The house is neither in the village nor very far from it," I reflected, "and this would be an advantage from *Resurgence*'s point of view. We need above all quick access to a post office. There is even a branch of Barclays Bank, which opens one and a half hours per week." "The cashier sits behind a round table beside an open fire, the small safe sits on the floor with its door wide open, and the customers sit comfortably on a row of chairs along one wall. There are no counters or security barriers," said John Moat. "And *Resurgence* has an account with Barclays, so it will suit us fine," I said.

CHAPTER 11

Hartland

T HE TWO JOHNS AND I ordered a drink at the bar of the Anchor Inn and talked about the house. I could feel a sense of trepidation in John Moat's voice. Although he was happy with the house itself, he was slightly concerned about the likely reaction of the village. John Lane said, "Wherever you go in north Devon, some people are bound to have reservations about outsiders. This is a fact of life for those who decide to live in rural areas. If you like the house, you should go for it." There was no more to be said.

I stayed with the Moats. The first thing I did was to phone Maurice Ash. "Maurice, we have found the house. The two Johns and I like it. The real estate agent's suggested price is £35,000. We will need an investment of £15,000 from Dartington Hall Trust." Maurice was sympathetic and promised to phone me back after consulting his fellow trustees. He talked with John Lane, Chris Zealley, and others over the telephone. Within half an hour he rang me back to say that the trust would be prepared to invest up to £15,000. Everything was going my way.

It was a Saturday, and the auction was to take place the following

Tuesday. "There is no point in you traveling back to Wales—you are welcome to stay with us," said Antoinette. That made sense, and I phoned June to let her know that I would be staying for the auction.

John and Antoinette live at Crenham Mill, a stone's throw from the Atlantic coast. They have thirty-six acres, including an ancient oak woodland. Their walled garden was filled with magnolias, wisteria, flowering cherries, clematis, roses, and all the flowers of early summer. The colors were a feast for my eyes. The garden was nature's poem: a piece of paradise, a perfect place for the poet and his wife, who tended it lovingly.

Every morning John left the house and went to his writing hut in the woods. Now I knew where he wrote his Didymus page for *Resurgence*. His satirical column was always hilariously funny and full of wit—it livened the otherwise serious and somber *Resurgence*.

Tuesday, the day of the auction, came. Accompanied by John and Antoinette, I arrived at Tantons Hotel in Bideford. This was my first ever experience of an auction, and I was feeling somewhat nervous and anxious. Fortunately John and Antoinette sat on either side of me. The room was rather empty: there were only two other bidders and a few onlookers, the vendor, and her friends. On the stroke of eleven, the auctioneer from Kivells read the terms and conditions of the auction and invited us to bid. Someone started with £30,000. John prompted me to join in, so I nodded at the auctioneer, and he announced my bid as £31,000. Bids continued to rise by £1,000 until my bid of £35,000. At that figure the bidding stopped, and the auctioneer proclaimed "Thirty-five thousand, one, thirty-five thousand, two, thirty-five thousand, three." He looked around the room, and seeing no further bids he said, "Mr. Kumar has the house." To my amazement, everything was over within ten minutes. I appointed a solicitor from Torrington to complete the deal, gave him the 10 percent deposit, and signed the necessary papers there and then.

The Moats and I came out of the hotel highly excited and happy. We went to a restaurant for lunch and celebrated the event with a bottle of champagne. As we toasted the success of *Resurgence* in Hartland, John said, "I know how expensive it is to move, to make the necessary repairs, and to pay the legal fees, so we would like to make a gift of £2,000 to *Resurgence* for this purpose." I was very moved by this kind and generous gift.

In the afternoon John said, "I would like to introduce you to a very dear friend of mine, John Jeffrey. He is a stalwart of Hartland: he runs the village grocery shop, is a professional bird photographer, and a man of profound literary and cultural taste. He will be a good introduction to Hartland for you."

At the foot of the cliffs, by the ruins of the medieval harbor, is the Hartland Quay Hotel. In the bar I met John Jeffrey. For the first time I talked with a man who spoke Devon English. I knew the difficulty of being an outsider and coming to live in Hartland, so I said to Mr. Jeffrey, "I need your help. I am coming to live in your care. Today I have bought a house in your village." "Yes, I heard from John; in fact, the house you have bought used to be in our family. It is a happy house, and I wish you well. If you need anything, don't hesitate to ask." This was a heartening beginning. John Jeffrey bought me a drink and introduced me to a number of other Hartlanders present in the pub.

ON THE LAST DAY OF JULY we hired a small moving van. Packing was painless. We had only a small number of possessions; back issues of *Resurgence* and our family belongings all fit in, and what did not, we gave away. Our friend, philosopher, and guide for the last three years, John Seymour, offered to drive us to Devon, since neither June nor I had a driving license. John had brought us to Pentre Ifan and now, with many regrets, was driving us away.

By the time we reached the outskirts of Swansea, the van came to a total standstill. We could not think what the problem was: the gas gauge for the diesel tank appeared to be full. We phoned the Automobile Association—the modern-day guardian angels of motorists. As we waited for the AA man, storm clouds gathered, and soon it began to rain cats and dogs. In the midst of the thunder and lightning, we saw a little AA van with its red light flashing. I got out of our van and waved to him. After checking the engine, the clutch, the gears, and various other parts, he looked at the diesel gauge, which showed the tank totally empty. "My goodness, how do you expect to drive a van on an empty tank?" We suddenly realized we had been looking at the wrong gauge. "And you know what," said the man, "there is a shortage of diesel at the moment and very little of it in this area, so don't be too surprised if it takes me some time to return with gas for you." He disappeared into the pouring rain. We waited about half an hour, and he came back with two gallons to get us on our way. He said, "There's no point in going to the garage where I got this—I took the last drop. I'll drive ahead of you into the city of Swansea in search of a garage which may have diesel." He was truly a helpful and kind man. We stopped at one garage and had to leave disappointed; we stopped at another, and again they had no diesel. At last the AA man stopped us and said, "Here is a garage which has a sufficient supply of diesel." Third time lucky, I thought. But as we drove in, the roof of our van hit the roof of the garage. Fortunately the garage roof was not damaged, but the roof of our van was badly dented. We filled our tank.

I had not expected such a rough ride. It was getting late and dark. We gave up all hope of reaching Devon that day, so I phoned Barbara and Herbert Girardet, who lived in Tintern, almost on our route. "Of course you must come. How can you think of passing by without seeing us?" said Barbara. Even though Barbara and Herbert lived in a small cottage, they found room for the four of us (Mukti was staying with his grandmother), together with four ducks and our cat, without a moment's hesitation. After a day of desperation, it was a great relief to spend the night in comfort. As soon as Barbara received my telephone call, she started to cook a special Indian meal. By the time we arrived the meal was ready, the table was laid, and several bottles of wine were waiting for us.

Our exhaustion and fatigue disappeared without a trace. Barbara and Herbert had been our neighbors in London when Herbert was a student of anthropology at the London School of Economics and Barbara was training to be a weaver. In the first issue of *Resurgence* I edited, I published Herbert's article on his idea of a radial house which would be built from renewable local materials and would incorporate a greenhouse and renewable sources of energy. Unfortunately, the idea remained on the drawing board, but I felt that it was quite a revolutionary design and that Herbert ought to build at least one such house. But Herbert's interests moved on. He had developed a great passion for forests in general and rain forests in particular. Also he had become much more interested in land use. He edited and published a book on the subject, while in the years since they moved from London, Barbara had developed her weaving into a fine art. Now she kept her own sheep and followed the whole process from shearing, spinning, and weaving to tapestry making. We had much to talk about. They wanted us to stay on for a day or two, but with the moving van standing outside, we could not accept their invitation and moved on the next morning.

The rest of the trip to Hartland was uneventful. When we arrived at the house, we were happily surprised to find a box full of oranges, apples, potatoes, onions, carrots, and cauliflower—a generous gift from John Jeffrey, deposited outside the front door. As we entered the kitchen, there were more gifts, this time a loaf of home-baked bread, a bottle of wine, a vase of flowers, and a welcome card from Antoinette and John Moat. And as we started to unload our van, Glen and Paul, grandsons of Henry Conibear, came to give a hand, and Henry's daughter Barbara brought a tray of tea and Welsh cakes. My fears that an outsider would find Hartland cold and unwelcoming vanished.

I realized that the idea of an outsider makes people close up. There is a fear of the unknown, but when they meet an outsider face to face, humanity triumphs. I could feel relief and joy. Having friends like the Moats and the Lanes living close to Hartland and neighbors like the Jeffreys and Conibears made me feel a sense of homecoming.

IT WAS AUGUST 1979, my birthday month as well as the month of *Sanvatsari*—the great Jain festival of forgiveness. During this month, all Jains celebrate the annual event of total reconciliation by forgiving and begging forgiveness of all creatures. This I had been taught as a way of healing wounded relationships. If I had harmed any man or woman, any animal or plant, I begged their forgiveness. If I had, knowingly or unknowingly, shown any disrespect or disregard for humans and nonhumans, I sought their forgiveness. Through this act I retrieved all my offensive and careless thoughts, words, and deeds. In a similar spirit, if I had been hurt by anyone in any way, I forgave them totally and utterly. I declared my friendship with all beings, I had no enemy.

Remembering this practice, I reflected on my relationship with Peggy Hemming. I had been upset and unsettled by her decision to disband our community in Wales, but as I looked back I realized that she had been a blessing in disguise. She had been an instrument of change in my life, and I was grateful. Without her, would I have moved out of London? Difficult to imagine. She came into my life for such a short spell but changed it fundamentally. She made me stand on my own feet and find my own solutions. She acted like a strong mother and forced me not to be dependent on her. My bitterness began to dissolve. It was a case not so much of forgiveness as of understanding her actions and being thankful.

Soon after our arrival in Hartland, I met a retired farmer walking by Ford House. He said, "Good morning to you." After I acknowledged his greetings, he looked at me with a certain surprise. "Are you the new owner of Ford?" he inquired. "Yes, we moved here only a few days ago." "Welcome then," he said. After a few moments' pause he asked, "Which church do you belong to? Church of England or Free Church?" I was taken aback. Certainly I was not Church of England. Perhaps I could be considered Free Church. "Free Church," I replied. I hoped this was a polite answer. "Which Free Church?" he pursued. Now I was in a bit of a fix. I took courage into my hands and answered, "Jain." After a moment's thought he said, "I'm afraid we don't have one of those in Hartland, but I am Wesley Heard, I play the organ in the Methodist Chapel. If you would like to come to our chapel, you will be most welcome."

This was an unexpected encounter. I was overwhelmed by the simplicity and generosity of Mr. Heard. He showed me the open heart of Hartland. This brief meeting on the road sowed the seeds of a lasting friendship. He kept his chickens and grew his vegetables in fields opposite ours, so we saw him often. Whenever I went away he milked our cow and kept an eye on the house. He advised us where we could buy hay and straw and generally helped us out from time to time.

One day he said, "I went to London once. That was on our honeymoon. I'll never go again. I am happy in Hartland. I have never been tempted to travel in a plane or across the ocean." "That is all right for you," I replied "as you were born in Hartland, but I had to walk all round the world to find Hartland."

Another day he told me how he came to be called Wesley. "After my birth, my father rode fifteen miles on horseback to Bideford and registered my name as John Heard. He rode back the same day. On arriving home he told my mother, 'I registered our son John, as we agreed, but I wish we'd called him Wesley.' My mother ordered him to ride back straightaway and register me as Wesley. So my father did. The registrar said, 'I can't change what is already written in the register, but I can add Wesley to John.' And so he did. And from that moment I have always been known as Wesley." "Your poor father. He had to ride sixty miles to give you the right name!" "But then he was a strong man, and a man of strong belief." Wesley was absolutely right. Unfortunately our modern living has taken away our strength, both physical and mental. Also the analytical and rational mind has diluted, if not completely destroyed, our faith. Wesley himself is a living example of the qualities his father had. Hartland has many people still continuing that tradition of using their own resources of body and spirit, rather than depending on external resources; but such people are now a threatened species.

People who have been highly educated, who are well read, well traveled, successful, and have a high living standard, often consider country folk uncultured and a little stupid. This is the arrogance of the urban mind. I felt envious of Wesley's uncomplicated and unstressful existence.

Colin Tiffany was a graphic designer who came regularly from Lampeter to Pentre Ifan to design *Resurgence*. He enjoyed working for *Resurgence* so much that he continued to travel down to Devon every two months. On his first trip to Ford House, he borrowed a horse box and drove our cow, Radha, and her calf, Hazel, down to us.

MY DAILY ROUTINE was not complete until Radha and Hazel arrived. No wonder the Hindus consider cows holy—they are such wonderful companions and guardians of the health of human beings, and that of the soil. They live simply on grass but provide us with milk and manure, and above all, for me, Radha was a supreme teacher of rhythmic breathing and prolonged meditation. She was also a teacher of the art of giving. The daily routine of milking was an unpretentious, spiritual practice for me. As I milked, I experienced her ability to relax completely. One cow at home as a member of the family is utterly different from the modern practice of mechanized milk production. In such a situation cows are no longer individual animals, partners in life, but are reduced to being walking milk machines. Cattle farming for beef is unquestionably an ecological disaster. When Hindus worship the holy cow, they have in mind the cow's qualities of patience, calm, the giving of oneself like a mother, and nurturing the land. The cow is a symbol of the animal kingdom. For Hindus, all animals are holy. In the same way, the Ganges is a symbol of all rivers; all rivers are holy. Mount Kailas is a symbol of all mountains; all mountains are holy. The entire natural world is holy. The role of religion and religious teachers is to help people to look at the world and see the sacred within it.

The Western world has recognized the importance of human rights and the sanctity of human life. It accepts that human life has intrinsic value, but Hindus and many other Eastern traditions have gone much further and recognized the intrinsic value of all life and the sanctity of nature. Darwinian theory creates a false notion that human beings are at the pinnacle of evolution and are superior to other forms of life; as a result, scientists, economists, and industrialists are bent on conquering nature, subduing it, and making it serve human beings. This linear development contrasts with the traditional wisdom of India, where the life force is seen as moving in circles, where human beings after death can be reborn as animals, birds, or trees. Similarly, animals, birds, and trees can be reborn in human form. Life does not end in death. We should be aware that we will be coming back to this world, and therefore we should not poison or pollute it, so that when we return to this world in our next life, we find it as habitable and beautiful as when we left it. Because today's human being may be tomorrow's cow and today's cow may be tomorrow's human being, the sanctity of human life and animal life is inseparable. Living with Radha and Hazel prevented me from forgetting this tradition.

Also my early morning appointment with Radha was a form of meditation. Meditation can take many forms. On the one hand, you can find a quiet place and sit cross-legged, with closed eyes, and chant a holy mantra or you can watch your breathing and heighten your awareness of your physical, emotional, and mental state. On the other hand, you can transform an activity of daily life into meditation by being totally mindful, fully present, and completely engaged in the activity itself. For me, milking was such a meditation.

When I started to milk, my mind would stop. Memories of the past and plans for the future would come to a standstill. I was only aware of the cow, her breathing, my breathing, and the sound of the milk hitting the bucket. My body would totally relax, and I would fall into a timeless trance.

CHAPTER 12

The Small School

Hartland was, in my view, almost self-sufficient as a village. Its 1,420 inhabitants included farmers, builders, a baker, a blacksmith, a chair maker, a cabinetmaker, two potters, dressmakers, printers, a type-setter, two doctors, a dentist, an accountant, and a hairdresser; there were three churches, three pubs, two garages, two cafes, two part-time banks, a newsagent–cum–sub–post office; and even a newspaper, *The Hartland Times*. In effect, there was everything essential for the community.

Hartland Primary School is an excellent example of how the children of a community should be cared for and educated, but it serves only children aged from five to eleven. Until 1961 the village had a school which educated children from five to sixteen years of age, with 198 pupils. But people who believed more in the economics of scale than in the vitality of the community and the future of its children closed the secondary part of the school in spite of strong local opposition. This has been the fate of small secondary schools throughout Britain.

This closure caused Hartland children to be widely scattered among other schools. Some went to Bideford Comprehensive, others went out of the county and into the comprehensive at Bude in Cornwall; and others went to private schools outside the village. So the children of one village community were uprooted and divided.

Some of my friends were deeply concerned about this state of affairs. Seeing their children travel one hour in the morning and one hour in the evening in unsupervised buses was disturbing. It was as if, for their children, a commuter's life started at the age of eleven, and this was particularly irritating for those of us who had moved to the village because we ourselves disliked commuting and valued the village way of life.

Removing children from the village on a daily basis not only wasted a considerable amount of their time—thirty-eight school weeks a year means they traveled on 190 days of the year, two hours a day, which is 380 hours spent on a bus—but it also gave children the idea that the village was not good enough for them as it could not provide the necessary education, and when they finished their education it would not provide them with work. So they were being led to believe that being born in a village was some sort of a handicap.

And was this traveling worth it? Devon Education Authority was spending £6,000,000 a year to take village children to town and city schools. The Department of Education in London had once stated that a sixteen-hundred-pupil school was an ideal size. No one knows how they arrived at this magic number. Did they think that by crowding more teachers and pupils together they would achieve higher standards of education? All these educational bureaucrats live in cities and have little understanding of rural requirements.

The more I heard and the more I thought about these questions, the more I became concerned and worried about the education of my own children. Am I going to send Mukti and Maya to a school of sixteen hundred children? Such a large school brings inner-city-type problems to a country town and subjects the village children to problems of drug abuse and drug pushing, violence and vandalism, bullying, indiscipline, shoplifting, and sometimes even sexual abuse, in a situation where it is difficult for teachers to know even the names of the children, let alone the names of their parents and their family backgrounds.

One teacher of a comprehensive school said to me that because of the size of the school and the classes, she had been reduced to becoming an administrator and baby-sitter rather than a teacher of creative and inspirational quality. This sent shivers down my spine, and I said to myself that it was no good cursing the darkness, let us light a candle. We can criticize the educational system until the cows come home and nothing will change. If we set an example of a good school and show that it is possible to provide high standards of education in a village community, then we will be in a better position to campaign and convince the authorities to stop closing small schools and help in the creation of new ones.

IT WAS FEBRUARY 5, 1982, when a friend dropped in at our house and in passing mentioned that the Methodist Sunday School was up for auction. June and I had just returned from India, where we had seen dedicated people engaged in village work and especially in education. We were inspired by the recent memory of those Indian projects.

The auction was on February 16. If ever we were to put our idea of starting a village secondary school into practice, this was the time. We went to see the building: two large halls, a small room, a garden, toilets, and adjacent to it a two-bedroomed cottage, to be auctioned as one lot.

Ideas started to explode, discussions got going. February 16 arrived. The auction was at 3:00 P.M. The lunchtime conversation was entirely taken up by the debate as to how much money could be bid. This was a somewhat academic question as in reality we had no money. The conclusion was that we should go to the auction and at least see what happened. If there was anyone from the village wishing to buy the property for a dwelling, then we should not bid against them. Second, although we had no money at the time, we might be able to raise £20,000. Therefore that figure should be our final limit.

With some friends, I arrived at the New Inn Hotel in Bideford. The hall was packed with Hartland people, which made us think there would be many bidders and we might not have a chance. The auctioneer read the terms and conditions and invited bids for a lease of five thousand years. I thought that he must have made a mistake and he must mean five hundred years, but no, it was five thousand.

A local builder started the bidding. His plan was to convert the property for resale. To my surprise, no one challenged him. I waited and looked around. The auctioneer was calling, "Is there any other bid? The property is going at £13,000." At that point I raised my head for £14,000. No one else joined the race. The builder and I kept going. When the builder's bid reached £19,000, I paused, thinking that the opposition was determined. However, I was encouraged by my accompanying friends to make my final offer, and this time I offered £20,000—and at £20,000 it stayed. The auctioneer invited the other bidder to come up with £500 more, £250 more, £100 more, but no, he was not willing to advance any further, and the property was bought for the school. Of course I had no money even for the deposit. So *Resurgence* made a temporary loan of the necessary 10 percent.

In the following issue of *Resurgence,* I included an urgent letter inviting readers to buy a share of £2,000 in the property or make a donation to *Resurgence* to enable it to buy a share. The response was terrific. We needed ten shareholders, and we got eleven. The eleventh amount of £2,000 enabled us to carry out basic repairs.

We went searching for a teacher. The applications came in from all over the country, but the right man was in Hartland itself. Michael Nix, who had been a teacher at our primary school but had given up the job in order to start the museum at Hartland Quay, and who wrote books on local history, seemed the most suitable candidate. He had been in the village for eleven years, knew the parents, had taught most of the children, and had covered with his feet almost every inch of the land of the parish. For a small school which is set up to focus on the community and the village, who could be a better teacher?

Now we had the building and the teacher, but what about the children? Some of the parents who supported the school did not have children of the right age. Others wanted to send their children, but the children themselves did not want to come because their friends were going to other schools. Still others who were dissatisfied with the big schools did not like to risk sending their children to a school which was still an unknown quantity. "Would it ever start, and would it start this year?" was the question.

Two sets of parents were most eager to see the school begin that autumn. Anna and Ian Morrison gave me a contribution of £100 for their son Adam, several months in advance, to show their faith and commitment. Adam was having to leave home at 7:30 A.M., walk to a picking-up point, take a bus part of the way, and then change to another, in order to be at school by nine. Once at school he had to carry his books and football gear all day. By the time he arrived home in the evening, repeating the morning journey, he was so exhausted he could sleep on the spot.

For Anna Morrison, the problem of educating children in large schools was not new. When one of her nephews was left behind in mathematics, she asked the mathematics teacher if he could spare some extra time to help the boy to catch up with some material he had missed through changing schools. The teacher's answer was straight and simple: "I have forty children in the class, and I cannot give special attention to any particular child." When she talked to the headmaster about Adam's long day due to busing, he replied that quite a few children who are bused in from the villages are sent to his office in tears in their first year. Because of this kind of experience, the concept of the Small School in the village was most attractive to her. She was born and bred in Hartland and has a younger child, Justin, who later came to the Small School.

Once Adam enrolled others came forward, and before long nine children from Hartland had formed the pioneer class of this new school.

On September 7, when the school term began in Devon, we opened the school. A *Guardian* reporter, Wendy Berliner, came to witness the first day and wrote under an eight-column banner headline, NINE VILLAGE CHILDREN GET A SCHOOL OF THEIR OWN. Other newspapers and radio stations also reported the opening.

Although we had only one full-time teacher, we had a strong team of part-timers. The subjects taught included French, rural sciences, biology, chemistry, physics, history, creative writing, pottery, fine arts, drama, folk songs, music, cookery, and gardening. By drawing on the community for our teachers, we were like traditional schools; these local teachers were not full-time, and only some of them had undergone teacher training, but all of them were very happy to pass on some of their skill and experience to the children of their community, many of whom they already knew. And for the children, these adults were examples of how it was possible to earn one's living in a great variety of ways.

I believed that the school should be an extension of home, and the relationship between teachers and pupils should be one of friendship and not of fear. One way to achieve this homely atmosphere was to involve children in the preparation of their midday meal. This worked extremely well and continues to this day. Two children, with the help of an adult, cook wholesome, vegetarian lunches. Cooking the lunch became a lesson in domestic science and nutrition. Children and adults laying the table, saying grace, clearing away, and washing up together strengthened the feeling of the school as a community where each individual was served and supported by others.

From the very beginning I was determined that the Small School should be non-fee-paying and be open to everybody from the locality. It should not be a privilege for those who can afford to pay, as happens in the public school system. Eventually, my aim was to convince the local education authority and the central government to finance the Small School as happens with such schools in Denmark, Holland, and some other European countries. In the meantime, I planned to approach charitable trusts, asking them to make a grant toward the salaries of the teachers.

I purchased a directory of grant-making trusts and sat down every evening marking those which seemed most likely to be interested in supporting our educational venture. I made a list of one hundred of them.

Jill Christie, who had come with me to the auction, gave invaluable support and encouragement in every aspect of the school. In particular she typed one hundred letters to these charities for me—a labor of love. Out of these one hundred letters, I received ninety-nine polite refusals, but the hundredth answer was from the Ernest Cook Trust. Their aim was to support education in rural areas, which fitted in well with our work. Three trustees came to visit me to find out more about our aims and the precise nature of our school. Jill Christie and Michael Nix joined the discussion. The trustees were of the opinion that the closure of rural schools was a mistaken policy of the government. And even if village schools were more expensive to run, they should be kept open. I argued that "expensive" was a relative term if one took into account the cost of transport, the cost of repairs due to vandalism, the cost of bringing in supply teachers to replace staff who were ill due to overwork and stress, and the cost of providing special education for those who couldn't cope with large schools and ended up psychologically disturbed.

Even if the trustees did not agree with every detail of my argument, they were sufficiently convinced to consider giving us a grant. "How much do you need?" one of them asked. "We need a grant of £5,000 to pay a modest salary to our full-time teacher," I answered. "We will discuss your application at our next meeting," the trustees assured me and left.

After about ten days I received a letter from the secretary of the trust saying that the trustees have agreed to give the School £5,000 a year for two years. It was more than I had asked for, and I was over the moon with delight.

Colin Hodgetts was an old friend. We had worked together in establishing the London School of Nonviolence in 1968, and we had kept in touch ever since. He knew from *Resurgence* that I had started the school and at that time he read an article in *The Guardian* by Dr. Rhodes Boyson, a minister of education, describing and supporting the Danish and Dutch systems, whereby a group of parents can establish their own school and the government will meet up to 80 percent of the cost.

Colin came down to Hartland with the article. "Why don't you go and meet Rhodes Boyson and ask him to put his money where his mouth is?" "What a splendid idea!" I said. Colin and I together composed a letter to the minister, although we were rather doubtful that he would be able to find time to see us. Something about our letter must have intrigued him, for his secretary phoned me immediately to make an appointment. Together with Colin and Dr. James Clarke, I went to see the minister in his office at Queen Elizabeth House, near Waterloo Bridge. He talked with us for forty minutes and listened to our arguments with sympathy and interest but said, "I would like to see parents having a greater say in the running of schools and also to have the right to establish their own schools, but as the law stands at the moment, I cannot see how the state can finance your school. It requires an Act of Parliament, so your best bet for the moment is to seek charitable grants and raise public awareness on this issue."

This was a diplomatic answer to our request. We came away deeply disappointed. However, I said to Colin, "It is too much to expect success at this stage. It is going to be a long haul and I would like you to join the campaign for state support of small schools. Michael Nix is planning to leave the Small School at the end of the year. We will be looking for a new head teacher. I would very much like you to have the job."

Colin was somewhat surprised at my suggestion but said he would consider it. He had a contract with the Save the Children Fund in connection with Vietnamese refugees and was a director of refugee action, but his work was coming to some kind of completion. The suggestion that he might move out of London and engage in a new campaign attracted him.

It was obvious that it would mean less than one third of his present income and masses of hard work, but after a certain amount of arm-twisting, he was persuaded to apply for the job, and eventually he was appointed to be head teacher of the Small School.

FINDING COLIN was perhaps the single most important thing I did for the school. He proved to be a competent campaigner, a dedicated teacher, a natural leader, and a man of many skills. Once Colin was appointed, I was freed from the worry of the day-to-day running of the school. I was able to limit myself to giving my advice on matters of policy as chairman of the Small School Trust.

The second most important action of mine was to persuade Kim Taylor of the Gulbenkian Foundation and Hugh de Quetteville of Sainsbury's Family Trust to visit the school and agree to make major grants which assured the viability of the school for the initial years.

Gradually the numbers of children grew, the commitment of the parents increased, and national publicity gave the school a high profile, which boosted everyone's confidence and made me feel that the Small School was here to stay. Colin developed a curriculum which allocated 50 percent of the time to academic subjects and 50 percent of the time to creative and practical skills; learning by doing became the ethos. For example, every Friday was devoted to practical skills like building; the children themselves built an extension to the school, which involved digging the foundations by hand, building the walls, which were faced with stone, and then doing the plastering, carpentry, roofing, plumbing, electricity installation, and everything else which made the extension a harmonious part of the school. It is now used as a workshop. This kind of education made me feel deeply satisfied and happy.

My son Mukti went to the school and was involved in this building project. When he left he was competent enough to help a friend renovate an old farmhouse during the weekends and holidays, and at the same time study for his A Levels in mathematics, physics, and communications. Thus the ability of the Small School to combine academic, practical, and creative subjects and educate children physically, intellectually, and spiritually was demonstrated.

CHAPTER 13

⊶∙∙∙⊷

Pilgrimage: Iona

Whan that Aprill with his shoures soote
The droghte of March hath perced to the roote,
. . . Thanne longen folk to goon on pilgrimages.
The Canterbury Tales

IT IS AN INDIAN TRADITION that when you are fifty you should go on a pilgrimage, so in the summer of 1985 I began thinking and planning for a pilgrimage to the holy places of Britain the following year. I put a small advertisement in the personal columns of *Resurgence* to see if there were any *Resurgence* readers who would offer me a bed for the night. There was such a tremendous response that when I set out I had an offer of hospitality in most of the places I was to visit.

My plan was to start at nine o'clock in the morning and to arrive at my host's house between 4:00 P.M. and 6:00 P.M. With a few exceptions, I aimed at walking every day, covering twenty miles per day on average, but a shorter distance for the first few days.

I started out with a small rucksack, one change of clothes, and the pair of Polish shoes I had on. I took no book, no diary, no camera, and as on my earlier walk from India to America, no money. Pilgrimage is best when you are traveling light, especially if you are walking.

On March 31, Easter Monday, I set off with my family toward St. Nectan's Holy Well at Stoke, two miles from Hartland. Two local friends, John Jeffrey and Wesley Heard, walked with us out of Hartland village. I was in my fiftieth year, John in his sixtieth, and Wesley in his eightieth. "Two old Methodists," they said, and I added, "sending off a non-Christian outsider to the holy places of Britain!"

For me there was no more auspicious place from which to start the journey than the Holy Well of St. Nectan, the patron saint of Hartland. Many hundreds of years ago, St. Nectan had to earn his living by working on the land and husbanding the cows. One evening when it was just getting dark, he saw from his kitchen window that two robbers were stealing his cows. The saint rushed out to stop the theft, but the robbers were cruel and chopped off his holy head. St. Nectan picked up his head, put it under his arm, walked to the holy well, and died there. This is the legend I was told by a former vicar.

To reach the well, we walked down a sloping, leafy track leading to the site. The well itself is housed in a domed edifice in stone, with a wooden door. I was moved by the song of birds as I opened the door. With a touch of water from the spring, and good-bye embraces from gathered family and friends, I began my journey.

Walking through stony bridle paths, tarmac roads, wet and muddy Brownsham Woods, and uphill fields to Clovelly, I experienced cold April showers and a steady wind against me from Bideford Bay.

I had hardly begun my walk, yet my toes were hurting, my feet were sore, my shoes and socks were wet. Finding it painful to continue, I stopped at the home of Fran and Sarah Sutton, who live in a converted chapel at Bucks Mills, exactly on my route. In a cozy seat by the fire, I collapsed in amazement at myself, wondering how I was ever going to walk two thousand miles when my feet were protesting after only ten miles. Was the weather going to be wet and cold all the way? But Sarah's soothing words lifted my spirits. She found a healing balm to massage my feet, and hot tea to warm my body. An hour's rest was enough to get me going. Fortunately, I had planned a short journey for the first day, which turned out to be a blessing for my unfit body.

THE FIRST NIGHT I spent at Sloo Cottages, by the sea at Horns Cross. The next day my hosts, Terry and Brian, came with me to guide me along the coast path to Bideford. As the crow flies, Bideford seems close to Horns Cross, but it is twice as far when walking up and down along the cliffs. As I walked on, the sight of the vast, deep sea raised my spirits. There is as deep a sea within, and my pilgrimage felt like the cliff edge from which I should dive into that inner sea. After a night's rest in Bideford and a walk, accompanied by a local musician, to Barnstaple the next day, I experienced a strong fear that I was standing on the cliff edge and wondering whether I would be able to jump.

As I progressed through the ups and downs of Exmoor, my knee was swollen, my ankle was hurting, and my feet were covered with blisters. Would I be able to make it?

On the fifth day I managed to walk from South Molton to Bampton, a stretch of twenty miles. My host for that night, Michael Cole, lived four miles off my route. So he met me at Bampton church, and I agreed to go to his house by car. I thought, "At last my legs can rest!" but Michael lives in a deep and secluded Exmoor valley and therefore had to leave his car on the road at the top; I had to drag my feet down the very steep, almost nonexistent, zigzagging path. Michael's plan was that an hour or so later a number of his friends would gather at the hilltop, and so we should walk up again to join them there to say the Prayer for Peace together. Although I did not want to disappoint him, I could not find the strength to go up and down that slope again in the same evening. Michael could see my desperation and went by himself to ask everyone gathered to come down to his house. I felt relieved and put my feet in a bowl of hot, salted water, as Michael's simple farmhouse had no running water to entertain the idea of a hot bath.

From Bampton, another stretch of twenty miles to Taunton was no less exhausting. After every few miles I had to sit down and apply balm to my feet and arnica to my knee, take a rest, and then walk on.

My Taunton hosts, Carol and Paul Zeal, live in a sumptuous Victorian house. On my arrival my first indulgence was to lie and soak in a hot bath. Carol is a homeopath; she gave me some remedies and a foot massage, which revitalized me for the time being. She said, "Take a day's rest," but that I could not contemplate. By the next morning I felt sufficiently strong to set off on the journey again. Later in Wells I was treated by Ian Pringle, an acupuncturist, in Mere by a healer, and in Salisbury by an osteopath. Every one of them urged me to take a rest, but my promise to myself was that I would walk every day, and if I stopped to give rest to my body, I wondered if I would be able to start again.

After giving me ultrasound treatment, the Salisbury osteopath suggested that I should put ice packs on my knee and ankle, and someone else suggested putting honey on after the ice pack.

Why, oh why are a pilgrim's legs lacking in strength? Walking was my birthright. From the age of five I had walked every day with my mother to our smallholding. Then from the age of nine to eighteen I had walked from village to village as a monk of the Jain order. When I left the Jain order and joined Vinoba Bhave, I was again a part of a walking way of life. And then I had walked almost around the world!

Walking was not solely a means to get somewhere. Walking in itself was an end, a form of meditation, a way of being. The journey was as important as the arrival. In fact the arrival was part of the journey. Growing up with such a training, I took walking as much for granted as breathing.

However, since that long walk I had become a householder, living in the world of motorized transport. I had, unknowingly, lost touch with walking and with my earlier self. But I was glad to go back to my feet and was glad to rediscover the pain and pleasure of walking on my own two legs.

Pilgrimage is best when you put your body on the pilgrim's path. The Tibetans go on pilgrimage by prostrating themselves every inch of the way. They start by standing, their hands held in prayer, then they kneel and, bowing down, lie facing the earth and touching her with their forehead in humility. Then they make a mark on the ground with their nose, stand up, and walk up to the spot marked by the nose (to ensure that they do not miss a fraction of the path). Then they stand and repeat the process, and this they do all the way to the temple, which might be one hundred miles away. For the pilgrim, every moment and every step is sacred. The holy places and temples are only symbolic destinations. By walking to the holy places a pilgrim is able to be free of speed, anxiety, and desire for achievement. Reflecting in this way, I gathered strength and kept going.

FROM TAUNTON I WALKED through the low-lying, willow-growing country of Kings Sedge Moor, passing by many of the basket-making workshops of Somerset. Glastonbury Tor appeared high in the distance, showing me the way I had to follow. My hosts, Ann and David Jevons, met me at the outskirts of Glastonbury and guided me to Chalice House, which they run as a guesthouse. David was an aircraft pilot and decided to give up his lucrative career so that he and his wife could devote themselves to Glastonbury and to the spirit of the New Age.

By now the rhythm of the day was established. After arriving, my hosts gave me much-desired cups of tea, a hot bath, a little rest, a big dinner, and only after that there was a gathering of people, whom I addressed and exchanged ideas with. By ten o'clock I went to bed. I read no newspapers nor listened to the radio.

The next morning, Ann took me to Chalice Well, which is beautifully kept by a trust. From the well the water flows out through a stone spout and falls into an ancient channel. Ann on the one side and I on the other washed each other's hands as a symbol of service and spiritual support. I held some of the holy water in my cupped hands and looking into it said, "Let all my desires, negative thoughts, fear, and mistrust dissolve in this water." Then I splashed it on the ground, saying, "Let it go, let it go, let it go." That was a stunning moment. My neck and shoulders felt unburdened. My heart felt light and free. I could see my anger and attachment melting away. This was the start of my inner journey. The outer journey had become a trigger for the inner journey.

As I was lost in the vast and infinite space within, Ann called me and said, "Now take some more water in your hands." This time, as Ann guided, I said, "Through this water let love and compassion, trust and hope, freedom and joy enter my being." I drank the holy water. It was an experience of being free in spirit and being part of the passing moment.

Ann told me that thousands of gallons of water flow from this well: there is an infinite source of water within it. We went to the actual well, twenty yards away, and lifted the lid with its two intertwining circles. The well is very small, not unlike a human body. I realized that the human body is also like a well, with an infinite spiritual source, if we can only let it flow. There are many holy wells, some hidden, some dried up, some ignored. Most of us drink processed, tested, treated, tap water, unaware of the ancient wells. Similarly we are trapped in quantified, measured, analyzed knowledge, unaware of the wisdom within us.

From Glastonbury I walked through Wells and over the Mendip Hills to the little village of Dean in Somerset, where I had been invited by Miranda and Nicholas Schofield. In spite of my hopes for the April weather, it was like winter: snow, wind, and bitter cold. When I arrived at Dean, the cottage of my hosts was filled with their friends who were waiting to receive me. Warmth came from the roaring Rayburn and from a hearty welcome—it was hard to say which was warmer. A sumptuous spread on the table gave no indication that I was staying with a not-so-wealthy young couple. When they showed me my room, I realized that Miranda and Nicholas had vacated their own bed for me. I was rather embarrassed to put my hosts out and make them sleep on the floor for my sake and I urged them, "No, please don't do this. I am very happy and very comfortable on a couch or on a mattress or even on the floor. Long practice as a begging monk has made my body accustomed to sleep soundly anywhere. Moreover, it will be good for my back to sleep on a hard surface." But no way could I persuade my hosts to let me sleep anywhere but in their bed. They themselves slept on the floor. Such kindness was expressed many times by different people during my pilgrimage. Who says the British are not hospitable?

Bed for the night and bread for the evening were the symbols of openness of heart, kindness of spirit, and natural generosity. I hope that I received this hospitality like a honeybee. A honeybee goes from flower to flower, takes a little nectar, and turns it into healing and life-giving honey. As it goes it carries pollen from one flower to another. A pilgrim transforms the love of people into pilgrim's tales, spreading the stories of a sacred journey. Like honey, sacred stories heal wounded souls.

As I went along I was told by people that my visit had put them in touch with old and new friends; my visit had been a good excuse to connect them with each other. I took it to be the pollinating effect of my pilgrimage.

From Dean my hosts accompanied me to Mere. Next day, joined by four others, I walked to Salisbury. And on the twelfth day, starting from Salisbury Cathedral, following the old Roman road, I came to Winchester.

As I walked the Pilgrims Way from Winchester to Canterbury, I was on the same path that many thousands of pilgrims had walked before. I had a sense that I was in the company of those people who had preceded me. As I stepped in their footprints, I felt I was in touch with their dedication, their purity, their sense of divinity.

The very beauty of the Pilgrims Way is refreshing. In most parts it follows the ridge of the North Downs. Even though Surrey and Kent are riddled with highways, suburbs, and built-up areas, in the woods of the North Downs I was able to escape the secular world. Now and then I had to cross the highways and expressways with their rushing trucks and speeding cars; I was amazed to see the madness of it all. The speed of my two legs and the speed of highway traffic are worlds apart.

In spite of our society's obsession with speed, I was impressed with the way this ancient path, over one hundred miles in length, is maintained. The Pilgrims Way is not the same as it was in the Middle Ages, as in some places industrial growth has swallowed it; but fortunately a new footpath, the North Downs Way, has been created, which goes all the way to Canterbury. It is clearly marked and well defined, and I met a number of people walking it.

THE TRADITION OF GOING ON A PILGRIMAGE is common to all religions. The Muslims go to Mecca, the Christians go to Canterbury or Jerusalem, and Hindus go to the source of the Ganges in the Himalayas. My mother used to say that if you haven't been on a pilgrimage by the time you are fifty, then your time is up: you mustn't put it off any longer. By the time you are fifty you have performed your essential duties in this world. You have paid off your mortgage to the building society and seen your children through school. You have given enough attention to your family and your business; now is the time to pay attention to your soul, your spirit, your imagination, and your creativity. From now on whatever you do should be in the service of the spirit. So pilgrims' routes have become established throughout the world. It was a great delight to walk that ancient path to Canterbury in my fiftieth year.

According to Jain custom, the birthday is the day of conception: you are born into the womb of your mother, and you exist from then on. So I was making my pilgrimage between the anniversary of the day of my conception and that of the day of my birth. If I was in India, I would have gone to the holy places of many Indian religions. I would have gone to Ajmer to be inspired by the teachings of the prophet Mohammed, the prophet of peace—Islam means "in peace." I would have gone to Bodh Gaya, the place of the enlightenment of Lord Buddha, the Lord of Compassion. I would have gone to Rajgir, where the founder of the Jain religion, Mahavir, taught the sacred nature of all creation. I would have gone to Kerala, where St. Thomas brought the teachings of Jesus, the Lord of Love. I would have gone to Gokul, the home of Lord

Krishna, the Lord of Joy and Celebration, and I would have gone to Ayodhya, where Rama, the Lord of Right Living, reigned. But I was not in India, I was in Britain, and therefore I went to the holy Christian places, to stone circles and ancient springs.

In India, before you enter a temple you go around it. There is a precinct for that purpose, and by going once, twice, three times around you prepare and center yourself. You leave your negative thoughts behind. When your body, mind, and heart are ready, then you may enter the temple. Similarly, I was making a journey around the temple of Britain, so that I might enter into its mysteries. This pilgrimage was a pilgrimage to Britain, to its rivers, hills, moors, dales, fields, to all its natural beauty. Walking every day would take me four months. In India people go on pilgrimage for a week, or a month, for a year, or even more; I know four women pilgrims who walked together the length and breadth of India, taking twelve years.

In Canterbury Cathedral there is an area designated for silent prayer and meditation where pilgrims light a candle. In this dark corner of the cathedral, lit only by the many candles, I too lit a candle and said the Prayer for Peace. After giving his blessings, Canon Brett led me to the chapel of Saint Thomas a Becket. Although modernized, the chapel has an atmosphere of martyrdom, the sword hanging above the altar speaking the language of power and pain. I stood in silence and astonishment as Canon Brett told me the story. King Henry II had wanted to break the power of the church and so had appointed his friend Becket as archbishop of Canterbury in 1162. But when Thomas took his place in Canterbury, his inner voice told him that he must be true to God, and being true to God brought him in conflict with the king. In exasperation, a drunken Henry said one day at dinner, "Will no one revenge me of the injuries I have sustained from one turbulent priest?" The archbishop knew that knights were coming to kill him. His monks urged him to hide or escape or to order them to resist. The archbishop was unperturbed. He said calmly, "Why should I hide? I am not afraid of death. One thing is certain, all of us will die one day; no need to hide or escape. As for resistance, we are not here to resist but to suffer. We will not take life, we will offer our life." And so Thomas a Becket died at the altar and became a martyr.

But when the king heard that his knights had actually killed Thomas, he wept. The sacrifice of Thomas à Becket transformed the king: Henry repented, and walking on his knees became the first pilgrim to Canterbury.

Listening to this story I felt my doubts and hesitation vanish, my pre-occupation with home, work, and worldly responsibility diminish. The tale of Thomas à Becket's fearlessness and detachment created a moment of breakthrough for me.

This breakthrough was further consolidated when I crossed the Thames Estuary by boat. Being in the water gave me the sensation of being away from the earth, sailing away, leaving the world behind.

There is no longer a ferry between Faversham and Southend-on-Sea. The usual route to Ely would have taken me to London and through the Dartford tunnel. I had all along tried to avoid walking through the busy streets of London. So, thanks to John Harrison, I was able to cross the wide Thames estuary on a personal ferry: *The Orcades,* the home of Andrew Kennedy and Stevie, who make their living as painters using watercolor and oil. *The Orcades* is generally anchored off Rochester, and it came to Faversham to take me across the estuary under sail. I was expecting a crossing of a couple of hours, but the weather was rough, the wind was blowing, the waves were high, and the rain was tapping on the roof. When we arrived at Southend Pier seven hours later, at 6:00 P.M., the sky was heavy with dark clouds. I was in the midst of a roaring thunderstorm, with dazzling lightning and heavy rain. Southend Pier had suffered from fire a few years before and was still black, charred, and deserted. There was only one rusty, broken, and slippery flight of steps left. With pounding heart and shivering body, I walked the one-and-a-quarter-mile-long pier.

By the time I arrived at the house of my hostess, Hazel Grimsdale, I could see a glimpse of the evening sun, which was about to set, and a patch of blue sky behind the clouds. The wind was dropping. Hazel said, "You couldn't have chosen a worse day to sail." But I disagreed, saying, "I would not have missed this experience at any price." When one is in a house, one wants to avoid the rain, the wind, the thunder and lightning. But when I was in that storm, the experience of the elements was physically and spiritually exhilarating.

FROM SOUTHEND, accompanied by a Japanese friend, Shigeo Koyabashi, and his twelve-year-old son, Sean, I walked to Chelmsford. From there

I continued north to Saffron Walden, Cambridge, and along the banks of the river Cam to Ely.

Almost six miles before reaching Ely I could see the faint outline of the great cathedral, and as I walked closer and closer, the grandeur of this magnificent holy place of pilgrimage slowly revealed itself. This day's walk felt easy. The riverbank was soft and level, but more than that I felt I was being pulled by the power of the cathedral. By the time I arrived in Ely, I was already so much immersed in the visual and emotional experience of the cathedral that I felt I knew it intimately.

Entrance to this holy place of pilgrims and visitors was no longer free, and when I urged the box office clerk to let me, as a penniless pilgrim, go and offer my prayers before the altar, I was told that no exception could be made. As I looked at those who were permitted inside holding their tickets, eating ice-cream cones, treating the building as a historic monument, a museum, reading up on its facts and figures, it seemed to me that spiritual experience was perhaps easier to find outside rather than inside its walls.

I followed the river Gapping Way to Ipswich, visiting the country churches en route to Brinkley near Newmarket, Ickworth Park near Bury St. Edmunds, and Bucks Hall near Stowmarket.

It was always an interesting exercise to seek and find little footpaths and narrow country lanes, sometimes tarmac and sometimes dirt tracks. The Landranger series of Ordnance Survey maps is excellent for this purpose. I could not carry all the relevant maps with me, as they would have been too heavy, so I would borrow a map from my host, and when I had walked off its edge, I would ask the next host to return it to the previous one and lend me the map of the next section. Sometimes if I did not have a map I would ask people the way. Strangely, people would try to direct me toward the main roads; when I said that main roads are not for walking on, that they are for cars and surely there must be a path for pedestrians, I would often discover that local people did not know their local footpaths. They would say: I wouldn't advise you to take the footpath—you will get lost; the paths are overgrown; it is much longer that way; or the farmer has plowed it up. But none of these answers would satisfy me, as I was prepared to make any amount of detour to avoid traffic, tarmac, fumes, and noise.

In fact I was much impressed by the number of long- and short-distance footpaths that exist in the English countryside. Three cheers for

the National Trust, the Ramblers Association, and various other countryside conservers who fight and maintain these lovely paths! By being
away from the main roads, I was much more intimately in the heart of
Nature, without disturbance. On these rural paths I met the trees, animals, rocks, rivers, and birds, and realized the sacredness of all Nature.
The churches, cathedrals, mosques and synagogues, shrines and temples
are not the only holy places, but the whole of creation is divine and
sacred. My pilgrimage was in every moment and in every place.

Sometimes I came across a tree which seemed like a Buddha or a
Jesus: loving, compassionate, still, unambitious, enlightened, in eternal
meditation, giving pleasure to a pilgrim, shade to a cow, berries to a
bird, beauty to its surroundings, health to its neighbors, branches for the
fire, leaves to the soil, asking nothing in return, in total harmony with
the wind and the rain. How much I can learn from a tree! The tree is
my church, the tree is my temple, the tree is my mantra, the tree is my
poem and my prayer.

Standing under a tree by the Gapping River, I realized that the law
of nature is to create energy and life by uniting. A seed united with the
soil creates the tree; water united with the earth produces crops. When
man and woman are united in love, they create a child. Wherever there
is unity, sacred and positive energy is generated. How absurd that our
modern materialistic mind is more accustomed to divide, to analyze, to
split and separate. The extreme example of the splitting mind is the
splitting of the atom. What do we get? Nuclear power and nuclear
weapons: a grotesque manifestation of negative energy. When two become one, the third emerges. When the one is divided and fragmented,
it brings destruction.

I had walked for about six hours, and as I was carrying no water I felt
thirsty. When I saw a small farmhouse not far from the river Gapping,
I left the path and walked across the field to it. I saw a woman in her
late thirties, her hair bound up in a scarf, making the most of this rare
sunny day—the first of May. She was absorbed in gardening as if in
meditation. I stood by the garden gate, slightly concerned that I should
disturb her, but fortunately for me she happened to look over her shoulder, her face serene and smiling. Looking at her I forgot my thirst; there
was a moment of suspense—neither of us knew why I was there. This
moment passed, and she said "Hello." Gathering myself together I said,

"I have been walking all day, the sun is hot, I am thirsty. Is it possible to get a glass of water?"

"Of course, do come in."

I followed her into the kitchen. "This man wants a glass of water," she said to her husband.

"Only a glass of water, or something stronger?"

"Anything, but not alcohol, would be fine."

"Cup of tea? Orange juice?"

"I would love a cup of tea."

"I would love one too," said the man, and offered me a chair by the long, pine table.

He was curious to know how far I had walked, why I was walking, and where I was walking to. When I told him that I had walked from Devon and was going to Lindisfarne and Iona and would be walking back through the mountains of north Wales, he said, "Rather you than me." But I could detect beneath his comment a little hint that he would also like to be free and on the road. When I told him that I was on a pilgrimage, he was even more intrigued. By the time I had told him snippets of my story and finished my cup of tea and homemade cake, he and his wife asked, "Why not stay for supper? Stay for the night?" I was touched. "It is very generous and kind of you to offer hospitality to a stranger like me." "But we don't get a pilgrim walking around Britain every day. Stay and tell us more of your story."

However, I had already arranged to stay with Brian Keeble in Ipswich that evening, and therefore I had to apologize for not accepting their spontaneous invitation. Hospitality is alive and well in Suffolk, but unexpected guests are rare.

One of the important elements of my journey was a pilgrimage to people. I had arranged my itinerary in advance so that people would know when I was coming, so they could arrange a get-together of friends. I considered that those involved in care of the land, peace in the world, and regeneration of spiritual life were all holy people from whom I could take inspiration, and it was to them I journeyed.

ONE SUCH INSPIRING PERSON was Lady Eve Balfour, who lived about twenty-five miles north of Ipswich. Some months before, Lady Eve had written to ask me for the recipe for chappatis—unleavened Indian flat bread. It is something of a miracle that with just flour, salt, and water you can create fresh, delicious bread within a few minutes. Earth, water, fire, and air come together to make a chappati. But it is hard to describe in words how to make it. Here is my attempt at a recipe:

Take two cups of whole-meal, freshly stone-ground, organically grown flour with one level teaspoon of sea salt mixed in. Add warm water to make a soft dough. Knead well and form into scone-sized balls. Roll these balls out round and flat and even. Place the chappati on a hot, dry, heavy frying pan (preferably cast iron). Cook the first side until it forms a dry surface, then turn over and cook the second side slightly more, until a few golden brown spots appear. Turn back to the first side, and with a ball of cloth press the chappati onto the pan and watch it puffing. Be gentle and attentive, don't let it burst or burn. When it has puffed up like a balloon, then it is ready. Spread a touch of butter on it. Serve immediately with cheese, salad, or cooked vegetables.

I sent this recipe to Lady Eve. She tried it and replied, "It didn't work; it didn't puff, and it was burnt all over." I tried to explain again: "Perhaps you didn't allow it sufficient time to form the crust on the first side, or perhaps you pressed the chappati too hard and broke it. In any case, it is a question of trial and error. Try again." Lady Eve tried again but still couldn't master it. So I said to her, "During my pilgrimage I will come and pay my respects to you and then I will demonstrate chappati making." She was thrilled and waited for the chappati session for three months.

When I arrived she had prepared a wonderful three-course meal for me, with fresh lettuce salad, the first I had tasted of the year, from her garden.

"You shouldn't have gone to such trouble, Lady Eve," I said. "I have to pay you a fee for teaching me to make chappatis, don't I?" She laughed.

We made chappatis together. I had never had such an attentive pupil. Although in her late eighties, she could learn like a child. She did as I told her. No ego and no pride. As Lady Eve was learning to make chappatis from me, I was learning humility from her. She made perfect chappatis, and we were both delighted.

Many years ago, when the wind of so-called technological progress was blowing hard and farmers were being persuaded to switch over to chemical farming, Eve Balfour stood firm for the principles of organic farming and launched the Soil Association together with the publication of her classic book *The Living Soil.* At the age of eighty-nine she was still a beacon for people engaged in maintaining the fertility of the earth. A lifelong gardener, she had perfected the techniques of growing fruit, vegetables, and flowers in all sorts of conditions. There was fruit under nets, small plants in cloches, seedlings in cold frames, and greenhouses of various sizes. In the first week of May 1986, when spring was late everywhere and everything was so behind, in the garden of Lady Eve everything was bursting with life. There were lots of little white flowers growing everywhere on the path.

"What are these flowers, Lady Eve?" I asked.

"Mind your own business," she replied. Taken aback, I wondered if I had asked something wrong, so apologetically I said, "I was only asking." "Yes, that is the name of the flower!"

We both laughed. "How do you manage to grow everything so well?" I asked. "I do nothing, just look after the soil, and the plants look after themselves."

What a pearl of wisdom, I reflected. Everybody is so concerned with plants and crops and yields. Lady Eve is primarily concerned with the soil, but she gets the crops anyway. We do not realize the importance or even the existence of the soil. We see trees growing, animals grazing, wonderful botanic and ornamental gardens flourishing, but underneath it all lies mother soil, largely ignored.

As I went on from the gardens of Lady Eve toward Norwich, I mused on the connection between the soil and the soul. As flowers, fruit, and grain grow out of the soil, intellect, arts, emotions, philosophy, thought, religion, and so many other qualities grow out of the soul. We are ever so busy in developing all the qualities and faculties without paying attention to the cultivation of the soul. We use chemicals to increase the output of crops, and we pour much sterile information and ideas into our heads.

An organic gardener like Lady Eve uses all waste such as weeds, autumn leaves, and kitchen refuse in a compost, and recycles and transforms waste into food for the soil. A seeker of spiritual wisdom can transform waste material such as anger, greed, lust, fear, and pride into energy for the soul.

MOTHER JULIAN OF NORWICH kept herself in a tiny cell to conquer her attachment to the flesh and cultivate the soul. She was able to overcome despair, writing, "All shall be well, all manner of things shall be well." This simple statement expressed a profound trust and faith in creation and in existence. My visit to the site of Mother Julian's cell, while I was contemplating the soil and the soul, made me make a connection between Eve Balfour and Mother Julian of Norwich: one, the soil mother and the other, the soul mother.

It is through the mother energy that our life is conceived, embodied, nurtured, and sustained. With a profound sense of gratitude, I went on from the cell of Mother Julian to the shrine of Our Lady of Walsingham. When I came into the dark inner room of the shrine, windowless with a narrow entrance, I felt as if I was entering the womb of the mother goddess. The room is lit only by candles and, as all pilgrims do, I lit a candle. As I stood in silence, eyes closed, I saw a white silhouette of a goddess against a gray background. The silhouette was not external—it rose from within. It was an expression of the experience of the power of the feminine. I came out of the womb room to the holy well of healing water. Water from the well is kept in a clay pot for pilgrims to drink: thousands have come to drink this water and be healed. Faith in water expresses the feminine aspect of healing. I took the water in cupped hands and drank, feeling the mother energy revitalizing me. How it was special I cannot tell, but certainly it was no ordinary water.

I could not leave Walsingham without visiting the Russian Orthodox Church about which I had been told by a *Resurgence* reader a few days previously. I was not disappointed. An abandoned British Railways station has been converted into a beautiful place of worship. A resident artist is with great dedication painting colorful icons of Russian saints and Bible stories, which fill the church. Within an aura of calm and peace, a pilgrim is effortlessly lifted into a state of prayer. Like walking by the river or in the woods, the atmosphere of the place helps to still the mind.

For ordinary mortals like me the physical atmosphere of calmness helps to encourage inner stillness. The wonder of Walsingham lies in its atmosphere of tranquillity. I don't know what happens when there are thousands of pilgrims crowding the streets, but on the sixth of May I seemed to be the only pilgrim there.

Between Walsingham and Crowland I had no place to stay. Molly Stiles of Norwich, an ardent champion of small schools, said, "You must go and give your support to the parents of Boughton village school, which is threatened with closure. I know it is off your route, but my friend Paul Coulten could pick you up in the evening and put you back at the same point the next morning."

Since I wanted to accomplish my pilgrimage on foot, it was with mixed feelings that I accepted Molly's suggestion. As Boughton was far off my route, it was not possible for me to walk there and keep to my itinerary, but at the same time I was keen to lend my support to this school in its struggle to survive.

After walking about twenty miles from Walsingham, I rang the Coulten household, reversing the charges. Mrs. Coulten answered. "Yes, Molly told me all about you. I will come immediately and pick you up." And so she did.

I arrived in the Coulten home and found myself in the lap of luxury. The house is set in an English garden of sumptuous size with flowering cherries, orchards, lawns, and tall trees. We sat surrounded by flowers in a huge, heated Victorian conservatory, drinking sherry. Paul Coulten runs a family insurance business started by his father and had never heard of anything like *Resurgence* or the alternative ideas represented in it. But that was no barrier between us. Mr. and Mrs. Coulten were warm, generous, and kind hosts.

Next morning they took me to see the primary school, which was set in the center of the village facing the village green, complete with a most beautiful duck pond. Children were happily playing, as if in heaven. How could the bureaucrats in the county town even contemplate the idea of closing such a superb school in an idyllic setting? The local government officers of Norfolk, sitting in their urban centers, concerned with economies of scale, were obviously taking no account of the human cost of closing such a village school and making little children learn to be commuters. Looking at the children playing, I could sense their inner security, which was surely due to the fact that they knew that their parents were just around the corner, their roots were there and they belonged there. To bus them away to a place they don't know, to a modern box-shaped building, where they will be instructed in an alien environment, is a totally misguided notion. What has become of England? Where have the sanity and wisdom gone? Have we not destroyed our rural communities enough already? Have we not alienated, disoriented, and displaced our young? Respect for the family, the community, and the natural environment is no longer part of education, it seems; otherwise, why should such schools be closed?

After our visit to the school, Mrs. Coulten said to her husband, "Darling, I am rather busy this morning. Could you take Satish back to his route?"

"Oh no, sweetheart, I have a meeting in Cambridge at noon. How am I going to manage?" Turning toward me, Paul Coulten asked, "Would you mind if I fly you there?"

I was slightly taken aback. This offer did not represent the simplicity I had planned for. I had seen Mrs. Coulten's Volvo, I had seen Mr. Coulten's sports car, but I didn't know that I, a penniless itinerant, would be offered a flight through the air. Mr. Coulten was obviously pressed for time, so what difference would it make if I were driven along a road or through the air? I agreed.

We flew over the Fens, the flat and treeless landscape of East Anglia. Mr. Coulten dropped me at an airstrip near to where I had left my path. What a difference of speed! What had taken six or seven minutes in the plane, and half an hour in the car, would have taken me perhaps six hours to walk. After being left at the airstrip, I had to readjust myself to my pedestrian pace. I had to walk through the Fens.

The fields were square, edged with drainage canals. There was not a bird, not an animal, not a human being. Occasionally a tractor or chemical sprayer in the distance, otherwise only the open sky with which to console myself. Miles and miles of level land, every inch shaped by human hands. Walking through such monotonous landscape, I felt bored and at times even frightened, reduced to an insignificant, lonely speck.

I AM USED TO DESERT. In the desert of Rajasthan, where I was born, the sands shine in the moonlight like fields of silver; here in the Fens I experienced an intensity of emptiness normally associated with the desert. It was an experience of exile, away from my home, my wife and my children, my friends and my colleagues, my neighbors and my village, the security of known and familiar surroundings, the cushion of set patterns, milking the cow and digging the garden and answering the phone.

Here, I was all alone on the road, with no particular place to go. I felt in exile from Hartland, but is Hartland really my home? After all, I have lived there only for seven years. I am in exile from my wife, but even that relationship is only fourteen years old. I am in exile from India, but in India where do I belong and to whom? My father died when I was four, I left my mother, my family, and my home when I was nine. The world is transitory, and I am just passing through, searching for my real home.

WALKING FROM CROWLAND via Spalding, I was making for Swineshead when suddenly a car stopped. As I passed by, the woman passenger asked if I would like a lift. I was deep in thought and never expected this offer. "Thank you for your kindness, but I am walking." "Where are you walking?" "To Swineshead." "We are also going to Swineshead. It will take you at least two hours to walk there, so why don't you get in the car, we will take you there."

At that moment, company would have been consoling and welcome, but I said: "You are very kind, but I must walk." The man said, "Just here people stand for hours showing their thumb and seeking a lift. Here we are offering you one, but if you don't want it, that's all right." They could not understand why I should refuse a lift and insist on walking. The man switched on the engine and was about to drive away. I quickly tried to explain that I was not trying to be rude or discourteous but that I was on a pilgrimage and had vowed to walk. The driver seemed unconvinced, and with a grumpy face he said, "OK, if that's what you want, good luck."

They drove off leaving me standing there, misunderstood. This I thought was the result of being on the road; looking again at my map, I discovered a dirt track leading toward Swineshead. I took it!

After about a mile a farmer came along on his tractor. "May I ask what you are doing here?" "I am making my way to Swineshead." "But you are trespassing on private land." "But this track is shown on the map and is not a dead end. Moreover I am harming no one and damaging nothing." "That is not the point; you are trespassing, and I don't want ramblers and hikers using my private land."

He was an example of some of the English country gentry who are extremely property-conscious. Offensive and ugly signs stating TRES-PASSERS WILL BE PROSECUTED; PRIVATE—KEEP OUT; GUARD DOGS PRO-TECT THIS PROPERTY; and BEWARE OF THE DOG are everywhere. I knew that there was no point in arguing, so I apologized. "I am very sorry, I didn't realize that this was a private track, but since I am already halfway along it, would you be kind enough to let me continue? I would be very grateful."

He was gracious enough to let me go.

At the point where the track joined a small country road stood the farmer's house, guarded by several Alsatian dogs. At some distance from the house they heard the sound of my footsteps and started barking loudly. With some nervousness I carried on, and as I came closer to the farm the dogs were frantic. On one side of the house there were two dogs chained, rushing up and down, straining to get at me but being jerked back by their chains. On the other side of the house a metal cage confined another two Alsatians trying hard, but unsuccessfully, to get out. They leapt up again and again at the bars of the cage, barking at the top of their lungs. My heart bled for these pathetic dogs. What has the farmer got that is so precious that he needs to imprison these poor dogs? This was not the only place where I experienced such a scene. People who whizz through cocooned in their cars may not realize it, but somebody who walks every day through the English countryside will experience the horror of farm after farm and house after house with imprisoned dogs to guard them. The anger and ferocity of these dogs was a regular irritation in my walking experience.

MY HOSTESS NEAR SWINESHEAD was Diane Moreland, who lives just outside the village of Fenhouses. It was not difficult to find her as she had written to me to say that she bred Afghan hounds, and there was a sign with a hound on the house. I entered the courtyard of the Coach House and saw in one corner, under a spacious covered enclosure, the Afghan hounds: tall and serene with silky hair, with golden puppies playing around. Here the hounds were not bred to guard but for their beauty and their company. This was a totally different and much more pleasant sight.

Diane opened the door and with a welcoming gesture took the ruck-sack from my back. As she put the kettle on and I collapsed in an armchair, she asked if I had had a good walk. The question was easier than the answer. Although physically I was not too tired, I felt as if I had been on the path and walking for a long, long time, much longer than eight hours. It was impossible to tell Diane what kind of walk I had had that day, and it is difficult to describe it even now, on paper.

Diane and I had not met before, and she was not a reader of *Resurgence,* so while we were enjoying a cup of tea I asked, "How did you come to know that I was going on a pilgrimage?" "Your hosts tomorrow, Biff and Helen Vernon, belong to the Healers' Network. They looked in the contact list to see if there was anybody between Crowland and Sleaford, as there was a gap in your itinerary, and they found me. Although I have never met the Vernons, they didn't hesitate to ask me to put you up. I said yes, and then on the same day I saw in the *Radio Times* that you would be featured on the program *Profile,* so I listened to it. I found your story interesting and wanted to meet you."

Next morning Diane walked with me for a few miles, and later Biff came on his bicycle to meet me and accompany me to his home. He is a teacher and lives with his partner, Helen, and their two children on a smallholding where they practice organic gardening and a life of self-sufficiency. They are part of a movement of young people who have left the cities to live a lifestyle compatible with their ideal of simple, wholesome, and harmonious living.

From their kitchen window I could see the high tower of Lincoln Cathedral, seventeen miles away. I had been invited to lunch by the bishop of Lincoln and therefore had to make an early start to be there by one o'clock. Helen and Biff were very kind to get up at six o'clock in the morning to give me breakfast and send me off.

In this flat land, the city of Lincoln rests on a hill, and the cathedral crowns it. The cathedral was guiding my path like a lighthouse. Sometimes I lost sight of it as I walked through villages and woods, but for the last seven miles the towers never disappeared from my view. It drew me like a magnet, through the drizzling rain. I walked without stopping for six hours, hardly noticing distance or time. I was half an hour early for lunch.

THE BISHOP, Simon Phipps, and his wife, Mary, welcomed me at their house situated at the East Gate of the cathedral. Seeing me wet through, he said, "As you have walked some distance, perhaps you would like to relax or have a bath while Mary is getting the lunch together?" I was delighted—I couldn't have thought of anything better than lying in the luxury of a palatial bathroom enjoying a midday soak. When I came down we sat together in the spacious living room, by the fire. "It is with great pleasure that I welcome you, Satish, to Lincoln and to my house," the bishop said. "Going on a pilgrimage is an ancient Christian tradition, but walking for four months around Britain to its sacred places is not so common." "I am honored to be your guest," I said. "I have indeed been inspired and renewed by being within many churches and cathedrals, but increasingly I am finding all places sacred and the presence of the divine everywhere." The bishop heard my comment with thoughtful silence and then said, "For us, God is above and beyond his creation. We aspire to reach God, but God and the world are not the same." "In the Hindu tradition the world is understood to be the dance of the god Shiva, and yet the dance and the dancer cannot be separated. The world is not like a painting, a finished object which when complete is seen as separate from the painter. The universe is a living dance, and God is in the heart of all beings and all things. We do not separate God and the world."

The bishop pondered and in a gentle voice said, "I believe that the world is God's creation and therefore it is sacred. Human beings must act as responsible guardians and caring stewards. We must love the land and look after the Earth in its glorious diversity. We have no right to plunder, pollute, exploit, destroy, kill, or in any way disrespect God's creation. Like in a family, God is the Father and we are his children, and all members of the family should live in harmony with each other. God's family includes the animals and the natural world. If we are sensitive and caring, we can live with nature rather than against it. The advance of science and technology requires that human beings live with greater sensitivity than ever before, since we are now equipped with extremely powerful and potentially destructive tools. This destructive impulse is not part of God. God is good and good only."

"For me, Divinity is neither good nor bad," I said. "It is like pure water and pure air. The human soul is also pure. Good and bad is a matter of perception. For example, from nature's point of view creeping buttercups or nettles are fine wherever they are; they will grow where the soil is right for them. From the human perspective, however, a gardener struggles to remove the buttercups and nettles; he regards them as weeds and complains when they overtake flowers. The rose and the thorn are part of the same plant—we cannot have one without the other. The analytical mind always attempts to separate the good and evil, the decorative and the ugly, the useful and the nonuseful, the weed and the flower. I have seen during my journey people pulling out foxgloves in one area and carefully planting them in another. If we are to live in harmony with God's family, we need to love the wilderness, the weeds, and the wet."

The discussion was getting deeper when Mary said, "It is all very interesting, but lunch is ready. Let's eat."

There was delicious food on the table: grapefruit and pineapple slices with chopped avocado and nuts in a delightful dressing for the starter, pasties stuffed with rice, cheese, beans, mushrooms, and herbs, served with cooked green vegetables, salad, and red wine. Then crystallized ginger chopped in cream with white dessert wine, followed by Earl Grey tea. This was the meal of the month! "Thank you very much for such a feast and for all the care and trouble you have taken in preparing it," I said. "When I first heard that you were a vegetarian I was taken aback," said Mary. "I had never cooked a full vegetarian meal in my life, but it was a challenge and I enjoyed it. And now I am glad that you are enjoying eating it."

Laughingly I said, "Yes, you need an Indian pilgrim to bring vegetarianism to the bishop's house." We all laughed and I said, "It is good to feast and it is good to fast. It is good to celebrate and it is good to undergo a penance. My pilgrimage is a kind of penance." "What do you mean by penance?" Mary asked. "Penance is a process of cleansing of the soul, undertaken entirely voluntarily. It is not a punishment or a penalty, it is not performed so as to achieve remission of sins, it does not arise out of contrition, it is not an act of self-mortification. As in the course of daily living our bodies require cleansing, as in the course of constant speech we need a period of silence, as after the company of others we need a period of solitude, so after fifty years of worldly life I needed to perform an act which would nurture my soul. Feast is food for the body, and fast is food for the soul. Being in a secure, homely, and comfortable environment is pleasant to the body and the emotions. Being on the road is hard on the body but is a state in which the soul can take wings and the spirit can be free." "That's a very interesting definition of penance," Mary replied. "As a Jungian analyst I understand it well, but such an act of penance must be absolutely voluntary. When it is imposed by someone else, even by a priest, it becomes a punishment." "We almost need a new word for the kind of penance I am talking about. A word to imply a purifying activity rather than a mortifying activity."

Simon and Mary were marvelous hosts. After lunch I was offered a comfortable bed on which to rest, followed by a guided tour of the magnificent cathedral. Once in the cathedral I could feel the dedication of the stonemasons, carpenters, and others who in previous centuries created this splendid edifice to the glory of God. In our times people build to the greater glory of banks and insurance companies! I was led to a small, intimate, and cozy chapel in the cathedral. In the tranquil calm of the chapel we meditated together, and I was brought to tears when Simon prayed for me and the completion of my pilgrimage. I felt like a baby held in caring hands.

Later I learned from a mutual friend that he was praying every day for me, and on my arrival back in Hartland, I received a postcard from him desiring to know if I had arrived home safe and sound. How could I not, when he was praying for me?

FROM LINCOLN ONWARD I pursued my journey with a settled mind and strong spirit. Now it was truly spring. Deep in the woods I found a bank covered with delicate yellow flowers. They were not primroses, and I had not come across flowers like these before. I wondered what they were, and with some hesitation I picked one and put it in my hat to ask later what it might be called. But I did not need to—the first person I met asked where I had got this "cowslip," as they are so rare. I explained that I had found a place in the woods where they were growing in abundance. Some inspired farmer had left a wide belt of woodland between plowed fields, growing willows, sweet chestnuts, ash, and alongside them flowering cherry.

This must have been one of the greatest years for cherry blossom. Never since I was in Japan in the spring of 1964 had I seen such a stunning sight. I stood there, spellbound, gazing at the glory of God. I was in an enchanted land where every single bud was in full bloom, flowering to its utmost perfection. All my walking from Hartland to here, all these forty-six days, was worth it to be at this moment under these cherry trees.

After an overnight stay with Gary Miller at Willingham-by-Stow, I followed a little-used path along the Weir Dykes in the direction of Barrow-on-Humber. The path was overgrown with thigh-high dewy grasses, so that, even though the weather was dry and sunny, my only pair of shoes were constantly filled with water and my trousers were saturated. The grasses are the colorful clothing of the earth; they hold the soil together and protect it from erosion. The soft caresses of the grasses contributed to the bliss of walking along this unspoiled and secluded path.

The bridge over North Kelsey Beck, which runs into Weir Dyke and interrupts the path, was broken: a sign said, DANGER—BRIDGE NOT SAFE TO CROSS. I could not contemplate turning back, which would surely have involved at least a ten-mile detour, so I risked it.

The path showed no sign of being in use, and I met nobody walking it. I enjoyed every moment in complete peace and solitude. Walking became a meditation, and every step was teaching me to be mindful. I relaxed to the sound of my own breath as it issued into the deep silence surrounding me. Breathing in I inhaled the warmth of the air, the smell of the wet grasses, the coolness of the water, the purity of Nature; I was breathing the universe into myself. Breathing out I was offering my energy to the universe. Breathing was my connection with the cosmos. I was one with the world.

As I breathe, I breathe the breath of God, the breath of all the peoples of the world. I receive a breath transfusion from existence itself. The birds, the cows, the sheep, the deer, the trees, and the grasses greet me by giving their breath to me as I pass them. My breathing is the sharing of life itself. Suddenly I found myself chanting:

> *Lead me from Death to Life,*
> *From Falsehood to Truth,*
> *Lead me from Despair to Hope,*
> *From Fear to Trust,*
> *Lead me from Hate to Love,*
> *From War to Peace,*
> *Let Peace fill our hearts,*
> *Our world, our universe,*
> *Peace, peace, peace.*

Again and again I kept chanting. Many other childhood chants from Sanskrit, Pali, and the Jain scriptures came to me. Chants which I had never used in thirty years appeared clear in my memory. The ecstasy of walking and chanting held me for hours. What freedom, being on the path. What a holiday does for your weary body and tired mind, a pilgrimage does for your soul and your spirit.

A night's rest with Betty and Ben Whitwell at Barrow-on-Humber well prepared me to be on the path again. I was always grateful to have night between the two days' walking. Without the night the day would be a burden; without the dark the light would be unbearable. Thanks to the night, every morning, no matter what the weather, wet or dry, sunny or windy, cold or warm, I was able to be on the road.

On the morning of May 15, as I set out from Barrow, I could see in the distance the huge Humber Bridge, a symbol of technological achievement. I followed the railway line to Burton-upon-Humber, from where I walked over the one-and-a-half-mile-long suspension bridge. The wind was particularly strong as it whipped up the estuary. My hat flew off, and I had to run after it—I saved it just before it fell into the river. Thereafter I had to hold my hat on my head tightly with one hand. After crossing the bridge I followed the river Humber westward to Goole. The gusty wind of the bridge was now followed by heavy rain. At one point, very near the path along the river, I sought shelter in a garage. Scarcely a moment had passed when a young woman opened the door of the house and with a big smile asked, "Are you all right in there? Isn't the rain dreadful?" "I'm sure it will soon pass. May I shelter in your garage until then?" "Of course you can," she said and went away. A little later she returned, this time with a cup of tea.

In Goole I stayed at the Natural Healing Center, where Kath Huddleston practices crystal healing. Members of the center were holding crystals in their hands. In every room crystals of all sizes, colors, and shapes, from all parts of the world, were displayed and gave out their healing influences. Kath told me that different people respond to different crystals and therefore it is quite an art to match the crystal to the person. For those who do not respond to crystal healing there were facilities for homeopathy, massage, acupuncture, and other forms of herbal and natural treatment, including spiritual healing. In the beginning of my journey I would have tried all these forms to alleviate the pain of my body; now I could observe these therapies with interest but without the need to try them myself.

I followed the river Ouse to Selby, and from Selby a disused railway line, recently converted to a bicycle path, bore me on to York. What a brilliant inspiration it was to bring back these disused and closed lines, which were still in perfectly good condition, for the use of walkers and cyclists! Free from the fumes of cars and protected on both sides by steep banks, I was able to reach York without the sight or sound of traffic on the road. I was told that the Manpower Services Commission (MSC) had provided the labor force to make it possible. I am sure that future generations will associate these paths with the period of the MSC and the great unemployment of the eighties as we associate so many bridges and railways with the Victorian era.

There must be thousands of miles of disused railway lines in the country, complete with bridges, lined with trees, and passing through most scenic countryside. If all of them were to be brought back into use for walkers and cyclists, it would reduce a lot of the congestion on the roads as many short-distance travelers would take to bicycles. It would also bring good health to the nation, as walking and bicycling are perfectly good physical exercise, and it would reduce the number of unemployed, as thousands of people would be required to work physically and with simple tools to adapt these railway lines to cycle and pedestrian use. I was only surprised that so few of these projects had been undertaken.

YORK IS A LOVELY CITY: the people have managed to keep out ugly modernization. Even the chain stores and department stores have been kept under control, with the old and the new standing side by side in harmony. It is usually a disappointment to come to big cities like Birmingham or Leeds—they don't look any different from one another. The same shops with the same goods, the same roads, the same houses, a monoculture of modernity that makes you wish you had stayed at home. Even as a stranger, I felt the friendliness of York's streets and houses and also the friendliness of those who dwell within them.

I stayed in St. Paul's Square, which is like a little hamlet or village: a community, closely knit together, everybody knowing each other, helping each other, and their children playing together on the open green of the square surrounded by magnificent trees towering above the tall houses. Although it is called a square, the houses in fact encircle the green. The roundness of the square makes it even more attractive, intimate, and homely. I remembered the American Indian Russell Means saying, "Roundness is equivalent to sacredness. The sun is round, the moon is round, the earth is round, the tree is round, the human body is round. Everything round is sacred." And I also remembered Ivan Illich saying, "You tell me where you live, and I'll tell you who you are." I wanted to tell Ivan that the people of York live in intimate squares like St. Paul's Square and they are very happy and human.

People were still talking about the lightning which had severely damaged a part of York Cathedral. Was it an act of protest on the part of the deity at the enthronement at York of David Jenkins, a man who disputes the Virgin Birth, as the bishop of Durham? Or was it a punishment to the church as a whole for discarding the principle of holy poverty? Or indeed both? Why did the lightning strike only the cathedral and nowhere else? It must have been an act of Providence. I heard the arguments with some amusement. What struck me was that the bishop of Durham was preferring history to myth. For myself I consider myth to be more capable than history of encompassing the complexity of truth. History is merely the accumulation of facts. Truth includes intuitive, experiential, and even irrational as well as rational aspects; fact is one aspect of the truth, but truth is greater than fact. How could a bishop be prepared to sacrifice truth to establish the facts? Apart from reflecting on this I could not offer any opinion on the act of the deity.

From York I came to the ruins of Fountains Abbey, which are well maintained by the National Trust, but more prettified than I would have liked them—presumably to please the tourists. The monks must have chosen this place for its wildness. By taming nature and turning it into a well-ordered park, some of the original magic of the place has been lost.

From Fountains Abbey I went to Rievaulx, and all my dreams of finding a ruined abbey in natural splendor were fulfilled. The ruins of Rievaulx stand in Rye Dale, a wooded valley of great power. Again the monks had chosen a magnificent site, and not an easy one. A canal was dug to connect the river Rye with the quarry so that stone for building the abbey could be brought to the exact spot, that most magical, inspirational, and holy place.

It is incredible to be in a monastery—built by human hands and with simple tools, and yet so ambitious a project. But in those days the monks were not obsessed with speed: they were not working for money, and the building of a monastery was an expression of their art, their craft, their livelihood, their dedication, and above all their good work in the service of the spirit. People told me that a lot of cheap labor was used, and the living conditions and the living standards of the workers were poor. But I couldn't help feeling that the quality of their life must have been good to produce such a monument of quality.

But of course when these abbeys and monasteries became centers of political power, and when material wealth and worldly possessions took precedence over spiritual seeking, their existence was threatened. The dissolution of the monasteries is not something over which I can shed any tears. Religion is an expression of the released spirit. When the Holy Ghost is imprisoned in monasteries, churches, temples, institutions, and disciplined orders, then it becomes frightening and haunting.

ACCOMPANIED BY MY HOST Otto Greenfield, Enzo, a novice of Tibetan Buddhism, and a young student called Neil, I walked along the river Rye and through Cropton Forest to Lastingham, to the crypt which was built by St. Ced of Lindisfarne fame. Thank goodness that St. Ced did not go for building great institutions like the abbeys of Fountains or Rievaulx but built a small church with a cavelike crypt conducive to meditation in the bleak surroundings of the Yorkshire moors. This crypt could not evoke envy; this small, simple space surrounded by stone walls embodies centuries of deep peace and eternal tranquillity—a perfect place to say the Peace Prayer.

From there Otto and Enzo turned back; Neil and I carried on through thick fog over the wild North Yorkshire moors. Neil, a student of architecture from Leeds, had joined me the previous day to walk from Fountains Abbey to Ampleforth. His intention had been to return home the same evening, but a day's walk had whetted his appetite. He asked my hosts, Otto and Rosemary Greenfield, if he could stay the night and walk on the next day.

As we walked over the wild North Yorkshire moors in the middle of May in thick fog, I was grateful that Neil had taken the decision to continue. Walking on my own would have been hair-raising. He said, "I love walking in the fog. I cannot see anything except the wet path under my feet, but I can imagine the rugged moorland around us. The fog is temporary. In a few hours, perhaps by evening or by tomorrow, it will be clear." I liked his relaxed, optimistic, and carefree attitude. There would have been no point in having someone complaining. He could easily have said, "How dreadful; we are only spending one day on this moor and it is foggy." But he didn't, and we walked as much in the land of the imagination as we walked on the moor. We had very little idea whether we were going north, east, or west. We believed that we were not going south since that was where we were coming from, but apart from that, we were totally in the lap of mist and mystery. The path was zigzagging and leading in all directions, but we followed our noses. I said to Neil, "We don't want to get lost on these moors, or our hosts tonight will be sending out helicopters in search of lost pilgrims." But Neil was much more adventurous and without worry. He reassured me that it wouldn't come to that.

After about an hour, which seemed like ages, I was able to come to terms with the fog, and I said to myself, "Whatever happens, we are in it, so why worry?" There are times in life when you don't know where you are and there is no alternative but to keep going in faith, trusting that in the end everything will be all right. Sure enough, by the time we approached the steep descent to Rosedale Abbey, the fog lifted and we could see the magnificence of the moor all around us.

Our stop for that night, the twentieth of May, was at Botton Village, a Camphill Community of the Steiner Movement. The village is spread along the south-facing slopes of the valley, where approximately three hundred people, the majority of them physically and mentally handicapped, live and work together. The community is divided into many households, each with ten to fifteen handicapped members and two houseparents. I stayed in one such minicommunity. I was much moved to see all the members cooking together, eating together, cleaning together, and supporting each other within the familylike environment of the household. What a world of difference between institutions where handicapped people are dumped, looked down on, and seen as a burden to society, and this thriving village, where they are participants in the whole range of daily activities and contribute a large percentage of the income.

I went to see the farm, the creamery, weaving, candle making, carpentry, glass engraving, printing, building, and numerous other activities where handicapped and nonhandicapped were working side by side. I was particularly inspired by a visit to the bakery, where the slowness of the handicapped bakers was no handicap at all. Rhythmic kneading of the dough by hand in a particular Steiner style was bringing everybody together. I could immediately feel that baking of bread for them was a sacred act. They were baking their daily bread for the whole Botton community as well as for a number of shops in the area. Baking bread was a source of healing the soul and feeding the body.

One of the members said to me, "If only people could learn to bake bread and share it with their family and neighbors, it would be a beginning of spiritual renewal in our society. We are what we eat. Bread is a staple and central part of our food. If we could bake bread with care and attention, our unhappiness, alienation, frustration, and bad relationships would diminish." This was a big claim. I looked into his face. "Are you sure?" "Yes, I am. I know what I am talking about and you can see it for yourself. Jesus Christ chose bread as the symbol of his own body— he could have chosen some other symbol, couldn't he? But he didn't, because bread is the real staff of life, and you cannot leave it to factories to make good wholesome bread for you."

I was impressed by his conviction. At home, my wife had always baked the bread. I decided that after the pilgrimage, when I returned home, I would begin to bake bread.

In the evening I was invited to speak about my journey to the residents of the village. I was warned that if any member of the audience should interrupt or distract me with noise or irrelevant questions, I should take no notice. When I stood in front of the packed hall, I was slightly hesitant and worried, but I started to speak in my normal way. As the story unfolded I could see beaming faces and eager eyes looking at me totally engaged. I spoke for an hour, and not once was I interrupted. Pure eyes and innocent faces in front of me with no trace of negativity, judgment, criticism, or skepticism made me feel that their handicap was only on the surface; their hearts are whole and souls unwounded. After my talk people were keen to come and thank me and shake my hands and invite me to their house. I was in tears with the warmth and love showered upon me. If these are the people whom we call handicapped, what is the word for the rest of us?

In the morning we climbed out of the valley and onto the moor again. Neil decided to walk with me for another day. We followed the Cleveland Way. The moorland here is rather boggy, so it was a great blessing to find this path studded with stepping-stones. I wondered how such beautifully shaped stones had been found—if they were brought here, it must have been a laborious task.

In the days of preindustrial Yorkshire, the people built beautiful stone walls, taking decades, sometimes generations, to turn their fields, farms, and landscapes into works of art. We make so much fuss about paintings, sculptures, and the art of building cathedrals, but people have unself-consciously nurtured and cared for their land, their trees, and their paths in such a way that now, and for generations to come, we can enjoy the fruit of their work and find sustenance for our living. On my way to Guisborough the landscape itself appeared as a great painting. Old stone walls, with moss and lichen growing in them, but still firmly holding together, follow the shapes and curves of the hillsides. Fields are rounded and of different sizes. Standing on a viewpoint and gazing at the land-scape was a fabulous feast for my eyes.

O Yorkshiremen and women of past generations, I thank you for leaving the land in such good heart and good shape. I hope that we also can leave the land in such a state that our children and grandchildren can be nourished by it.

Drunk with the beauty of the moor, Neil remembered the saying "Live as if you will die tomorrow, but farm as if you will live forever." The shepherds of Yorkshire still live through every stone, every wall, and every field.

FILLED WITH FEELINGS OF AWE, we reached the Beacon near Eston and from there looked down to see miles and miles of concrete and tarmac— the smoke-filled metropolis of Middlesborough and Billingham. What we humans do to the Earth! Yet the Earth is so tolerant, forbearing, and forgiving. Neil and I held our breath and, without much looking around, rushed through Middlesborough. The situation was much eased when a group of peace activists holding a welcome banner, met us on the bridge of the river Tees: they had organized a prayer meeting and reception for us in Billingham Church. We spent the night enjoying the warm hospitality of the minister of the United Reform Church and his wife.

I was not sorry to leave Billingham behind; I followed a disused rail-way line that had been converted to a footpath and cycle track. Although the path lasted for only a few miles, it was good to be on it, and when I left it I found myself in the midst of fields and woods. I was struck to see a herd of deer. I stopped walking and hid behind a hedge, curiously watching their swift movements. They were extremely alert and at once noticed my presence. I saw some kind of nervousness erupting, and they ran in all directions. One of them moved across the field like lightning and leaped over a high hedge. What a shame that Neil had left this morning and was not with me to witness the leaping deer on the way to Durham! I was astounded by the sight of it. What energy! What suppleness! They live on grass and leaves alone—perhaps that is why they have such pure energy and innocence. Yes, innocence. When I was watching, before they ran away, I saw no sign of sin or ego in their eyes. They looked at me deeply, directly, and penetratingly. I saw some signs of confusion and perhaps fear, but that is all.

I ARRIVED IN the Durham of St. Cuthbert, a great Celtic saint. His remains are in the cathedral, and yet he lives in every corner of this splendid city. St. Cuthbert embodied the innocent divinity of a deer. He had no difficulty in communicating with birds, otters, and other members of the animal kingdom, as well as with human beings. He was a healer of wounded souls and a teacher of deep compassion.

Along the river Weir at Finchale Abbey, I saw a gypsy man who seemed to me an incarnation of St. Cuthbert. As I approached the abbey I was stopped by him for no apparent reason. "Where do you come from?" he asked with a tremendous force. "From Devon." "Now tell me the truth. Where do you come from?" "From India, then." "There you are. Where in India?" "Rajasthan." "There you are. The queen of Rajasthan is the world queen of all Romanies and gypsies. And as a gypsy, my people originate in Rajasthan. Now, hello, brother." He put out his hand to shake mine. "In my wagon I have rice and spices. Will you come and eat with me?" "It is very kind of you to invite me, but I must keep on the road. I have a date with people in Newcastle." "Never mind, next time. Tell all our people from Rajasthan that their brother lives here and has rice and spices for them." Then he opened the buttons of his jacket and showed a waistcoat which he claimed had been given to him by the queen of Rajasthan. "We gypsies believe that all boundaries, racial, national, or religious are fake. That is why we do not make boundaries and we do not live within boundaries, that is why we follow the free spirit. We will go where the wind leads us, we will go where the clouds lead us. All men are brothers, and all living creatures belong to the same family."

I heard his words, which were spoken with deep emotion, and could not help but conclude that St. Cuthbert would not have said anything very different. Walking in the land of St. Cuthbert, I felt he was accompanying me in spirit and showing me the way to Lindisfarne, which was only about one hundred miles away, five days' walk.

I left the river Weir as it turns toward Sunderland and walked through Chester-le-Street to Newcastle, where I was the guest of the Catholic chaplain, Tony Battle. In Tony's house a young man in white robes suddenly walked into the room. "Hello, I am a Buddhist novice, and I would like to walk with you tomorrow, if I may." "Where do you live?" I asked him. "In the newly founded Buddhist monastery of Harnham. I would like to invite you to our monastery, but unfortunately we are a few miles off your route."

So far I had been to Christian centers only, and therefore a suggestion of taking my pilgrimage to a Buddhist monastery immediately grabbed me—I decided to make the detour to Harnham, next day.

The monastery is in an old farmhouse, situated on top of a hill which falls away steeply on all sides. It reminded me of the Potala Palace in Lhasa, the former residence of the Dalai Lama of Tibet. I was welcomed in the main hall of the monastery by the monks. A great brass statue of the Buddha stood in the background. All of us sat down on cushions on the floor. "It is a very new monastery, and we are pleased to welcome you here," the monks said.

Hardly a moment passed before two novices in white robes brought a chair and a bowl full of hot water with mustard powder in it. I was asked to sit on the chair and soak my feet in the bowl while we drank tea and talked. "Our founder the Venerable Sumedho spent twelve years in a forest monastery in Thailand, where he practiced a life of deep meditation, totally removed from the modern world. For the purpose of self-realization, it is essential that we do not spend our energy in trivial matters and distract ourselves from the profound task of bringing an end to all suffering," one of the monks said. "How can one bring an end to all suffering?" I asked. "Not by thinking about it, not by analyzing it, not philosophizing or speculating about it, but by being fully aware of it. A total awareness of our situation will bring about a natural and appropriate action, and that will bring an end to all illusion and suffering. But unfortunately, people indulge in mental gymnastics and theories, and miss the point. Once the Buddha was responding to a similar question; he said, 'If someone is hit by an arrow, what do you do? Do you spend your time asking from which direction the arrow came, what the arrow is made of, or what is the size and weight of the arrow? All these questions are irrelevant, a waste of time. The only appropriate action is to remove the arrow immediately from the wounded body.' There is a right action for every situation and for every form of suffering. Right action is accompanied by right thought and right living. Although there are no rigid rules for everybody to follow, if we are motivated by compassion, we will be able to help reduce and eventually overcome our own suffering and the suffering of others. Compassion is the key to open the doors of enlightenment. When you are filled with feelings of compassion, there is no room for ego, for anger, greed, or desire. These four are the cause and the source of suffering," the monk concluded.

By now my legs were revived and I was ready to walk around the buildings and woods of the monastery. No wonder that the Thai monks believe in living as forest dwellers, close to the earth. Dwelling in the forest, they derive their inspiration from the earth and the trees. The Buddha himself sat under a tree meditating. He believed that from a tree he could learn compassion. What an act of giving the tree performs when it sheds its leaves, part of its own body, so that the earth may receive nourishment! The Buddha also believed that the true answers to our deep problems come not from the mind but from the earth. What forgiveness, compassion, and forbearance the earth shows! It is dug, plowed, built upon, but it never denies anybody anything. It does not refuse or protest. We put one seed into the earth and it returns a hundredfold. When philosophers, intellectuals, and sophists came to the Buddha with skeptical questions, often he would not answer with words—his answer would be to touch the earth. He would sit in meditation for hours in his renowned posture of *Bhumi Sparsh Mudra,* the posture of touching the earth with the fingertips of both hands, which symbolizes reverence for the earth and recognition that all and everything, our body, our knowledge, and our wisdom, comes from the earth and returns to the earth. We disregard the earth at our peril. The monks of the forests are the embodiment of the earth's spirit.

Having been inspired by the living example of these monks, I found it a wonderful experience to spend the next day wandering through the woods along the river Coquet to Alnmouth.

That night I stayed in a Franciscan friary. St. Francis too, very much like the Buddha, took his inspiration from nature. He is without any doubt the patron saint of ecology. The Buddha gave up princely possessions and went with his begging bowl, practicing holy poverty. St. Francis also discarded the trappings of wealth and welcomed Lady Poverty. The lion and the deer sat side by side listening to the words of the Buddha; birds and the beasts of the field and forest came to talk to St. Francis. Thus St. Francis is the Buddha of the Christian tradition. The friars of Alnmouth follow their great master and live by the sea of nature without and the sea of faith within. They spend many hours in prayer. One of the friars said to me, "I need many hours of prayer to arrive at that perfect moment of prayer in which I am one with God." "You said it!" I replied. "It has taken two months of pilgrimage for me to arrive at some inkling of that state." The friar said, "Often people start to pray or meditate and they get impatient. The first lesson is to learn to be patient. You have to paint many paintings, and only one or two of them will be the ones you feel satisfied with. You need to play music for hours to get to a moment of ecstasy. The Japanese spend twelve years in order to learn flower arrangement. A student spends seven years learning medicine. But when people seek to learn meditation or the art of praying, they want to do it in one day. The path of prayer is not for the impatient. Prayer is not just kneeling down in a chapel and saying the words; one's whole life is prayer. When St. Francis was feeding the birds, that was his prayer—prayer was his way of life."

The friar was quite at home connecting prayer and nature in this manner, as the whole of the Northumbrian coast is vibrant with this connection. This is the coast and the country of St. Cuthbert, whose love of birds and animals evokes the memory of St. Francis.

BATTLING ALONG THE NORTH COAST with the wind blowing in gusts of ninety miles an hour, I came at last to Lindisfarne, the Holy Isle, the Isle of St. Cuthbert. I arrived in time before the tide closed the causeway. I was in a sacred temple of which the sea is the keeper. Twice every day the sea opens the gates of the temple to let the pilgrims, the visitors, and even the tourists in. Tourists generally return before the sea closes the gates, but pilgrims are in no hurry. They stay the night or a few nights, to be soaked in the tranquillity and purity of the place. The monks who chose to build the priory here were very wise; there are very few such sacred sites where the sea is the guardian of the soul. The moment I stepped on the white sand I was free of the busy world. Here I was in the company of the sun, the sky, the sea, the sand dunes, and the spirits of saintly souls. St. Cuthbert prayed and meditated in solitude, totally surrendering himself to the sacred sound of the sea. Every night after midnight when all his fellow monks were asleep he would get up and go out. On one occasion, a curious monk, a light sleeper, noticed this and followed him. He found him in the sea up to his armpits, where he spent the night, occasionally singing hymns, and with only the waves for accompaniment. At daybreak Cuthbert came out of the sea and knelt on the sand to pray. Two otters followed in his footsteps, licked his feet, and warmed them with their bodies. This is the island where humans, nature, and religion are one.

The enchantment of being on this sacred island was further enhanced by the presence of my wife, June, and my children, Mukti and Maya, who had come to see me after two months' absence. I was making my pilgrimage by being away and June was making a pilgrimage by staying at home, taking responsibility for *Resurgence,* the house, and the children, by herself. The longer I was away, the more I became aware that my voyage was only possible because June had stayed at home, and released me: her letting go was a gift of love to me. I am deeply grateful to her for this. Leaving June, children, and Lindisfarne behind felt like traveling on without a ticket. But the Cheviots on my left and the Lammermuir Hills in front were like a gravitational force pulling me toward them.

EMERGING FROM the Lammermuir Hills on the thirtieth of May 1986, I stood on the northwestern slopes gazing at the form of King Arthur. There he lies on his back, almost filling the horizon, his forehead, pointed nose, and broad shoulders resting on the land, but his feet deep in the sea. From there he rules Edinburgh, and yet eternally he is asleep. As I walked closer, the shape of the sleeping giant appeared even more clear, until I was almost under his shadow, at which point he was transformed into nothing more than a large hill known as Arthur's Seat, frequented by Edinburgh citizens for walks and for meditation. Arthur makes Edinburgh so attractive that people of arts and culture, poetry and music, education and religion have gathered around him. Edinburgh embodies the spirit of the court of King Arthur and his round table.

Arthur and his ambience make Edinburgh the most attractive city of Britain. Not too big, not too small, not too commercial, not too crowded, it is a city graced by the sea and Arthur's Seat. A night's sleep in the midst of a living tradition and ancient myths renewed my spirit for the eternal quest. Leaving Edinburgh I followed the Union Canal, now disused but still a path to paradise for walkers. Never mind, O Canal, my sister, if the longboats have deserted you! Trees and birds and green algae can flourish in peace now that you are a romantic wilderness. Weeping willows embrace you, water lilies adorn you, and herons keep you company. How happy I am to be walking at your side.

I was deeply immersed in thought when I was suddenly stopped by a Scot holding an umbrella in the drizzling rain. "Do you know what the date is today?" "It's the first of June, isn't it?" I replied, wondering why I was being stopped to be asked such a mundane question. "And it is raining, and it is cold!"

Pointing his finger at me he said, "You must be from India. Now you have too much sun, which you don't want, we have too much rain, which we don't want. Is it fair?"

I could hardly be held responsible for Nature's unfairness, but I wanted to defend her. Before I could get a word in, the stranger asked, "What are you doing in Scotland?"

The moment he knew that I was on a pilgrimage to Iona he said, "O, a pilgrim? I want to tell you a strange experience I had—please bear with me. Perhaps a pilgrim may be able to understand me. Not long ago I went to the Lake District, camping with my family. One evening, as my wife was cooking and my children were amusing themselves, I went for a drink. On my way back from the pub, as darkness fell, I saw a face, a head without a body, sitting on a stone wall peering at me. It was a saintly face, compassionate eyes, most serene. I had never seen anything like it before. I stopped. Was it Jesus Christ, I wondered. I could not move—my legs were frozen. I was taken over by fear and amazement, but within seconds I recovered. Summoning my courage, I went to the head and lifted it with both my hands. I carried it a few steps. I heard a voice, 'Why are you carrying me away? I belong here, to this place, to this wall, to these surroundings.' The voice made me shiver. I put the head back exactly in the place from which I had taken it. I retreated, and all the time the face was smiling at me.

"When I arrived at our camp, I told my wife and children what I had just experienced: an encounter with Jesus Christ, an encounter with the all-embracing smile. My family laughed at me. 'It must be a hallucination; perhaps you are drunk,' they said. There was no point in arguing. I have told this story to my friends, but they have all received it with skepticism. As you are a pilgrim, you will understand. Forgive me if I am detaining you. Although that encounter happened some time ago, I am still stunned by that most wonderful smile. Jesus Christ sat there on that wall telling me that if you can smile you can love. When you smile you are free from stresses and strains and worries of life. When you smile you please everyone and hurt no one. That experience changed my life, and that is why I am no longer shy of speaking to strangers."

Terry, and two other companions who were walking with me, stood in silence listening to his story. It was his true experience, and we were honored to celebrate the transformation of his life. "I know you have to go a long way, and perhaps I am talking too long. Thank you for listening to my story, and I wish you well in your journey." He smiled, shook hands, and said good-bye. The rest of the day our minds and our conversation were filled with the man and his remarkable story.

Terry and the two companions who had joined me were not used to walking twenty miles. In the evening they found that their feet were blistered, their hips were hurting, and their legs aching, but during the day the influence of that strange encounter carried them along.

We arrived at the house of Hazel Wood, who lives on a council estate in Larbert. When Hazel found that although she had offered hospitality to just one pilgrim there were now four of us, surprise showed for a moment on her face. But she showed no reluctance in having us all. While we drank tea and rubbed our feet, she made arrangements. She herself would sleep at her mother's house, her son would stay with his friend, her daughter with a neighbor, and the whole house would be at our disposal. "No, you can't do that," I protested. "You stay in your own rooms, and we will sleep on the floor in the living room. Pilgrims don't need the luxury of beds." "Do you want me to spend the whole night in agony and without sleep? I will not be able to bear to sleep in the comfort of my bed while my guests are on the floor. In any case, you are my guests, and you have to do as you are told!"

We all laughed. How grateful I was to Hazel and to my hosts every-where who, night after night, gave me their love and made me feel at home. For the last sixty-three days I had stayed in sixty different homes. Sometimes in a flat, sometimes in a mansion, sometimes in a council house, a farm cottage, a bungalow, but everywhere the same warmth of welcome. My hosts had included retired military men, civil servants, clergymen, small farmers, headmasters, businessmen, media people, doctors, lawyers, opticians, students, a few communities, and several monasteries. Wherever I went, I was received with love. Hazel Wood embodied all the great qualities of Scottish hospitality. We were comfortable, relaxed, happy, and we had a good night's sleep.

HOWEVER, THE PINE FORESTS of Scotland were not so hospitable. On our way to Callander, Terry and I followed a footpath, west of Aberfoyle, into the forest of Achray: a large commercial forest with many tracks, utterly confusing, each tree identical and every track the same. We followed a track which seemed to us right according to the map. It led us higher and higher to a viewpoint on the Menteith Hills, from where we could see magnificent mountains and highlands but could recognize none of them. We could see one or two lakes in the distance but were uncertain which ones they were on the map. We should have returned the same way as we had come but, reluctant to waste time and hoping that we might be heading in the right direction, we came down a steep slope. We met another track and, being without a compass, tried to guess which direction we should take. Naturally we followed what we thought was north, but after about a mile the track came to an abrupt end. This time we had to return, as it would have been foolish and impossible to venture through the thick forest without knowing where we were going. For about two hours we kept wandering round and round, up and down, backwards and forwards, frustrated, exhausted, and lost. Suddenly from the top of a hill we recognized the town of Aberfoyle and realized that instead of moving west toward Callander we had regressed and were east of Aberfoyle. "Let's sit down and eat our lunch," Terry said in a worried voice, "and thank goodness we still have most of the afternoon in which to find our way."

We sat down, had our lunch, and looked at the map as hard as we could. None of the tracks through the forest was on the map. We reflected that we were lost only because we wanted to go somewhere! We could easily build a small shelter from the wood around, and there was plenty of fresh water in the streams. We were surrounded with delicate flowers and delicious berries. We could clear a bit of land and grow food. This would be a perfect place of peace, meditation, and the simple life, but we were bound with our plans, with our ideas and illusions, and therefore we wanted to get out of this paradise. We lacked courage to pursue this vision.

After about half an hour's rest, we decided not to spend any more time there but to try to find our way. The search for the path was not easy without knowing what it looked like. In the maze of the forest, neither sitting down and resting nor looking for the path seemed to do much good; nevertheless, the only course left to us was to keep searching. We came to another fork: one branch was heading marginally northwest, the other turning northeast. We took what seemed to be the northeast fork, heading—we thought—toward Loch Venachar. The path again came to an end, but this time we were faced with tall deer fencing and a new plantation. We climbed the eight- or nine-foot fence and ventured through the boggy ground between the waist-high lines of Sitka spruce. The light and air made us feel that we were coming out of the forestry land and gave us a ray of hope. Further along we had to climb another deer fence, and we found ourselves on a high hill. We saw a lake, compared the shape of it with the map, and decided that it must be Loch Drunkie. "If it is Loch Drunkie, we are not too far from Loch Venachar," Terry said. We saw a lookout tower, and near it a small lodge; we breathed a sigh of relief. Perhaps we could go and find somebody there who might be able to help us. As we headed toward it, we soon found ourselves on a tarmac road—a sign of civilization again. As we approached the lodge, a man appeared. Before we had any chance to ask him the way he shouted, "What are you doing? You are trespassing on private land!" Terry and I could not help ourselves—we shrieked with laughter. Here we were lost in the forest for hours, what had seemed an eternity, and the first person we meet is screaming at us to go away. "We are very sorry, but we don't know where we are. In fact we are lost." But he was not interested, and he would not help us. The tarmac track led to another tarmac track and eventually to Loch Venachar and to Callander.

WE WERE IN THE LAND OF LOCHS: Loch Katrine, Loch Lubnaig, Loch Voil, Loch Earn, and most glorious of them all, Loch Tay, which is the Gaelic word for peace. Spending a couple of nights in Killin, overlooking Loch Tay, was truly an experience of living in peace. If the gods were to choose an abode for themselves, they couldn't do better than the mountains surrounding Loch Tay. Those who dwell in this land, breathing pure mountain air, drinking water from pure streams, and immersed in the true wealth of nature, are living in the neighborhood of the gods. If I were to judge the people of this area by my host Renwick Russell and his neighbors, who do not have power, position, or the trappings of modern living, then I would conclude that their life is one of contentment, harmony, and happiness.

Walking the hills and glens on the footpath of the West Highland Way, Terry and I were joined by Lorenzo, lovingly called Enzo, who had hitchhiked from York to join us for a week on the last leg to Iona. Enzo was both a good hill walker and a good map reader, and therefore I could leave him to guide us through the Grampian Mountains. We passed through Tyndrum and the Bridge of Orchy, from where we followed a small road by Loch Tulla, which brought us on a footpath along Glen Kinglass. There we were in the midst of mountains and away from any sign of civilization or population. The mountain stream of Kinglass was the purest stream I have ever seen in my life. I looked down into the stream, the water ten or fifteen feet deep, and still could see the rocks underneath, crystal clear. Not a speck of dust or dirt could I see anywhere. We put our rucksacks aside; sitting by the pool, praising the wonder of water, we washed our faces and drank as much as we could. We filled our bottles and wished we could live there forever. Before this experience I could never have imagined that water could be so clear and delicious. No wonder Scotland produces world-famous whiskeys with this water. If you live by Kinglass stream, you don't need to drink whiskey, the water itself is intoxicating enough—it is an elixir of life, so sweet, so soft, so gentle. It quenched our thirst, we could put it on our eyes, and yet it is so powerful that the rocks have eroded and given way to its speed. But the water takes no pride in its power and strength. It is so humble that it always finds the lowest level. We were honored to be walking by the stream of Kinglass; it led us to Loch Etive, where we were sad to leave its company.

Following the river Lonan, we arrived in Oban, where we were the guests of Jeremy Inglis. Jeremy does bed and breakfast in his own flat and runs a restaurant in the town. For him, helping young visitors by providing simple, inexpensive, self-help accommodation is more important than money. There were Americans, Australians, French, and Welsh travelers staying there, all using a small kitchen. We were quite happy helping each other and being friendly. The atmosphere was much more of a community center than of a place that offers bed and breakfast. On the kitchen shelf there was a line of teas: Assam, Darjeeling, Lapsang

Souchong, Orange Pekoe, Jasmine, Chamomile—you name it, it was there. Different varieties of jams, chutneys, and pickles made by Jeremy were on another shelf, which made us feel at home. He lives in one room of the flat, which serves as his study, office, bedroom, dining room, living room, and the common room for the guests. By keeping his establishment to the basics, he can run it on a shoestring and charge a very modest fee of £4 a night. And when pilgrims like us arrive, he can offer his generous hospitality without charge. "Jeremy, are you sure you can afford to let us stay for nothing?" I asked. "I never gave that a thought. I want you to stay with me. If I keep worrying whether I can afford it or not, I can't afford anything, but if I don't think about things, they take their own course and keep ticking over. Having pilgrims to stay here is a rare honor."

I was touched by his sentiments. As we were talking, Jeremy said, "There is a letter for you." I opened the envelope and saw that it was from Janet Banks of the Erraid Community near Iona. She wrote: "I wish I could join you to walk across Mull, but am not able to do so. I will join you on the day you walk to Iona, but when I think of you, a pilgrim without money, I wonder whether the boat company is going to let you cross the Firth of Lorn and the Sound of Mull. I hate to think that you will be stopped at Oban and unable to come to Iona. So, please allow me to send you a small present of the enclosed boat ticket."

Until then I had been so absorbed in my walking that I hadn't given any thought to this problem. How considerate it was of Janet to send me this essential gift!

MULL LIVES IN THE SHADOW of Iona. Every step I took, I meditated on Iona. The sweet sound of the word became my mantra; Iona, Iona, Iona. Walking through the sparsely populated island of Mull, we came across a house with barns and outbuildings, where we decided to shelter from the rain. A young woman in her teens answered the door and readily allowed us to rest in one of the buildings. After only a few minutes a Land-Rover drove up to the house. Soon a man came in. "Who are you? What are you doing here?" "We are pilgrims traveling to Iona." "And where do you come from?" "My friend Terry is from Edinburgh, Lorenzo is from York, and I have walked from Devon." The man looked at us in surprise, and his face softened. We carried on this conversation for a few minutes, then he said, "If you were not invited into the house by my daughter, that is because she is not allowed to let strangers in when she is on her own, but please come in and have a cup of tea. It is warmer in the kitchen." We were feeling rather tired and thirsty, so we were very grateful for his invitation. As he led us to his house, the farmer explained, "I look after sheep on about three thousand acres of land here. The owner lives in Kent. Sometimes it can be lonely and bleak, but in the main I enjoy being on the road to Iona, and the quietness of Mull."

As we drank tea and ate biscuits, a collection of walking sticks in the corner of the room caught my attention; gnarled and twisted, well made, well polished, works of great craftsmanship. Loving hands had shaped them. Each one was individual. The man said, "In the wintertime, when I have less work, I enjoy playing with them, paring the bark, polishing the wood, and joining intriguing handles to the sticks. As I walk the hills, chasing my sheep, I come across these pieces of wood. When I find them they look rather ordinary, but I can see their uniqueness beyond their rough state. In fact all sticks have the potential of being a perfect stick. They need caring hands to bring out their special quality. These sticks give me a tremendous sense of fulfillment. What would I do without them? How would I be able to spend long winter evenings? I don't know. As I work on them, so they work on me." "Do you sell them, or are they just a hobby?" "They are more than my hobby, they are my love, but occasionally I do sell them. They can fetch anything from thirty to fifty pounds, but many of the sticks you see here I cannot bear to sell. They are part of me."

The evening was drawing near, so we had to say good-bye to our stick-making shepherd and find Willow Bank, the house of Graham Martin, where we were invited to spend the night. "You can't miss Graham's house, it is very near. About three or four miles. You will see a log house, which he has built himself." And so it proved to be.

Graham is a *Resurgence* reader and had gathered together a number of his friends for the evening. I discovered to my surprise that here in the middle of Mull there were quite a lot of *Resurgence* readers. "*Resurgence* is particularly helpful in this rather remote island as it keeps us informed and in touch with kindred spirits elsewhere," said one of them. "*Resurgence* always uplifts me," said another. "I have come to say thank you for what you are doing," a third voice added.

I was pleased to know that so far away, so many people appreciate what we do. It was encouraging.

While we were talking, Lorenzo made a brilliant suggestion. "We must prepare a present for the community of Iona, an offering to them for their work of renewal of the spirit—which is after all not dissimilar to the work of *Resurgence*. And there can be no better present than bread, which we can bake tonight, keeping Iona in our minds."

The rest of the evening we spent together baking bread. Graham devoted himself to getting the Rayburn oven up to the right temperature. Enzo looked after the yeast. I kneaded the dough, and other friends watched and advised when the dough had sufficiently risen. Graham plaited the dough into a Celtic knot. The outcome was a wholesome and handsome-looking loaf of bread, which we packed in fine white tissue paper and put in a box. I was made responsible for carrying it with care and devotion.

NEXT MORNING AT EIGHT O'CLOCK we started to walk to Iona. Gray and black clouds hung low in the sky, resting on the brown hills. Waves came toward us, pounding the seashore, loud and strong, affirming that the waves alone rule Mull. Cold wind and a steady drizzle knew not that it was the beginning of summer. Trees were still gray and leafless. The spring and summer of 1986 were far too late in Mull. But the severity of the weather and landscape was no obstacle to us: we moved on full of vigor and anticipation. The long winter, which had held on right into June, must come to an end soon. The thought of Iona made me feel the coming of the spring in my soul. Iona, Iona, Iona!

Helen Steven, a member of the Iona Community, met us at midday. Janet Banks from the Erraid Community, by whose courtesy I had crossed the Firth of Lorn, also joined us. Similarly a number of local people had come to be pilgrims for that last stretch. Helen led the singing of songs of Iona, which further raised our spirits and warmed our hearts. As we approached Fionnphort we saw the abbey, the sacred site of Iona. The abbey was hardly distinguishable from the hills surrounding it, a modest monument of great charm, built from local stone, blending with the landscape so harmoniously.

It was the ninth day of June. St. Columba's Day. The moment I took my first step on the white sand of Iona I was overcome, unable to walk or move. Stunned by the spirit of Iona, I was in tears. Helen held my hand, and Terry put his hand on my back, and they helped me to walk slowly to the abbey.

Before we entered the abbey we walked around its perimeter. That circumambulation helped us to leave all thoughts behind and to enter as light as feathers. Entering the abbey was the peak moment, the peak experience, the peak of the pilgrimage. We reached the green altar of Iona marble, shiny and pure. We sat down together in silence, in peace, in prayer, at one with the place. In the evening Helen spoke about the life of St. Columba. He was a prince of Ireland. He was a scholar and a devoted student of the scriptures, but only priests and monks could have free access to the holy books. One night, in his passion for learning, Columba entered the abbey library and in the candlelight started to copy the Bible. But he was discovered and taken to the king for his due punishment.

Columba was found guilty of stealing the scriptures and disobeying the church, but his pride prevented him from submitting to the judgment of king and court. As a result a battle was fought. Many men were killed. When Prince Columba realized what he was doing to save his face and pride, he repented. He accepted exile and left Ireland. He pledged himself to go as far away as not to be able to see his beloved country and to save at least as many souls as the number of men who had been killed in battle. When the boat drew away from the shores of Ireland, he came to several small islands, but everywhere he was within sight of his country. In the end he arrived in Iona, and from here Christianity spread far and wide.

I presented our gift of bread to the community, and they shared it with the congregation. Someone came to me and said, "How good the taste of real bread is. What a shame that the church has given in to the convenience of wafers. Jesus could not have dreamt of giving wafers as his body and Coca-Cola as his blood! He gave real bread and wine, and we must revive the old tradition." Another person said, "After tasting your bread, I don't think I can eat Mother's Pride white sliced anymore. How did you make it?" "Water, flour, yeast, and salt," I said. "That's all you need. The rest is simple. People don't bake bread not because it is difficult to do but because they are too busy to do it. So say to yourself that when God made time, he made plenty of it; I have plenty of time to make real good bread." "But I haven't got very much time." "Yes, this is where Mother's Pride comes in. If you don't want to eat Mother's Pride anymore, you will have to take your focus away from the time which has passed in which you could have done a lot of things but didn't, and turn your attention to the time which is coming, flowing endlessly towards you. An eternity of time awaits you: not only of one lifetime but of many lifetimes. The magic of St. Columba is still working, although apparently his life ended long ago. The message of Iona for me is not to want to do too many things at once. So when you bake your bread, just bake your bread without worrying about anything else." "It is all very well, but what do you do with salt, water, yeast, and flour? Of course I ought to get a bread book," the man said. "A book will certainly help," I agreed.

Walking on and around Iona was like walking in the land of dreams. The entire island is an embodiment of tranquillity and peace. People walking, standing in shops and doorways, smiled at me and waved their hands. They were kind, confident, self-reliant, and relaxed. Their houses were simple, modest, and yet friendly and warm. Nothing extravagant, nothing out of proportion, nothing grand, and yet people in them are happy and well. There is nothing in Iona to arouse envy, apart from its serenity and sanctity. If people of the world lived on the scale and in the simple ways of Iona, there would be no burden on the Earth and no risk to its ecology. Iona is a dream island, a community where people live in harmony with themselves and with their natural environment. Through the centuries people have come here to revive themselves and their spirits. Many of them come once a year as a retreat. Here pilgrims come and find what is timeless and eternal.

IN THE SHADOW OF IONA there is another island, the Isle of Erraid, which hosts a community of people in the old lighthouse keepers' cottages. This island, with its terrace of cottages, belongs to a Dutch family who live in Holland. The community has made a remarkably sound arrangement with the family, by which the community is the steward of the buildings and the land for eleven months, and the family come for one month for their summer holiday. This arrangement frees the community from the responsibilities of ownership and capital investment. The Dutch family also benefit in that throughout the year the buildings are cared for, looked after, maintained, and lived in, at no cost to them.

This is where Janet Banks lives; I stayed there for one day with the community. When the tide was out, Janet and I walked to Erraid from Mull in ankle-deep water. "We are a more or less self-sufficient and self-reliant community," Janet said. "We grow most of our vegetables, we make compost from the seaweed, and we have a few cows to provide us with plenty of milk, butter, cheese, and yogurt. We have weaving, knitting, and various other crafts. I make candles and stained glass. Visitors come to stay for a week or more, and contribute to the cost of living here. As we pay no rent and share everything, the cost of living is very low." "How do you organize the work?" I asked. "Every morning we meet for half an hour, and we have developed a way of planning the day quickly and efficiently." There was no doubt that the community was functioning efficiently. The whole place looked clean and loved: the garden full of vegetables, the kitchen full of good food. Before members begin any activity or work, they hold hands together, stand in a circle, and attune themselves to the fulfillment of their tasks in harmony with each other. This way they create a positive flow of energy and mutual support, which is the backbone of any community. "Only with open and generous hearts and care for others can a community flourish," said Janet.

In the evening the community gathered around the fire with tea and cakes and listened to stories of my pilgrimage. They were keen to ask details of my journey. We kept talking late into the night. A young mother with a baby in her lap said, "I am a very practical woman. Can I offer to wash your clothes?" Everybody shrieked with laughter. "Since you walk every day, and while walking you must get sweaty and sticky, I thought I must offer you washing." "It is most kind of you," I answered, "but I have left most of my clothes with Graham in Pennyghael for washing as I will be walking back and staying with him tomorrow." "All right then. I am a hairdresser. Would you like a haircut tomorrow morning?" This time there was an even bigger shriek of laughter. Everybody could see that my mustache and beard and hair were overgrown. I accepted her offer with heartfelt thanks.

The next morning I duly had my haircut. A few days later, when summer suddenly arrived, I thought with gratitude of the community of Erraid and its hairdresser, as I walked under the hot Scottish sun.

I was pleased to have completed my pilgrimage to Iona, the spiritual capital of the north. Now I headed back to the homely south.

CHAPTER 14

Pilgrimage: Return

I HAD A DATE with readers of *Resurgence:* there was to be a weekend gathering in Edinburgh, with Kathleen Raine as guest of honor. So after seventy-four days of walking, I reluctantly took the train from Oban to Edinburgh. My only consolation was that I had walked over this ground on my way up to Oban.

It was strange being in the train and looking at the magnificent Highlands through the glass of a window. These were the hills, rivers, and woods among which I had wandered: feeling them, smelling them, tasting them, touching them, and being one with them. Passing them now at speed, I could only get a fleeting glimpse. This hurried journey removed any possibility of experiencing the sacred beauty of these hills. I felt a betrayal of my pilgrimage, which was still with me on my arrival in Edinburgh that evening. Those mesmerizing moments of looking at Arthur's Seat and walking step by step closer to it a fortnight ago were only a memory. Now from the railway station I could not even guess in which direction Arthur's Seat was.

My spirits lifted next morning when I saw Kathleen Raine. With a colorful shawl from Kashmir thrown over her red silk dress, she looked the queen of all the poets—happy, charming, and full of vigor. It was the fourteenth of June, her birthday; a bouquet of flowers from Rosalind Brackenbury, and from me a copy of *Learning by Heart,* which was rushed hot from the press for this day, added to her joy. She received this beautifully produced poetry anthology, to which she had contributed, with surprise. She had the first of the one hundred and seventy-five numbered copies which had been specially produced in aid of the Small School. Having read some of the poems and seen the list of prominent poets who had contributed to it, and the beautiful illustrations by Truda Lane, Kathleen said, "I am delighted with this anthology. There is so much rubbish being written in the name of poetry that I am often appalled. I am all too familiar with the universal banality of most modern poetry. Of course it is good for people to express themselves, but I wonder if it would not be better if people were to read more and write less. Read real poetry, I mean. Poetry is a craft, a vocation, a dedication, a commitment, not something people can do in their spare time— except, of course, for their own pleasure."

Kathleen has made that commitment. She has dedicated herself to the renewal of the sacred in poetry and the arts. In the hurricane of modern materialism, most traditions of art and poetry, which relate to the human soul and the universal spirit, have been uprooted. Kathleen Raine is one of the few who has stood her ground. Her latest act in the fight against declining values is the publication of *Temenos,* a review devoted to the arts of the imagination. The true function of the arts is to nourish the soul, and through *Temenos* she has been able to do exactly that.

At seventy-eight Kathleen is a dynamo of energy, busy at editing, writing, speaking, and participating in seminars and conferences around the world. It has been a feat of willpower and tenacity to bring out each issue of *Temenos.* She has sold her furniture and her paintings to pay the printing bills and keep the arts alive.

She has many friends in Edinburgh, and it was a rare occasion for them to have her in the city on her birthday. The evening sun shone until late; the garden of the Salisbury Center was filled with guests. She spoke and read poetry with eloquence and authority, and we heard her in an enthused silence.

A weekend with the readers of *Resurgence* heartened me. It is always surprising to know who they are. Artists, craftspeople, poets, and smallholders are the expected subscribers to *Resurgence,* but here I found that a number of them were involved in computer technology, city finance, fashion design, and shopkeeping. Outwardly they came from varied backgrounds, but they all had one thing in common: spiritual values were fundamental to their personal and social life.

THE PREVIOUS WEEK in Iona I had met Jeanne Knight, a student of theology from Cambridge, who wanted to walk with me for a few days. After a brief discussion we agreed that she would meet me in Edinburgh when I resumed my walk south.

I set off again on Monday morning together with Jeanne and a few other pilgrimage enthusiasts. As soon as we were out of the city, we found a pleasant path to walk on. In the midsummer warmth, blessed by the hot sun, I took my shoes off. With bare feet on the ground, touching the grass and soil, I was in my element once more. Following a small burn through an ancient woodland, we became immersed in the magic of the natural world. "This is the kind of untamed landscape which inspired those saints, St. Francis and St. Seraphim," Jeanne remarked. "I know of St. Francis, but who was St. Seraphim?" I asked. "He was a Russian saint of the eighteenth century who lived in the woods. He wished for no distraction from his total devotion to God, so he chose the wilderness; by so doing he was able to heighten his awareness of God's presence in creation." "When did he live?" I asked. "He was born in 1759, the son of a builder but deeply religious: he entered a monastery at the age of nineteen. The monastery was situated in the midst of the immense forests of central Russia. At the age of thirty-five, Seraphim had an inner call to go deeper into the forest. He built a little log cabin as his hermitage by the river Sarovka, with a table, a log for a chair, an icon in a corner, but no bed. He grew vegetables, kept bees, and lived in holy poverty. As St. Francis of Assisi had his falcon and his wolf, St. Seraphim had his bear. When St. Seraphim came out of his hut, foxes, hares, and snakes would gather round him."

After about three hours' walk we arrived in Roslin, where we visited the House of Transfiguration, an ecumenical and contemplative community. Brother Jonathan received us warmly, even though he was not expecting us. As he showed us around the community, to our amazement we came upon a cell dedicated to St. Seraphim. "He is the patron of this community," Brother Jonathan said, pointing to the large icon of the saint which hung on the wall. I had neither heard of St. Seraphim until that morning nor knew that the House of Transfiguration had any connection with him; it was an extraordinary coincidence that Jeanne's introduction to this saint should be followed immediately by our visit to a community dedicated to his path.

The members of this community live in utter simplicity. Each brother has a wooden hut approximately eight feet by six. In each hut there is an icon, a table, a chair, a bed, and nothing more. The brothers have a minimum of clothes and books; they have reduced their needs to the very basics so that maximum time and attention can be devoted to prayer and silence. Their food, which they prepare and share in the communal house, is simple.

In answer to our apology for not telephoning him to let him know that we were coming, Brother Jonathan said, "The telephone is a great distraction. We have thought much and long about whether it is necessary for us to have a telephone. Even our bishop suggested that we should have one in case of emergency, but we said to him, jokingly, that God doesn't send His messages over the telephone! When we are at prayer, when we are sharing a meal, when we are having a meeting, the telephone could ring and disturb us. So a telephone was never installed." He added, "Not only the telephone but all modern machines are intrusive. They make a constant noise in the background. Silence is the casualty of gadgetry. The more possessions we have, the more time we have to spend in looking at them. They are all a distraction. The teachings of St. Seraphim tell us to keep our lives as simple as possible."

It was a refreshing relief to be in a Christian community which has returned to first principles. In a world of cathedrals, bishops' palaces, and rambling rectories, it requires great courage and commitment to return to a life in a cell with minimum possessions and no modern conveniences. One of the members commented, "We are at a loss to understand how it is that in spite of being a Christian, Western society leads the world in its rush to capitalism, high living standards, economic growth, and increasing personal wealth; whereas the teaching of Jesus is that it is easier for a camel to go through the eye of a needle than for a rich person to enter the Kingdom of Heaven."

Roslin is an ancient place for pilgrims. From here they used to begin their journeys, walking and riding to Santiago di Compostella in northwest Spain. They visited holy places along the route, and on their return to Roslin they brought shells, the symbol of St. James, and placed them in the church to mark the completion of their pilgrimage. Now the church is desacralized, a sight for tourists but nevertheless a very mysterious place where the past is strongly felt.

From Roslin, Jeanne and I picked up a little-used track over the beautiful moorland of Hare Moss and Auchencorth Moss, many miles of unpopulated wilderness. For Jeanne, not being used to walking long distances, the twenty-five-mile trek to West Linton was long and tiring. But in spite of blistered feet and aching legs, she kept up the pace in a determined way. That determination is the very essence of Jeanne's life. At the age of twenty-five she has taken a vow of lifelong celibacy so that she can dedicate herself to God and to the service of people. I asked her: "Isn't it better to realize God not by turning away from the world but by living through the world?" "This wonderful world is not a monotonous creation. There are many kinds of landscape—rugged mountains and moorlands, lush valleys and woodlands—all of them are part of the glorious tapestry of creation. Similarly, celibacy is one of the many colors of that tapestry. A life of celibacy is not turning away from this world; it is a way of serving the world with all my energies. Through this one form of denial, I am more able to accept the world. To me, celibacy is the key to a life without fear. Celibacy channels the energy in such a way that I can act with full vigor," explained Jeanne. "To many people a life of celibacy appears to be bare and harsh," I commented. "But bare mountains and deserts have always attracted saints and seekers. The very quality of harshness inspires thoughts of divinity. A life of celibacy attracts me for its bare simplicity. For me all children are my children, the whole of humanity is my family. I have transformed my romantic love into love of the divine. It is the universal love I am seeking through celibacy." These were strong words, and they were coming from her mouth with passion.

Jeanne paused for a moment, looking at the Pentland Hills. She said, "The hills have their heads in the clouds, but they create the valleys, attract the rain, and are in no way removed from the ground; they connect the heaven and the earth, and for me that is ideal. If you get bogged down in the world of bodily comforts, you become isolated in your own corner. If you remove yourself totally from the workings of the world and live only in the vision-world of abstract thought, then you too are in a corner. But like the Pentland Hills, if you can be in the clouds and on the earth at the same time, then you are a bridge. Celibacy is a bridge." This was Jeanne's firm conviction, and I salute it.

The hills are a source of inspiration to many religious people. The lamas of Tibet say the mountains are the abode of the goddess Tara. Whenever the lamas needed clarity and upliftment, they went to the mountains. Some of the lamas who were displaced from the mountain monasteries of Tibet during the Chinese invasion of the 1950s came to Scotland and searched for a landscape with the same soul. They found it here, in Eskdale in the Lothian hills, and started the community Samye Ling at Eskdalemuir.

But, alas, this community of the Tibetan order was not on my route. When I expressed my sadness to my hosts, Bill and Peggy Bartlett of Elvanfoot, they said, "It may be off your route, but it is not very far to drive. It is about forty miles away. It would add four extra days to your journey if you walked there and back, but if you can delay your departure by one day, we will take you to Samye Ling." Bill added further, "We have been living here so close to the community but have never been there, so taking you will be a perfect opportunity for us to visit the lamas as well." That was enough to persuade me.

Jeanne, Peggy, Bill, and I got in the car and headed toward Eskdale: over the fast-flowing river Annan, through the old town of Moffat, and past the Black Esk River, we followed the White Esk River. No wonder the Tibetan lamas chose to be here, as these mountains look so much like a Himalayan range, and yet they have a Scottish serenity.

Bill had already phoned and made arrangements for our visit; we were warmly received by one of the members, who took us to the central hall of the temple, where morning meditation and chanting takes place. The smell of sandalwood incense filled the air, and a larger-than-life statue of the Buddha gave off a golden glow. In front of it a large bowl of fruit and flowers lay as an offering. The walls were resplendent with intricately painted Tibetan *tangkas;* the floor was covered with thick pile carpet on which lay cushions, drums, gongs, and other ceremonial equipment. The atmosphere of the place was rich and luxurious: I could not help making a mental comparison between the austerity of the community of St. Seraphim, which I had visited only the day before, and the splendor of Samye Ling. The young man who showed us around had been living at Samye Ling and practicing the dharma for some time.

The teachings of the Buddha were evident on his face and in his being. He talked and walked at a slow and settled pace, as if all problems were under his control. He seemed immune to anger, panic, frustration, and anxiety. "What did you do to become so calm, composed, and happy?" I asked, being impressed by his demeanor. "Nothing very much," he replied. "Surely, you must do something to achieve this state? Otherwise, why aren't we all like you?" "I do meditate morning and evening." He was self-effacing and reluctant to speak about his personal practice. "What do you do while you meditate?" I pressed. "Nothing very much. I sit quietly, gaze at the Buddha, and listen to the lamas." And he quickly moved on to explain various practical activities of the community. If years of meditation can help you to find your true self and a state of equilibrium, then time spent sitting in the lotus position is well worth it.

The young man took us to the site where the lamas and volunteers, with the advice of professional builders, were busy building a new temple in Tibetan style. "Everyone was amazed that the planning department could be so courageous as to allow such a monumental building, in such an alien, though elegant, style to be built in this part of rural Scotland," our guide told us. "Lords, Ladies, MPs, civil servants, farmers, and city dwellers have all joined to raise money, which has amounted to over one million pounds, for this temple." "How did you find this wonderful place?" I asked. "Many years ago, when hardly anyone had heard of Tibetan Buddhism, Chogyam Trungpa was offered this beautiful house and land. He was taken aback. The house was situated at the confluence of two rivers, the White Esk and the Black Esk. The meeting of these two waters, as he saw it, would facilitate the harmonious coming together of the Orient and the Occident, of the masculine and the feminine, of the spiritual and the material: all dualities would end at Eskdalemuir. Moreover, when he looked at the breathtaking mountains surrounding this place, so evocative of Tibet, he could not refuse the offer. Ever since, thousands of people have come here and learned a way of compassion and detachment."

As we walked and talked we came to stand under a tree; I immediately felt the close connection between trees and Buddhism. The Buddha received his enlightenment under a tree. He had said, "The *Bodhi* tree under which I sit is a perfect example of compassion and detachment." Ashoka, emperor of India and a passionate follower of the Buddha, instructed every citizen to plant five trees a year, to look after, nurture, and respect them, not only as a means of food, wood, and shade but as a source of inspiration and enlightenment. Ashoka had said, "Go and sit under a tree. You will become calm, you will become still, and, if you sit there long enough, you will be enlightened."

Now it was lunchtime, and we were invited to the members' simple and yet sumptuous meal. While we were relishing the wholesome brown rice with stir-fried cabbage and soya sauce, our conversation moved from subject to subject. Bill Bartlett was keen to find out about the importance of Tibetan chanting as part of daily practice. A Tibetan nun, who had joined us at the table with her young son, came to our aid. "The mind makes you leap either into the past or into the future— it is like a wild horse. The sound of the chant is used by the Self as reins to guide the mind. Meditating on the full meaning of the mantra which we chant, we can come to the realization of our true being. For example, we chant 'Om mani padme hum,' which means, 'I am the jewel in the heart of the lotus.' Now, we don't need to *think* of the meaning of the words *linguistically*. The real meaning is in immersing our whole being into the pure sound of the chant. When we are enchanted by the chant, we need not indulge in the intellectualization of concepts. We simply become the chant, we become the jewel, we become the lotus, we become ourselves. It may take long practice, but the journey begins with the first chant. The more you chant, the more powerful and charged the chant becomes."

This reminded me of the image used by Eknath Easwaran, an Indian teacher, about a *mahout* taking his elephant through the market. The elephant is bound to be attracted to the fruits on the stalls. So the mahout gives the elephant a stick to hold in his trunk. No matter how delightful are the goods along his path, the elephant cannot be distracted. The stick acts on the elephant like a mantra on the human mind.

But Samye Ling is by no means a community of meditators, sitting and chanting all day long. The members here work with their bodies as much as with their minds. "Sitting in a corner and contemplating is only a starting point," we were told. "Eventually all our activities should become meditative." As we visited various workshops of pottery, printing, woodcarving, and other artifacts, we witnessed that meditative quality. Everyone was truly engaged in the work without appearing to be frantically busy or being under pressure. "As my hands turn the clay into a pot, I realize the process of change taking place within me. When I came to this community, I was like raw clay. With the help of my teachers and with the help of meditation, I am turning myself into a useful pot," said the woman who received us at the pottery. I understood her. It was clear to me when I looked in her calm and mellow eyes. "How do you feel being in Scotland?" I asked a Tibetan member of the community. "I feel fine. Sometimes blessings come in disguise. We were getting a bit lazy in Tibet. The Chinese invasion woke us up; we had to get on our feet and start moving. We had to come out of hiding and offer ourselves in the service of the world, particularly the West." "Why particularly the West?" I asked. "It is very simple. The West leads the world in the religion of materialism. But materialism is reaching its limit. People are looking for something which will satisfy their inner needs. Perhaps we can make some contribution in this field with the teachings of the Buddha. We Tibetans need to learn a bit of materialism too! It will be a balancing act, a two-way process."

Our day at Samye Ling was an inspiring experience. As we drove back to Elvanfoot, we reflected on the life of the community which seemed to us like "a laboratory of rich experiments."

THE NEXT DAY Jeanne stayed with the Bartletts, as her burst blisters meant that she could not manage any further walking. I continued alone, along Daer Water to the dramatic Dalveen Pass. Here Steygail stood close on my right, 575 meters above sea level, and Well Hill loomed up on my left at 606 meters. Step by step, like a human figure in a Chinese painting, I kept moving on this road, which wound like a snake. Although it is an A road, there was hardly any traffic on it; fortunately the newly enlarged A74 trunk road had taken the through traffic away and left these mysterious mountains all for me! Mountains are Nature's cathedrals. I put my rucksack down and sat on a stone, gazing at the glorious rocks. Sheep grazing in the foreground, birds flying above them, and a stream flowing below. There was no sense of time or space, just a slow movement in the eternal stillness. I understood the words of the woman lama about the "enchantment of the soul." She had said, "When intellectual concepts end, life becomes a constant flow."

I walked to the picturesque village of Durisdeer and then followed a minor road to Drumlarrig Park and Poets Corner. I kept moving along the river Nith to Thornhill, where I was met by Richard, the son of Maggie Sale, on his bicycle; he led me to his home in Penpont, where I was to stay the night.

Appropriately, my bedroom resounded with the sitar music of Ravi Shankar, the air perfumed with the scent of incense. No one was to disturb me until I had my bath, rest, and dinner. I was treated as an honored guest, with the utmost care and consideration.

Maggie's home is a refuge for those who need help: battered wives, drug addicts, and the homeless. Maggie receives them with an open heart, consoles them, counsels them, and gives them help and advice as appropriate. Maggie is a giver of love: she gives and gives, and seems to have an endless store of energy, and time for everyone. In the kitchen she keeps a pot. Anyone staying for the night or having a meal can put a contribution in this pot, if they are able and if they so desire. The pot has been there for many years, and it has never been found empty. Some give more, some give less, some give none, but as the Indian proverb goes: "Annapoorna, the goddess of grain, keeps the pot full."

I stayed two nights at Maggie's house, meeting many of her friends, who, like her, are involved in the movements for peace, education, ecology, and social justice. Some of them accompanied me as I continued my walk from Penpont to Lothlorien community and then on to Dumfries.

Of Dumfries I knew nothing, apart from the lines in the T. S. Eliot poem "The Railway Cat," which my daughter, Maya, recites with relish: "But you saw him at Dumfries; Where he speaks to the police."

Alistair Warren, my guide in Galloway, had told me that this town has a much closer and greater connection with another great poet, Robert Burns. So my first desire on arrival there was to make a pilgrimage to the newly created Robert Burns Center in a converted mill on the banks of the river Nith.

As Alistair and I were looking around the museum, we came to a room in which there stood a life-sized statue of Robert Burns, the handsome poet, dressed in elegant clothes of velvet and lace. The sculptor had achieved a tremendous feat in putting life into the statue, from which grace was pouring out. To our amazement, Burns was being embraced, caressed, and kissed by a beautiful woman of about twenty, also elegantly dressed in black and white. Alistair and I stood astounded a few feet away, gazing at the sight of a couple in love. "The statue is luckier than I, isn't it?" I said laughingly. The woman overheard me and also laughed. "Don't look so sad and sorry," she said, and to my pleasant surprise, she embraced me and gave me a warm kiss on my lips. Then she said ecstatically, "Burns is my love and my hero, he can never die. He lives through his poetry. He wrote for the people. When working people got their weekly wage, they would divide it between bread, beer, and Burns, buying his latest book. I read him passionately, I come here often—I love him, for me he is the greatest poet."

A land where people love poetry and dance to the rhythms of Robert Burns is a sacred land. I felt uplifted by meeting this woman who valued poetry above all else.

I WAS INVITED to narrate the story of my pilgrimage to a gathering of people at St. Joseph's, a school in Dumfries run by Catholic brothers. The gathering took place in the building where the brothers lived. They had very kindly offered the room. About fifty people of all ages had come to listen to "A strange story," as Maggie Sale described it, "reviving the ancient tradition of pilgrimage by depending on the freely given hospitality of people. Here is someone who finds spiritual nourishment through walking in nature and meeting people."

I spoke for about forty minutes. "Carrying no money," I said, "gave me the opportunity to stay with people and receive their help and support." As I sat down, one of the brothers was provoked to stand up and comment. "It's all very well for you to go without money, but if everyone went on such a journey, where would we be? Under the guise of spirituality, there are far too many people living off others. A true traveler should be self-reliant and not take food from others." His words came like a bombshell, and the audience was stunned into silence. The enthusiasm I had generated was dampened as if cold water had been poured over it. I felt as if I had received a physical blow. The last person from whom I had expected to receive such a comment was a monk! It took me a few moments to gather my thoughts together. And then in a hesitant voice, I offered my explanation. "It is hypothetical to ask what would happen if everyone did the same thing. It is extremely unlikely that everyone would go on a pilgrimage without money at the same time."

The brother stood up again and asserted, "But one should set an example which anyone can follow. If something is good for you to do, then it must be good for everyone else to do. I don't see how everyone can go without money, seeking shelter and sustenance from others.''

The point seemed logical, but there was something not quite right about it. Alistair Warren came to my defense. "Giving hospitality to pilgrims is an old Christian tradition. Those who were on a pilgrimage would receive hospitality from those who were not, and at another time their roles would be reversed, so all could receive mutual hospitality. Christian monks and priests have always depended on the generosity of the community.''

The doubting brother would have none of this: he stood up again and persisted, "I teach children here in this school, and by this I am earning my living. Christian priests perform a particular service to the community; it is their job, and therefore they earn their keep. In my view people wandering in the name of pilgrimage or peace are just taking advantage of other people's goodwill, and by calling yourself a pilgrim you make other people gullible.''

Obviously the brother and I were on very different wavelengths. I said, "You are a brother, you have taken a vow of celibacy. Can everyone take such a vow? If you are saying that nothing is valid unless it can be practiced by everyone, the first thing you need to do is go out, find a woman, get married, and have children, because if everyone became celibate like you, the world as we know it would come to an end!''

There were shrieks of prolonged laughter from the audience, and the brother himself joined in. The ice was somewhat broken. "I take your point," the brother said smilingly and gave way to other questions. But the atmosphere of that meeting remained uneasy and negative. There were few questions after that. Even tea and biscuits could not do much to lift it. As we talked informally, one of the older brothers said to me, "I am sorry that you were put to such harsh questioning." That apology from a fellow brother put some balm on my wound.

When Maggie, Alistair, my hostess, Kathy, and I returned to her house, we spent the rest of the evening discussing the matter. A potent seed of doubt had been planted in my mind, and no amount of kind words from Kathy, who is an Irish Catholic, could comfort me. I retired to bed early, leaving my friends still sorting it out.

Going to bed was easy, but falling asleep was not. My mind kept spinning round and round. Thoughts, arguments, counterarguments, questions, more questions, and even possible answers kept me awake.

As I tossed and turned, I felt pain in my back and sat up in bed trying to calm my mind. The words of the brother were like a barb in my flesh. I thought of my whole past, I thought of India, which I had left behind. Was it right to leave India and come to live in the West? Shouldn't I have stayed close to my own culture and my roots? Then I thought of June, my wife, Mukti and Maya, my two children—was it right to leave them alone at home and go around wandering like a pilgrim? Perhaps the brother was right—I have always been escaping from my duties and responsibilities.

I lifted the edge of the curtain and looked out of the window. The sky was dark, no stars, no moon, no light. Everything seemed without life. I lay down once more, trying not to think about the dark outside and doubt inside me. I concentrated on my breath and started to count. That seemed to work. My legs, arms, and body began to feel heavy. My eyes, cheeks, and lips began to relax. I was half asleep and half dreaming. I became aware of a hand coming toward me, which then lay soothingly on my forehead. Then I saw the arm and then the body. I looked into the kindly eyes of this person. For a moment I could not recognize her, then I did. It was no one else but my hostess, Kathy, saying simply, "It is past midnight, you must go to sleep." "Did you think the brother was right?" I asked. "No, the brother was wrong. Everyone has their own pattern of life; you are your own pattern. The brother was trying to make everyone fit the same pattern. That cannot be right. So go to sleep." Then she became silent, kept looking unblinkingly at me. I felt as if she was trying to mesmerize me into sleep.

I woke up. There was no person there. The light was coming through the window, it was morning. I was still feeling tired, but it was time to get up and be on the road again. I got out of bed, washed, dressed, put my rucksack on my back, and came down to the kitchen. Kathy had laid the table for breakfast; orange juice, porridge, toast, marmalade, tea, but I did not have any appetite. I drank a cup of tea.

Kathy said, "I will walk with you for a while, then my daughter will come in the car and bring me back. Quite a few people who attended the meeting last night have phoned to say that they want to give you lunch and be with you again at Ruthwell Church." I heard this in silence.

We walked through the well-kept and beautiful gardens of the Royal Hospital, full of old, mature, and graceful trees. Kathy suddenly came to a stop. "Satish, don't you think that this is the most wonderful tree of all?" We stood before a magnificent oak and gazed up at its lofty branches. I stood there feeling the protection and magnanimity of this great tree. Kathy began to sing:

> *I think that I shall never see*
> *A poem lovely as a tree.*
> *A tree whose hungry mouth is pressed*
> *Against the earth's sweet flowing breast;*
> *A tree that looks at God all day,*
> *And lifts her leafy arms to pray;*
> *A tree that may in summer wear*
> *A nest of robins in her hair;*
> *Upon whose bosom snow has lain;*
> *Who intimately lives with rain.*
> *Poems are made by fools like me,*
> *But only God can make a tree.*

Listening to Kathy's sweet voice, my worries receded. I hugged the tree, strong, solid, firm, and unconcerned with the ways of the world. Whether someone sings songs of praise or blame, the tree takes no notice.

We walked on. Past Rosebank Farm, we turned right and followed the road alongside the river Nith. My dream of the previous night came vividly to my mind, of Kathy coming into the room and putting her healing hand on my forehead. But I was not able to talk to Kathy about it. Instead I repeated the question I had asked her in my dream, "Was the brother right?"

Kathy said, "The tradition of pilgrimage is practiced in different countries and different cultures in different ways; some people have gone on pilgrimage with money and some without it, one does not invalidate the other. What surprised me is that he expressed his opinion in such a harsh way."

The only thing I could gain from this experience was to learn to practice right speech. According to the Buddhist tradition, speech which causes pain is against the principle of right speech, one element of the eightfold path. Right speech means that we should speak words that will bring about love, friendship, unity, and harmony and never say things that may bring about hatred, enmity, disunity, and disharmony among people; we should speak pleasant words and never those which are rude and insulting. We should speak only useful and meaningful words and not waste time in idle or foolish babble.

We were so engaged in our thoughts and talk that our arrival in Glen Caple took us by surprise. Kathy said, "Gosh! This is not where we are supposed to be—my daughter will be waiting at Bank End, which is miles away, and the people who have offered us lunch will be waiting at Ruthwell, which is even further. And the vicar of Ruthwell, who is expecting you to visit the church and its ancient cross, will be waiting as well. Where did we lose our way?"

Looking at the map and asking people, we found that the path had been lost in Dumfries itself. Maggie Sale came to the rescue. "I hope you are not too inflexible to give up walking a few miles. Since people are waiting for us, we had better take a lift."

I felt frustrated and irritated. Why hadn't I been alert? We had been on a direct road to Bank End. What had possessed us to turn away from it? It is no good traveling with a disturbed mind.

With some trepidation I agreed to Maggie's suggestion. She remembered some friends who lived in Glen Caple; we went to their house, and quickly a lift was arranged and we were put on the right road to Ruthwell. Happily we started walking again, through Dock Ridding Wood and Comlongdon Wood, and arrived at Ruthwell Church, to meet the vicar and a dozen or so people for lunch. We were late, but everybody cheered when they saw us coming. It was nearly half past two, and we were hungry.

A large cloth was spread on the ground, and we sat in the cool shade of a tree. People had brought salads, soup, quiches, bread, cheeses, a variety of puddings, and all manner of drinks. It was a feast and it was a celebration. With much joy and high spirits we shared the lunch. This was all Maggie Sale's superb organization. She had even invited my host for that evening, Dr. Barry Dale, to meet us there so that he could guide me to his home on the estuary.

After the lunch everyone from Dumfries said good-bye to me and returned. Only Tom, frail and fragile looking, decided to accompany us to Powfoot. I could see concern on Barry Dale's face. He said to Tom, "We will be walking along the sand of the estuary, on Priestside Bank; the terrain will be difficult—marshy, muddy, and wet." But Tom was determined to come. "Don't worry, I have come prepared with my Wellington boots. I may look slight, but I can walk long distances." So we set off at a brisk pace, Barry with his long staff leading the way. He looked like St. Christopher, the patron saint of travelers, reassuring and confident, giving us a sense of safety and security. When we reached the estuary we realized that Barry's warning was no exaggeration. We were confronted by the enormous expanse of the Solway Firth.

I stood there, overwhelmed, looking at the wide stretches of water where four great rivers, Eden, Esk, Annan, and Nith, meet the sea. The power of water had created a landscape of sand, mud, marsh, and sand dunes. I could see the struggle taking place between land and sea, almost a battlefield. As we started to traverse the marshy surface of Priestside Bank, we were constantly jumping various pools and streams. One of the streams was quite wide. Barry plunged his long staff into the middle of the water and, using it as a pole, jumped over; then he passed his staff to Tom to follow his example. But unfortunately Tom landed in the middle of the stream, completely submerged in exceedingly cold water. Seeing him fall, I felt as if a snake had crawled up my back. But he was swift to stand up in the waist-high water. Barry took his hand and pulled him out, a true St. Christopher. Tom was shocked and shaken but undaunted. "Don't worry," he said, "I'll get dry as I walk with you," but Barry was too concerned to allow it. "You are shivering—you'll get pneumonia. We have to walk three more hours at least before we get home. I will walk with you back to the road from where you can take a lift or a bus to Dumfries." But Tom was unwilling to give up: "I was not expecting an easy path, and a pilgrim's path is not an easy path." Barry and I were a bit bewildered. We did not feel that Tom should risk continuing for several hours with the wind blowing on his wet body, but we did not wish to hurt his feelings either. "You are with us in spirit, but please take Barry's offer. I will wait here until Barry returns." At my request, Tom agreed.

After about half an hour, Barry returned and we carried on. Walking on the wet sand was slow, and hard on the knees. Barry took my pack, as he was so at home and at ease on these sands and scars. By the time we got to his house in Powfoot, it was after nine and beginning to get dark. But his children and his wife, Sue, were waiting for us with a hot dinner in the oven and the table beautifully laid. I had been on the go for thirteen hours. But once I arrived, the warm welcome of the Dale family dispelled all my fatigue.

The next day was going to be even longer. I rose early and, equipped with a great pack of sandwiches, I departed alone. I traveled north and east to meet the bridge over Annan and then south again along the footpath at the estuary's edge through Gretna, zigzagging down to pick up the footpath along the river Eden. From my map I could see that there was a railway bridge at Stainton: the railway line had been dismantled, but there was a bridge over the Eden. I decided to cross the river at that point, but when I arrived at the bridge it was fenced off with a wood and steel structure about twelve feet high, covered with all sorts of signs, prohibiting trespass, declaring the bridge was unsafe and illegal to use.

I could not afford the time to change my route and walk a few more miles to the next bridge, so I had to ignore the prohibitive notices. The bridge looked strong and in good condition, and I saw no reason why it wouldn't take my weight; my only fear was that someone would see me and try to stop me. I looked around carefully. There was no one in sight apart from a couple of anglers down below the bridge. So I climbed the fence with some trepidation and walked over the bridge, excitedly looking at the fast-flowing river Eden below me. As I started climbing a similar fence on the other side of the bridge, I felt a tremendous sense of satisfaction and achievement, and no fear anymore: nobody had seen me, and even if they saw me now, it was too late to stop me.

I walked through the city of Carlisle alongside the river Caldew, on the beautifully kept public footpath, the Cumbrian Way. Sometimes it was overgrown, but I pushed my way through with pleasure. The quietly flowing Caldew was shaded by trees, and branches hung low into its waters. On the other bank, where clumps of wildflowers were scattered between the trees, I could hear the constant hum of the honeybees. I could not see any hives, so I wondered if these were wild bees and whether I would come across a wild hive on a tree. I kept looking in the branches of every tree: I had a strong urge to find wild honey but was not lucky enough to find any.

I came across a small clearing with shafts of sunlight warming the ground near the water, so I sat down in the sunny spot to rest. As I opened my sandwich box, I heard a sweet yet strange sound. It was very near, above my head. I looked up. There was a bird flying this way and that, sometimes high and away and then back low and near, making louder and louder sounds: *koor-lyou, koor-lyou, koor-lyou.* It had an elegant gray body with a long, curving beak. I felt the bird had some message for me and that was why it was keeping so close on this secret and sacred riverbank. Not being a bird-watcher, I did not know what it was, but I certainly felt that it was a brave and courageous bird, without fear, and later when I described it, people said it must have been a curlew.

After walking beside the Caldew for several hours, I felt its presence as a friend, and I had to part from it with some reluctance.

At about five o'clock in the evening as I was marching along at full speed, a car stopped; out stepped a woman with fair hair and a big smile. She was my hostess for that evening. By this time, having walked alone all day, I was certainly in need of some company. How pleasant it was that she had met me on the road, how reassuring that I was on the right path and could not now lose my way, and how comforting to know that my destination was only a couple of hours away.

Jacky had come equipped with very detailed maps of the area, and therefore we could leave the tarmac track, follow a plowed up footpath to the river Ive, and walk along it to her home at Thomas Close. Her husband, Tony, was cooking the supper. They live in Dufton farmhouse, practicing some of the principles of a lifestyle which is in harmony with the Earth and environment.

Our conversation went on late into the evening. In spite of having walked over forty miles, perhaps the longest walk yet in my pilgrimage, I was feeling quite relaxed and comfortable in my body. Next morning I walked only a short distance, about ten miles, to Penrith. Ana and Nick Jones of the Water Mill at Little Salkeld were my companions and guides for the day. They are old friends, so being able to walk with them and come to their mill gave me great pleasure.

Nick and Ana are living examples of people who practice the values in which they believe. In spite of many difficulties of all kinds—personal, financial, social, and cultural— they have created a means of right livelihood in the Buddhist sense. They are earning their living through milling flour, baking and serving wholesome bread to the community, and cultivating the land. They do no harm to their own being, to others, to animals, or to the natural environment. This is the kind of blameless profession commended by the Buddha. Nick and Ana gave up their steady, well-paid jobs and bought the mill when it was disused and derelict. They restored it and brought it back to life through a terrific amount of perseverance and endurance. Eventually they were able to create a situation such that neighboring farmers could grow organic grain to be milled locally, and thus strengthen the local economy and the community. The mill has become a beacon for their area, where people gather for spiritual, intellectual, and physical sustenance.

By the evening train, June arrived. I had not seen her since she came with the children to Lindisfarne. Although I knew that I was wandering in the wilderness of Britain with the blessing of June, the fact that she had come to walk with me for a week gave me a sense of great satisfaction—it was proof of her endorsement of my wandering. "It is good, June, that you have come to walk with Satish," said Ana in her smiling way. "This pilgrimage is going to be the talk of the family and friends for a long time to come, so I didn't want to miss the experience myself," said June. "Yes, we were talking about you and wondering how you have been getting on," Ana commented. "It's been hard. But ever since I first knew Satish it was clear that he would do something at the age of fifty, and at least he hasn't disappeared into the Himalayas," June replied. "I could not go to the Himalayas leaving a young family behind," I interjected. "By the time the householder departs for the Himalayas, the children should be grown up and able to take on responsibility."

ACCOMPANIED BY JACKY, we took the most glorious path into the Cumbrian Mountains, following the river Caldew to its source in Skiddaw. Surrounded by magnificent mountains, there stood Skiddaw House, desolate and derelict, telling the story of the past when men and women lived in the solitude and simplicity of these mountains, keeping sheep and gathering food as gifts from nature. As far as we could see there were bare, brown hills, but under our feet was soft, green grass tended by the sheep; it felt like a cushioned carpet, cooled by the waters of Caldew. The previous evening we had arranged to meet our host, Alan Hankinson of Keswick, in this wonderful place. We sat, lay down, and rested in anticipation of meeting Alan, but almost an hour passed and there was no sign of him. We wondered whether we had misunderstood him. In the end we decided to walk on without him.

We followed the Cumbrian Way along the edge of Lonscale Fell, toward the town of Keswick. The rough, stone-strewn, rocky, irregular mountain path made it hard going for us, but then came light relief in the form of a figure running at full speed toward us. He was quite a sight; we stood motionless watching this Fell runner who was so at ease with the rugged rocks. He passed us and for a while disappeared in the distance but then reappeared down in the valley, crossing the bridge over the beck and up again on Blease Fell, still at full speed.

From the slopes of Jenkin Hill, we looked at the much-awaited sight of the two great lakes, Derwent Water and Bassenthwaite. It was breathtaking:

> *Who comes not hither ne'er shall know*
> *How beautiful the world below*
> —Wordsworth

There is nothing more beautiful to see, there is no better place to go, all and everything is here. Here is the grandeur of God's creation. Everything in balance, all in proportion, the hardness of the blue water, the flexibility of the swaying trees, the gentle movement of the breeze. This was a place of total peace, and yet we had to keep moving and come down from the heights to find Alan Hankinson and his house in Skiddaw Street.

I was anxious about missing Alan, but as we descended through the woods of Ormathwaite we saw him coming toward us, curly wild hair, weathered face, deep eyes, and fit body. "I'm sorry to be so late, but I was leading a group of walkers and, as I am sure you well know, you can never determine how long a mountain walk will take," he said.

Alan was to lead us the next day. I was up and about early, and my feet were itching to be in the lap of Lakeland, but my excitement did not impress him: he was taking it easy. For him, being on the fells of Cumbria was a familiar affair, so it was after nine when we left the house. But once we were on the move, Alan shot like a bullet, up and up and up, following Brockle Beck and then to Falcon Crag. From here we could see the spread of Derwent Water and Bassenthwaite and umpteen streams and rivers between the two lakes.

I loved the lakes, but I wanted to move into the mountains. The path, a sheep track between the heather, led us up to High Seat, over six hundred meters high. From here onward there was no path, only endless boggy marsh. "If you walk on the hillocks and mounds of tough grass, avoiding the water between, you will be all right," said Alan. June and I looked at him doubtfully. I was concerned about the bogginess of the terrain: I had once sunk up to my knees in a similar bog on Exmoor and did not wish to experience that feeling again, but there was no alternative route. We followed the line of the sheep fence, which kept flocks in one valley from wandering into another. How did farmers bring posts and netting to this remote place and manage to put the fence up, I wondered. Our pace was slow, and the path meandered; my excitement and enthusiasm turned into anxiety and frustration. We reached the hilltop of High Tove and sat down there for a drink of water and a look at the map. I felt reluctant to keep zigzagging over the hillocks and bogs, so I suggested taking a right turning and going down into the valley of Watendlath. From there a marked public footpath would bring us up again. Alan warned us that we would lose hundreds of feet in height, but because of my anxiety he agreed, since this was not territory which he knew well.

We started to climb down. There was a steep slope of scree and stones, loose and risky. One stone dislodged by my foot rocketed down. I stood holding my breath, aghast, pressing my fingers to my lips, hoping it would not hit anyone down below. Eventually we managed to get to Watendlath, where there was a group of houses and a lovely lake fed by five small streams. This was surely the time to stop, rest, and have lunch, which we did, and we then looked at our maps again to make sure that we found the public footpath going up the fells. When we had determined where the path was going, we put our rucksacks on and set off. Although the path was clearly marked on the map, within ten minutes it had petered out into the heather, in spite of it being National Trust land. Now I regretted losing height, as Alan had warned us. We had to walk up and up again on the steep hill in the same kind of terrain as High Tove. I should have paid more attention to Alan's experience. Seeing June stagger behind, Alan kindly took her rucksack, and we kept up a fast pace. After an hour's walk we came to Blea Tarn, a large pool of clear water held in the shoulders of the hills. When I saw Blea Tarn I felt a sense of relief; we had regained our height and met up with the sheep fence. Now if we kept to the ridge we would soon be at Greenup Edge, from where we would descend into the valley of Easedale. This thought spurred me on and put me in a more optimistic mood.

We stood at the high point of Ullscarf, 726 meters high as described in the map, and looked around:

No habitation can be seen; but they
Who journey hither find themselves alone
With a few sheep, with rocks and stones and kites
That overhead are sailing in the sky.
It is in truth an utter solitude

—Wordsworth

All the bogs and jumping on hillocks were now behind us, and this solitude was ample reward.

PEOPLE LIKE COMPANY and the gods like solitude. We build towns, villages, and communities, but the gods stay in the mountains. From the house of the gods in the Cumbrian heights, Alan, June, and I descended into the valley of Easedale, which was sleeping peacefully, sheltered by cliffs and crags and covered with a blanket of green grass and mountain ash trees.

The valley brought us to Grasmere, the home of the poet Wordsworth, who spent his life singing of the grandeur of this landscape. He used to walk to Keswick to lunch with his friends and return in the evening without much ado. The distance we had covered, walking hard all day, Wordsworth would have done as a matter of course: through quiet valleys which now are filled with roads, crowds, and cars. In the nineteenth century, country people would not have thought twice about walking twenty miles in a day, whereas we in modern times seem to behave as if we have lost our legs.

Arriving in Grasmere and hitting the A59 was quite a shock. After the solitude of the hills we were in the midst of souvenir shops, gas stations, cafes, and superstores. We spent the night in Ambleside, which was bustling and busy with tourism, and next morning I experienced a sense of relief in setting off for the towering hill of Jenkin Crag. As we climbed up and up, I felt high and superior, glad to leave the world down below. But when I looked back at the old stone and slate houses of Ambleside nestling on the shores of Lake Windermere, the clear water stretching along the valley as far as the eyes could see, my desire to escape into the hills was tempered by the attraction of the world I had left behind. How wrong I was to see the height of Jenkin Crag without relating it to the great lake and the land which rest down below. Jenkin

Crag and Lake Windermere are aspects of the same reality. There can be no high without a low. I remembered the Taoist principle of polarity, which is not to be confused with opposition or conflict. High and low, pleasure and pain, life and death, positive and negative "are more like lovers wrestling than enemies fighting . . . The art of life is more like navigation than warfare" (Alan Watts, *Tao*). These thoughts flashed through my mind like lightning, and therefore I was as happy descending from Jenkin Crag as I had been to climb it.

We followed a footpath which went alongside the river Kent and met the river Sprint near Burneside. There used to be a working mill here, which was shut down and left to fall derelict—the same fate as thousands of other mills. A few years ago Edward Acland saw the potential of this beautiful mill and borrowed the money from friends and family to buy it at a low price.

We arrived there in the heat of a late summer's afternoon. Our hosts were enjoying a swim and play in a deep pool of water beside the mill house, where the river Sprint emerged out of dense woods onto large slabs of rock and rushed its way past. We put our rucksacks down, threw our clothes off, and plunged in to join them in the river. The experience of our hot bodies meeting the cool waters created shudders of delight! This place was like paradise: the rocks, the river, the woods, the people, the house all in perfect harmony.

A good half hour of submersion had more than cooled our bodies, and with perfect timing a tray full of tea and cake appeared on the wooden table outside the house. We went from hot to cool and then to hot again. "Once upon a time, this was a great mill, serving many communities," Edward said. "Now the milling is no more, but I have used the huge space of several stories for my collection of antique tools and artifacts." Edward is a lover of things old and well made. He is a collector of items which other people have found useless and superfluous but he sees as objects of beauty and craftsmanship. "These objects have an immense value and long life because people put their skill, ingenuity, and love into making them with their own hands. Modern gadgets, made quickly by machines and lacking the human touch, are used today and thrown away tomorrow," said Edward as he showed me around. "Where do you find these wonderful things?" I asked. "I go to old farms and mills, to auctions and sales—there is no one source. Quite often these tools are rusting away unused or discarded uncaringly. When I see that, my heart bleeds, so I bring them here and make use of them in my work."

Edward is a woodworker and carpenter. He particularly likes to repair old doors, windows, and broken furniture. Conservation and recycling are his great passions. "Waste not want not" is his dearest motto.

He has many skills and many interests. Not long ago he gathered together a group of friends to make a large Indian tepee. This involved men, women, and children working together over many months—finding the right material, designing, cutting the canvas correctly, sewing it together, searching for poles of the right size in the woods, and working out many other fine details—needed a tremendous amount of imagination, cooperation, and hard work. "You have a choice: either you can sleep in the house or in our tepee, which we erected this afternoon with you in mind," said Edward. For June and me, it was not a choice but a matter of pleasure and honor to sleep in the tepee.

We walked several hundred yards on a freshly mown path through long, lush undergrowth of grass, nettles, and pink campion. As we came to a meadow by the river, I was struck by the magnificent sight of the beautiful white tepee surrounded by friendly green trees. I wanted to stand still and gaze at the purity of its shape, which pointed toward heaven and yet was firmly grounded on earth. I had never seen anything like it before. How could our architects take no notice of this rounded dwelling, and make square boxes for our homes?

I slowly walked to the tepee, went around it, looking upwards, downwards, sideways. It was so simple yet so mysterious, beautiful in every detail. It offered shelter for most human needs and protection from the elements, and yet it had the magnificence of a noble sculpture which fitted so naturally into the spirit of the landscape. "The culture of America's native Indians, which gave birth to the tepee, is a culture close to the earth. We call those people primitive, savage, and uncivilized, but they understood intuitively the workings of nature, and respected the laws and principles of the cosmos more deeply than our clever civilization of modern times. If we were able to seek the wisdom of the Indians, we would find joy, contentment, and comfort in simple things and consider ourselves an element of nature, not separate from it, not superior to it, but part of it. American Indians believed all beings were relatives, members of the same family, sharing the planet in a spirit of mutual support and receiving sustenance from each other, held together by the Great Spirit," said Edward. "But progress has come to mean the separation of the human and natural worlds," I interjected. "Yes," Edward replied, "the ever-expanding modern culture sees everything existing for the benefit of human beings. The bonds between all creatures have been broken, and nature has become merely a resource . . . Even environmentalists advocate nature conservation on the grounds of self-interest and human benefit, whereas the Indians considered the living elements of earth, air, water, and fire as the sacred limbs of the Great Spirit, existing in their own right, irrespective of human need."

We went into the tepee; the interior was unexpectedly spacious. Edward had lit a fire in the center to keep insects out. The smoke ascended and found its way out through a hole in the roof. Edward explained, "The design of a tepee is such that the hole will let the smoke out without letting the rain and wind in. The two ends of the canvas at the top are attached to separate poles, which can be moved according to the direction the wind is blowing. In any case, when the tepee is erected it is set with the main entrance away from the prevailing wind."

He left us in the tepee to settle down but returned soon after and said, "Do you mind if we also sleep here?" "Of course not, your company is welcome." As Edward spread his sleeping bag, his children arrived and then a few more friends who had joined us for dinner. They were followed by Hans, the potter, and Mary, the oak swill maker, who live in a cottage by the mill. Although the number of people grew in the tepee, I was only very dimly aware of their presence. I was amazed at how comfortable, relaxed, and informal the atmosphere was; the space seemed infinite. Lying by the flickering fire, Edward and I continued talking late into the night while our wives slept blissfully.

I CAN BE ACCUSED of being a pastoral romantic, but it is in the woods and hills, meadows and river valleys that my soul finds nourishment. Therefore, parting from Sprint Mill was like parting from a lifelong friend, even though my love affair with this piece of earth was only one night long. The river Sprint kept us company until we met the river Kent near Kendal. We followed the footpath alongside the Kent as long as we could, and from there we crossed fields and farms to follow the Lancaster Canal.

It was a sorry sight to see this magical waterway abandoned in favor of tarmac roads. Now, only a few pleasure boats move between the locks. A section of the canal has been blocked and filled to give way to even more roads. Fortunately stretches of footpath are still used by ramblers and naturalists, for in other respects the canal has become a rural backwater, evoking nostalgia but leading nowhere; history stands still.

We left the canal after a few miles to go to Gressingham. Early the next morning, June left to return to the children in Hartland, and I followed a path along the river Lune. Being no lover of big cities I skirted around the built-up area of Lancaster and came back to the Lancaster Canal, which took me comfortably to Billsborough and thence to Preston. Now I was in the grip of the urban sprawl of Liverpool; it was no longer possible to avoid that concrete jungle. The smell of burning gasoline from the exhausts of speeding cars and the sight of the derelict, dusty docklands was the treat of the day! I would not say that everyone should live in a rural idyll, but when towns and cities become industrial wastelands, they lose their human scale. The majority of people in Britain live in cities. Why do they have to be subjected to such unconvivial atmospheres?

When I had endured the long and lonely road to the center of Liverpool, I found some sense of relief. I was among people enjoying the sun on the promenade of the Crosby Channel. The expressions on the faces of people were friendly and gentle; the harshness of the road along the dockland had disappeared. Joining people in prayer at the Anglican and Catholic cathedrals gave me a sense of peace and rest.

Continuing to walk through the poorer part of Liverpool, I was intrigued. Although an atmosphere of poverty prevailed, with the houses run-down and the streets full of litter, I saw many smiling faces. People were standing engaged in relaxed conversation, children were playing in the middle of the streets scarcely aware of the traffic, and the cars were going at a slower pace, minding the children.

Next morning I took the ferry over the river Mersey to Birkenhead. Rosemary Fitzpatrick had gathered members of the Soil Association, local peace groups, and a number of environmentalists to give me an unexpected welcome and lead me through the Wirral and then to the walled city of Chester, from where next day I headed west into Wales, following the river Dee.

MY FIRST NIGHT IN WALES was spent at Llandyrnog near Denbigh, in the valley of the river Clwyd. My hosts, Guy and Molly Clutton-Brock, were living high in the hills in an old stone cottage without electricity or running water. Guy and Molly are living examples of voluntary simplicity. They run an old car to help them move about in their old age and keep them in touch with friends, but that is one of the very few concessions they have made to the twentieth century's technological age. The living room was warmed by a wood-burning stove, for which they had collected wood from the surrounding hills and sawn and split it themselves.

It was the fifth of July and yet still cold in the Welsh hills, so I sat near the fire, eating my supper of bread, beans, and beer, which Guy and Molly had kept for me as I had arrived long past dinnertime. Nothing is sweeter than hunger satisfied, and even a very basic and simple meal prepared with care and imagination can be most delicious, especially when it is home-baked bread, beans cooked with herbs and spices, and home-brewed beer.

The living room we sat in was also their study and workroom. Next to the living room was their kitchen, and above the kitchen was the guest room where I was to sleep. "It is much easier to look after a small cottage, especially at our age. A large house, a lot of furniture, and many gadgets do not necessarily add to comfort. They give an illusion of comfort. We have been living in this cottage for nearly ten years, and we are quite happy."

Guy and Molly had learned the lessons of simple living during their time at Cold Comfort Farm in Rhodesia, now Zimbabwe. They never joined the colonial club. They lived close to the earth, working with their hands, laboring in the fields, identifying themselves with the native African people. Their white skin was no barrier, and their farm became a refuge for freedom fighters. But because of their support for Robert Mugabe and the movement for independence, the farm was confiscated and they were exiled by the Smith regime under the charge of supporting terrorism. Since Zimbabwe became independent, the Clutton-Brock cottage in Wales has become a place of pilgrimage for Zimbabwean politicians, diplomats, and intellectuals. When they visit Britain they invariably come to Llandyrnog to pay their respects to the Clutton-Brocks. "They are always surprised and shocked to see us living in such a small cottage, in what they call primitive conditions. They ask us to return to Zimbabwe. They offer us a big house, a car, a pension, but we say to them that we are fine as we are, thank you. But why have they forgotten the poor peasants and become, so soon after independence, slaves to the creature comforts of high living? It is not us who should be offered cars and comforts, it is they who should live a life which is more akin to the ordinary people in Zimbabwe. When I say this to them they laugh at us. They think we have grown old, idealist, and impractical."

There was sorrow in the voice of Guy when he spoke these words. His love for Zimbabwe, as shown by his support for its independence and his admiration for the freedom fighters, had turned to sadness. "When there is the taste of power and position, it is very easy to forget the promises made to the people."

When I was ready to go to bed, Molly showed me how to light the paraffin lamp. In the room she showed me a flask of hot water, a jug of cold water, and a beautiful large Victorian china bowl to wash in. There was a chamber pot under the bed since there was no flush toilet. "Everything comes from the earth and must be returned to the earth," said Molly, explaining how all the organic waste from their household, including our excreta, was put on the compost or buried in the earth. "Nature creates no waste. Even the dead old leaves fallen on the ground are the source of new life."

Early in the morning, Thomas Brown from a Quaker community in Llanderfel came on his motorbike to the cottage of the Clutton-Brocks to guide me to his home. He left his bike, and we started to trek through the hills of Berwyn. The austerity of the Clutton-Brocks' life was echoed by the austerity of these Welsh mountains; bereft of trees, they were bare, magnificent, and somewhat daunting. Thomas and I kept stopping to gaze at the vastness of these mighty mountains.

From Llanderfel we crossed over the river Dee and followed a dismantled and overgrown railway line. We had to climb and jump over many fences that farmers had erected over the line, thinking that no one was going to use the railway anymore. There must be hundreds of miles of such disused railways, the legacy of Dr. Beeching, who massacred them in the interest of apparent economy and encouraged the building of new roads through the beautiful landscape of rural Wales. We followed the little-used line beside the river Dee, which brought us into a wide open valley.

Suddenly we arrived at the beautiful Lake of Bala—Llyn Tegid, long and slim, lying like a sleeping beauty between the handsome hills, fed and nourished by rivers from all sides and ornamented by tall trees. My feet stopped, my eyes widened with amazement as they drank in the wonder of the water. It was a real surprise to encounter it. After having seen great lakes and mountains on my journey, I was under the illusion that I had seen the best of nature's glory, but being confronted with this quiet, clean, and unspoiled stretch of water, I was taken aback. People had talked about the wonderful Welsh mountains, but nobody had ever mentioned the name Lake Bala. Perhaps the Welsh have in their wisdom wanted to keep this lake a secret, unexposed to tourism.

This was the court of nature at its most festive and exuberant. I dangled my feet in the water, experiencing the ecstasy of the moment. As I sat there, I had a strong sense that I was an intruder, interfering with the lives of the lovers and disturbing the stillness of an eternal embrace. Bala belongs to Bryn Bedwog, and I should tread gently in their house.

And so I left the lake behind and headed on toward Cadair Idris, nearly three thousand feet at its peak, overlooking the entire breadth of North Wales. Roaming up and down in the mountains of Meirionydd, once more I was one with nature; I was dancing the dance of Shiva.

Past Dolgellau, I followed a stream through woods, walking on a dirt track barely wide enough for a small tractor or a Morris Minor. Sure enough, a thousand feet up on this remote edge of Idris I saw a young woman holding a baby in her arms beside a lonely Morris. I could not resist speaking to her. "So the good old Morris has made it to this height on the bumpy track!" The young woman stared at me fixedly, wide-eyed for a few seconds, and did not answer. Perhaps I was being discourteous to approach a woman alone in such a wild place. Feeling apologetic, I was passing by her when she put her finger to her lips and inquired, "By any chance, are you Satish on pilgrimage?" It was my turn to be amazed. I could not believe my ears, hearing my name being pronounced by this unknown woman standing in long grass in a clearing overlooked by Penygadair. I stopped and wondered, looking at this woman of silky hair and sweet smile. "How is it that you know my name?" "I read *Resurgence*. Seeing you here it occurred to me that I might be meeting the pilgrim, by some act of providence." "I am pleased to meet you too." "When I first heard about your journey, I wondered whether you would pass through my village, as I wanted to offer you a bed for the night. I live on the border of Wales and England, but to my disappointment I learned that your route did not bring you to my place. But ever since, I hoped that I would meet you somewhere on your way, and today my wish is fulfilled." Her voice was filled with emotion. I stepped toward her and offered a handshake. She gave me a kiss on the cheek. "What brings you here?" I asked. "We are here on a day out. My husband is interested in orchids—he is over there, in the woods." I wanted to see the orchids too, so we set off to find her husband.

EVERY AGE CREATES new places of pilgrimage. There was a time when people built stone circles and erected standing stones as a spiritual focus. In the Middle Ages, the relics of saints and martyrs drew people for inspiration and healing. In India, the presence of religious teachers and ascetics by riverbanks and in the mountains has for centuries drawn people to those holy places. In our own age the birthplaces of Shakespeare and Tolstoy attract people who look for renewal and inspiration; the grave of Gandhi has acquired similar significance.

For me, the Center for Alternative Technology at Machynlleth has a similar attraction. Intermediate technology has a spiritual and religious dimension because it is a gentle technology, compassionate to the environment and frugal in its use of the earth's resources. This spiritual dimension makes Machynlleth a place of pilgrimage. Spirituality is not about beliefs—it is about the way we live and conduct our day-to-day activities. When Lord Krishna pleaded with the warrior Arjuna to practice steadfast wisdom, Arjuna protested saying, "I do not understand these big words and difficult concepts. Tell me in simple language. How does a steadfast person walk, sit, eat, talk, and live?" This immediately made Krishna relate his teachings to the mundane practicalities of life; by performing simple actions such as walking, sitting, and talking in a compassionate manner, one is able to lift ordinary activity into a form of yoga. If we were able to grow our food, produce energy, and obtain water in the spirit of yoga, we would never attempt to create a technology which is harmful to humans or to our habitat.

People such as Mahatma Gandhi, who advocated the use of the spinning wheel, and E. F. Schumacher, who invented the terms *intermediate* and *appropriate* technology, were intensely religious people; the reason they promoted the ideas of simple technology was that it was conducive to the spiritual as well as material well-being of all—rich and poor alike. Without this dimension, alternative technology has no philosophical basis.

As I descended from the heights of Cadair Idris and entered into the valley of slate quarries, my feet speeded up with anticipation. Many years ago, a number of enthusiastic ecologists came to this area. They found an abandoned slate quarry, overgrown with bracken and brambles. Surrounded by tall trees, this wild and remote corner of Wales was exactly the kind of site they were looking for. The mountains, deserts, and wilderness have always attracted pioneering spirits because in such undisturbed settings they are able to give form to their eccentric experiments without being interrupted or interfered with by the established order. They negotiated easy terms with the owner and camped in harsh conditions to lay the foundations for a community which would demonstrate by example how life can be lived when based on the use of renewable energy, organic methods of producing food, and nonhierarchical relationships. I was received by Peter Harper, who took me around the center on a guided tour. All sorts of windmills, solar panels, water wheels, and composting systems were on display. Peter himself lives in a house which uses no electricity from the mains. This was a convincing example of how it is possible to fulfill all one's basic requirements with locally available and renewable sources of energy. He then took me to see the greenhouse and vegetable garden. Gardening is his passion. The principles of rotation, companion planting, and organic husbandry are practiced here.

When the center was established it was a step in the dark, but now 100,000 people visit it every year, and it has become a thriving community whose members are driven by idealism and dedication. Running the center as a successful business as well as a community requires a difficult and delicate balance. Somehow I got the impression that they have managed to achieve it. On the one hand, an efficiently run office gives you the impression of being busy in the world, and on the other hand, goats, chickens, community kitchens, and children playing in the yard created a relaxed atmosphere. Peter took me to the Hightech workshop with some trepidation, which I could quite understand. Here a number of computer programmers and silicon chip experts were working with sophisticated technology to be used in the Third World. I doubted that this kind of progress would liberate the Third World. It would only make the recipients more dependent on Western science. For me there could be no reconciliation between alternative technology and high technology. However, the force of the computer age seems to be so strong that it has engulfed even the ecologists and low-impact technologists. So perhaps I should not be too critical; after all, in every other way, this center is a beacon of new thinking. When people realize that oil reserves are finite and nuclear power is dangerous, they will return to live by the sun, the wind, and the natural potential of the Earth. At that time the Center for Alternative Technology will become the center of life and society.

Andy and Catherine Evans-Rowland, and their few-months-old baby, Gwen, are members of the center, and I stayed in their home for the night. The next morning Catherine said that she would like to walk with me and bring Gwen. Gwen had already stolen my heart. Watching her play, smile, and gaze was so engaging that I could enjoy it for hours. Catherine packed the picnic and the diapers and we were on the road.

We walked through Machynlleth, which once upon a time was the capital of Wales. Catherine told me that Wales was the first country to have the parliamentary system of government, and Machynlleth had the first parliament. So it was not England that had brought forth the mother of parliaments but Wales! We stopped for a few minutes at the original building, which stood as a charming monument. "Now the English dominate our thinking, our language, and our way of life," said Catherine with a voice of anguish. "The English come to enjoy the mountains, but they don't like our language; they come to have their holidays in these beautiful valleys, but they don't want to know about our culture. They like the splendor of this landscape, but they wish they could have it without the people who inhabit it. I have nothing against the English, I only wish that they would come respecting our people, our history, our culture, and our language." I totally sympathized with her. When will the dominant cultures of the world stop dominating peoples who are economically and politically weaker?

We sat in a field under a tree, a cool breeze blowing. Gwen was hungry. Catherine put the baby in her lap, supported her head on her right arm, the red nipple between Gwen's lips. Here was a harmonious union of mother and baby, each being nourished by the other. Catherine's sense of fulfillment and joy in feeding her baby was clear on her face. The giving and receiving were mutual. After a few minutes she moved Gwen from her right breast to her left. Milk was bursting from her breast. When one is prepared to give, there is always plenty. When one is hesitant, worried, under pressure, then even the milk in the breast dries up. As we started walking again I asked Catherine if I could carry Gwen on my shoulders. She was happy to agree. Gwen was the youngest pilgrim to be with me, and it was a joy to carry her.

After spending a comfortable night in an old Welsh farmhouse in Stay Little, I carried on my walk to the south. Wandering through the Hafren Forest, I found myself in Cerrig yr Wyn mountain range, the source of two great rivers, the Severn and the Wye. I followed a forest path toward the river Wye, flowing southward. In the Wye Valley there are many unspoiled small Welsh farms and farming families where generations have carried on their lives for hundreds of years. Here modern farm machinery is defeated, as it cannot climb up the steep slopes and narrow dirt tracks.

Past Llanngurig, on the east bank of the Wye, is the A470 trunk road—an old and forgotten minor road, which naturally I followed. The gentle flow of the river Wye on my left and the hard, rugged, and rocky hills on my right presented me with a perfect setting for my ruminations. I was alone and at ease. For centuries this valley has served humans, animals, birds, trees, plants, and numerous forms of life; it has been a mother. The Wye makes the way and the Wye is the way, the way to all destinations and no destination. It takes you everywhere and nowhere. You can swim in it, float in it, dive in it, and drown in it. The Wye is the giver of life and death. It moves mysteriously; it embodies power, and yet it follows the lower path.

I stopped for the night at Rhayader. In the morning Lawrence Golding, hill walker par excellence, came to lead me away from the valley and into the hills. "When you are in the valley you appreciate the hills, and when you are in the hills you appreciate the valley, but I love the hills most. When you are up here you are in the company of the sky, and you reach the source of the valleys. Without knowing the beginning you cannot know the end," said Lawrence. "The mountaintops have a purity about them: here no paths reach. It is a virgin landscape, and so my heart longs for it." He led me from hilltop to hilltop, into remote regions, away from built-up civilization.

After our twelve-hour-long journey, we descended from the hills about dusk. We came to a farm gate. A herd of sheep were passing through it, so we stood aside by the hedge. Then there was a pause. Another group of sheep, with a shepherd, was still some way off. We thought that perhaps we could pass through before the next lot of sheep reached the gate. But the shepherd saw us coming. He advanced, brandishing his stick and shouting, "Stop there, will you." Lawrence was not to be deterred. "It will take us only a second to pass through, and your sheep are still yards away."

That threw the farmer into a fit. "I have seen many vagabonds like you who do no work, idle away your lives, and interrupt others when they are working. What do you do for a living?" "I do not need to tell you what I do for a living! Mind your own business. I am on a public path, and I have a right to be here." Walker and farmer, both insisting on their rights, were near blows. I pulled Lawrence away saying, "Never mind, let him bring his sheep through first." And the farmer drove his sheep through, still abusing us.

Lawrence spoke of his dislike of farmers who plow up footpaths, erect barbed wire across paths, and show no courtesy to walkers. "Land is not merely a source of food, it is also a source of spiritual and emotional nourishment. If people are deprived of contact with their countryside, their spirit will die." Lawrence pleaded passionately for a new relationship between people and land.

AFTER A NIGHT'S REST at the home of Richard Booth in Hay-on-Wye, I set off alone again, walking through the landscape and villages of the gorgeous Golden Valley of the river Dore. Glenn Storhaug with his wife, Liz, his children, and five other friends met me at Arthur's Stone, where we all walked together through woodland. Glenn and Liz were my hosts for the night. A poet and printer, Glenn is a magnetic person, attracting people interested in the good things of life, the arts, crafts, education, and a healthy environment.

We sat in the front garden, cooled by a breeze coming from the Forest of Dean, enveloped by apples, fuchsias, roses, beans, and many other kinds of fruits, flowers, and vegetables. Glenn and Liz had prepared a large meal for an unspecified number of people who might turn up to meet the pilgrim that evening. We enjoyed a hot vegetable stew made with produce from the garden, which was served with coarse brown bread. Overlooking an open view of Herefordshire and marveling at the magnificence of the meadows and fields, I realized that it was only through our ancestors' deep reverence for nature that we could inherit this abundant wealth.

Glenn and his friends celebrated the simple beauty of life and lived in harmony with their surroundings. They made relatively few demands on the resources of the Earth and found joy in their creative work. Glenn himself was involved in the hand-printing, typography, and designing of books which embody the beauty of simplicity. Art for him was not an end product but an absorbed involvement in the process of doing things well and making things which are good in themselves.

Modern civilization induces us to do things for material gains, for money, power, fame, or comfort. Because of this we have been taking and taking from each other, from the environment, and from our own souls, without any thought of giving back or of replenishment. Glenn believes the teaching of Coomaraswamy: that the artist is not a special kind of person, but that every person is a special kind of artist.

That evening I was invited to give a public talk in Hereford, city of Mappa Mundi fame. I talked about the way of replenishment. "In India we are required to practice three principles: *yagna, dana,* and *tapas.* These are the three replenishing relationships. Through yagna we replenish the earth and nature. Through dana we replenish culture and society, and through tapas we replenish our soul and our spirit.

"Our food and water come from the earth, our homes and clothes come from the earth; in fact we are made of the earth. If we keep on taking from the earth without giving anything back, the earth will be denuded. Therefore the Indian saying is 'If you cut down one tree, you must plant five.' We must always be alert and thoughtful so that we repair any damage we do to the earth. That is yagna.

"From the very moment of our birth we take sustenance from society: from our parents, from our neighbors, from our teachers, from our friends and colleagues. We enjoy the fruits of the work of our ancestors in literature, architecture, painting and music, roads and railways, schools and churches. This reservoir of culture will dry up if we do not give something ourselves for future generations. If we see our work as a gift to society, the quality of our work and its meaning will be enhanced many, many fold. That is dana.

"As we replenish the earth and our society we also need to renew ourselves. We spend a great deal of energy giving expression to our intellectual, emotional, and spiritual being, sometimes negatively, other times positively, sometimes in anger, sometimes in love. Unless we pay attention to the healing of our souls, we cannot be whole. By meditation, by fasting, by watching the river flow, by gazing at a flower in bloom, by walking in nature, by going on a pilgrimage, we replenish our souls. That is tapas."

As I spoke I realized I was interpreting the three ancient Indian principles in a modern context. Rather, these ancient principles were as relevant to our modern times as they were in the days when nobody had heard of ecology and sustainability. My pilgrimage was a form of tapas.

Next morning I went to see the Hereford Waldorf School, which Glenn and his friends have helped to establish. This school takes its inspiration from Rudolf Steiner's educational ideas, according to which children up to the age of seven are not required to pursue intellectual activities such as reading, writing, and arithmetic. This preseven period is a time to develop emotionally and intuitively, and children are helped to learn through stories, colors, games, and plays. Only after the age of seven do children engage in intellectual activities.

I was delighted to visit this school of sixty children, which had a friendly, enthusiastic, and dedicated group of teachers and a warm atmosphere. One of the biggest problems in running this kind of school is finance. The British system of education is so monolithic that either you have to be part of the state-maintained comprehensive schooling, which is organized on a large scale with little regard for the particular needs of any group of parents and their children, or you have to send your children far away to private schools, confusingly called public schools, which are expensive and elitist. There is no alternative. In Germany, Steiner schools are financed by the government. There they recognize the importance of plurality, parental choice, and new approaches in education. If a similar principle could be adopted in Britain, then education would be liberated from the shackles of monoculture. The problems faced by the Hereford Waldorf School sounded only too familiar to me after my work at the Small School.

From hereford I continued my march through Gloucester and on to Taelna Community, near the Benedictine monastery of Prinknash Abbey. Here I stayed with George Ineson. This stage of my journey had become a pilgrimage to people from whom I had drawn inspiration; George is one of them. During the Second World War he and his friends pioneered a pacifist community, which still continues and has grown to become almost a small hamlet. Farming, silversmithing, pottery, carpentry, architectural design, and woodcarving are the principal activities of this community. In the age of individualism and materialism, where self-interest is pursued to the exclusion of everything else, Taelna has been a shining example of how to overcome narrow personal ambitions in favor of the common good. The community has drawn people from all over the world to experience its spiritual and shared way of life.

George has been one of the leading spirits of this community. He has kept a hospitable and welcoming house, open to all visitors. After showing me around the various workshops and the farm, and outlining the impressive history of the community, he explained, "When we began living together, we held almost everything in common. But as the community developed, we learned certain lessons. There are certain activities better pursued in solitude and in an atmosphere of individual freedom, such as study and meditation. Other activities are more appropriate to the family, such as bringing up children, but there are other activities which are enhanced by sharing in a community and through cooperation with the whole group. There is a tremendous waste of energy, talent, and resources when every individual pursues his own ends and competes with each other. The cult of individualism has been the curse of Western society."

From George Ineson I moved on to Roger Franklin; it was like sailing from one lighthouse to the next. Roger met me in Stroud and said, "You have already walked for four hours under the scorching sun—would you like to have a dip in our splendid, newly opened swimming pool?" I happily agreed to this. After the swim, Roger relieved me of my rucksack and drove it to his home, where he prepared a dinner to welcome me in the evening. Veronica Ross, an old friend of mine from London who also lived in the neighborhood, guided me along a newly formed bicycle path through lush Cotswold countryside to Roger's house.

A small dinner party had been arranged, attended by a group of people who had helped and supported Roger in his untiring campaign against nuclear weapons. He has spared no effort in his work for peace: his whole life has been one continuous struggle for disarmament and the dismantling of the war machine. I know no other person who has devoted his or her life so passionately and single-mindedly, day and night, to world peace.

One of his most courageous actions to register his intense dislike and disapproval of the arms buildup was to refuse to pay the percentage of his income tax which went to the defense industry. He explained to me, "In 1849 Henry David Thoreau refused to pay tax in protest against an unjust war and the continuation of slavery. His essay 'Civil Disobedience' is a classic statement of conscience. We are in the same predicament now. Our governments are spending incredible amounts of resources on war preparations and armaments. It is a colossal waste. My conscience will not allow me any longer to willingly pay to help the building of genocidal machinery. I can no longer bring myself to write a check to the Inland Revenue as though the expenditure to which I am contributing had my approval. I have gone on a tax strike."

People like Roger are the salt of the earth and the conscience of the community. I salute him, his dedication and his commitment.

From Stroud it was two days' walk to Bristol, where my hosts were Jean and Stephen MacFarlane, a Quaker couple, both strong supporters of the Schumacher Society. They have been involved with issues of sustainable development in Africa, and removing the yoke of debt and exploitation forced on the Third World by Western industrialized nations. Together with John Pontin, Jean and Stephen have been generous hosts to the illustrious thinkers and activists who have come to give the Schumacher lectures. I have always been able to depend on them for their help in getting the event known and publicized.

During more than a decade of Schumacher lectures, I have come to know and love Bristol very much, because of friends like the MacFarlanes who have drawn me to Bristol year after year. From my bedroom window at their home, I had a wonderful view of the Clifton suspension bridge, built by one of the most brilliant engineers of the Victorian age, Isambard Kingdom Brunel. I have been around the world and I have crossed many small and great bridges, but none compares with the shape, size, architectural quality, and beauty of this bridge.

Next day I was delighted to discover that my path went over Brunel's bridge. In the cool and misty morning, I stood in the middle of the gorge, looking down at the gushing waters of the river Avon. It was a magic moment.

NOURISHED BY NATURE'S BOUNTY, I continued on my path: sometimes on big roads, sometimes on country lanes, ascending the hills and descending into valleys, refreshing myself in brooks and streams, over winding and wide rivers and along many ditches and dikes. Walking by day, resting by night, I crossed the Somerset levels, within sight of

Glastonbury Tor; mostly alone, sometimes accompanied, I climbed the Quantock and Brendon Hills.

Arriving at Exmoor was like entering a beautiful new world. A herd of deer grazed on Dunkery Hill, a troop of horses and riders trekked across Porlock Common, and I made my way to Watersmeet near Lynmouth, owned and protected by the National Trust. Now I was within sight of Hartland Point.

My last night on the road was spent in Barnstaple on July 31, 1986. I headed home. June came to welcome me at the bridge over the river Yeo, near Bideford. On the one hand, I felt a sense of completion and satisfaction that my four-month pilgrimage was coming to a conclusion, but on the other hand, I also felt the loss of the freedom of the road. At one level, I kept wishing to remain a walking pilgrim for the rest of my life, but at another level I was drawn to be with Maya, Mukti, and June.

I was filled with feelings of gratitude to June, who had enabled me to make this pilgrimage by staying at home, looking after the children and guests, and managing the magazine and the house. In truth June had made a greater gesture than me. I was indebted to her. What had I done to deserve this? I could only imagine that in my previous life I must have sown the seeds of good karma—perhaps by enabling someone to go on a pilgrimage?

A FEW DAYS AFTER I had completed my pilgrimage, our friend Clara Erede came from Florence to visit us in Hartland. "I have been thinking of you while you were on your pilgrimage," she said. "Although I missed my chance at fifty, I would like to make a brief pilgrimage to mark my sixtieth birthday, and would like you and June to come with me." This request came out of the blue and I was flattered to be invited. "Of course," I said. "Where do you want to walk?" "To Assisi—I live so close by, but have never been there, although people come on pilgrimage from all over the world," Clara said. "I have never been to Assisi either. St. Francis, who considered all creatures of the Earth members of one family, and called the sun and the moon his brother and sister, has been one of the greatest inspirations for me. What a good idea!"

June's instant agreement sealed the matter, and upon hearing of this plan, John Lane, Veronica Ross, and Barbara Girardet also decided to follow Clara to Assisi.

The English party flew to Pisa and took the train to within about a hundred kilometers from Assisi, from where we met Clara and started walking. Step by step for seven days we meditated, chanted, and read stories of St. Francis and Santa Clara. James Hillman's essay *Walking in Paradise and a Paradise in Walking* added to our inspiration. We arrived in Assisi on a stormy and thundery afternoon, with a heightened sense of the spiritual mystery of the place.

In the basilica, the life of St. Francis is vividly and compellingly depicted by Giotto in his arresting frescoes. As an ecologist, I responded to the paintings, Francis feeding the birds and talking to them.

Soon after we returned from Assisi, a Spanish friend, Amparo Aracama, came to spend a few days with us in Hartland. "No one could be more authoritative than you, Amparo, to guide and lead us on a pilgrimage to Santiago de Compostela," I said. Amparo was not expecting such a request, but knowing well my enthusiasm for pilgrimages, she readily and generously offered to come with me. Having already tasted the magic of Assisi, June, John, and Veronica again decided to form the party.

By plane and boat, we arrived at Lugo, about 130 kilometers east of our destination, and walked on the Camino de Santiago. In Assisi we had hit rainstorms, and here on the way to Santiago we were enveloped in a heat wave. We walked through unspoiled medieval villages and natural woodland, eating traditional Spanish soups, bread, cheese, and fruit, drinking red and white Rioja, and taking our siestas on a heap of freshly cut hay. As we walked, we engaged in discussions on the seven deadly sins, even if we did not manage to avoid them.

On arrival at St. James of Santiago we were given certificates by the priest as a proof that we were indeed walking pilgrims. In the presence of St. James, the savior of Spain, we felt a sense of spiritual mystery, as we had in Assisi.

These pilgrimages have taken me to places of antiquity and landscapes of splendor, which are great attractions to large numbers of tourists. Pilgrimage is, among other things, a spiritual form of tourism, whereas tourism has become a secular form of pilgrimage. When we journey as pilgrims, we go with a sense of the sacred, without making demands—and indeed, we expect a certain amount of inconvenience and hardship on the journey, whereas secular tourism expects the world to be arranged for it. In the age of ecology, perhaps pilgrimage and tourism need to come closer together.

CHAPTER 15

Japan

WALKING AROUND BRITAIN, experiencing the freedom of the road, being out under the open sky and in touch with the vast earth beneath, gave me a new lease on life and new burst of energy. This led to the establishment of Green Books, a new venture to publish books on ecological and spiritual matters which would help to create the consciousness needed to replenish soil, soul, and society (yagna, tapas, and dana).

Jonathon Porritt was the first to support this venture, giving us £1,000 on behalf of Friends of the Earth, with the Council for the Protection of Rural England following suit soon afterward. As momentum gathered, many readers of *Resurgence,* Maurice Ash among them, came forward with money, manuscripts, and ideas. In order to accommodate the office of Green Books, we renovated some outbuildings to Chris Day's design, which had an organic warmth to it.

I felt as if I had gone over a hump. Before going on my pilgrimage, I was feeling physically and emotionally at a low ebb. Roger Hills's acupuncture treatment, Misha Norland's homeopathic doses, and Mrs. Robinson's Special Mixture all helped to a certain extent, but not enough to give me any zest for life. Walking to the holy sites did it. I decided that life begins not at forty but at fifty!

While I was in this invigorated mood, I received a flood of invitations from abroad. Accompanied by my son, now fourteen, I went to America at the invitation of the Chinook Community in Washington State. That was a four-week lecture tour of a country which on the one hand is leading the world to an abyss, in the form of unchecked industrial and military expansion, and at the same time trying to save it by means of vigorous alternative ideas represented by writers and thinkers such as Wendell Berry, Hazel Henderson, Lester Brown, Joanna Macy, Nancy and John Todd, the New York Open Center, the Esalen Institute, and many others.

Mukti and I found America immensely engaging, hospitable, and yet bewildering. If there was any human habitat which considered itself un-challenged master of everything, human or nonhuman, it was America. The arrogance and stupidity of establishment America in handling and wasting natural resources was beyond our comprehension, but we could not help but bow our heads to the courage and determination of ecolo-gists, bioregionalists, and decentralist minorities, including the native American Indians who were, against all odds, attempting to stem the tide.

Another invitation came from Spain, from Cortijo Romero, where Nigel Shamash had established a center for rest and renewal. Situated in the foothills of the Sierra Nevada, not far from the city of Granada, this center offered a great attraction to many English people who wished to combine their holiday with learning to live in a new way. I gave a two-week course, combining the ideal with the practical, showing that pleasure need not be the enemy of simplicity and spirituality.

A further invitation came from the government of India itself. Kath-leen Raine had persuaded Mrs. Indira Gandhi to hold a conference around the theme of *Temenos,* the review of the arts and imagination edited by Kathleen. This time I traveled with my daughter, Maya, who was nine at the time. Kathleen fell in love with Maya and kept her on her lap most of the way in the plane. Kathleen said, "She is like my granddaughter." John Lane and Keith Critchlow traveled with us. We received a splendid welcome and sumptuous hospitality as guests of the government in New Delhi. The conference was attended by many out-standing writers, artists, and intellectuals from India and abroad. The bone of contention for the Indian intellectuals was that by speaking against modernity, progress, economic growth, and urban industrial development, the West was trying to keep India backward, and the likes of Kathleen Raine were falling into that trap; whereas Kathleen and I were reminding them of Mahatma Gandhi and saying that the world has much to learn from the traditional wisdom of India. The successful materialism of the West is hollow, and unsustainable in the long term. There must be a middle way by which India can retain its ancient culture and yet overcome its poverty and degradation. That middle way may go through large-scale revival of handicraft, cottage industry, small-scale farming, small-scale irrigation, and intermediate technology; but to many Indian participants this seemed like an impractical dream. Alas, it seemed to me that India will have to go through the dark tunnel of industrial squalor and ecological destruction without finding a way out of grinding poverty. The only outcome of this conference for me was a sense of frustration, but for Maya it was wonderful: she was given dresses of silk and satin, she watched parrots and peacocks in the garden, admired the lotus flowers in the pond, enjoyed the visit to the Taj Mahal, and was deeply impressed with the classic Indian dances. So, all in all, the journey was well worth it.

THE LAST INVITATION of 1987 was from Japan. Alex Stuart was a student of tea in Kyoto. As an avid reader of *Resurgence* and a staunch supporter of the Small School, Alex wanted to share his enthusiasm for Japanese culture with us. "You can stay with me in Kyoto. You might find enough material to produce a special issue of *Resurgence* on Japan, and you might earn enough fees from your lectures to cover your travel costs." We did not need much persuasion. June and I decided to go.

The travel agent warned us, "Although Aeroflot is cheaper by almost half, it is not a comfortable or reliable airline. You get what you pay for." But I said, "Since we are two, we will be saving almost £800, and we are prepared to rough it. Let's go with Aeroflot."

To our surprise, the check-in and entry into the aircraft was smoother and quicker than with many more prestigious airlines. Here we were not among four hundred passengers on a jumbo jet; the Aleutian is a small aircraft, and we much preferred it.

It is true that Aeroflot service is not as flashy and slick as that of British Airways, but in a sense the standard is higher. The food they served was in durable, heavy-duty dishes, and the Armenian wine, which came free, was served in glasses. It was obvious that things were going to be washed rather than wasted. I could not complain at the quality of the food: they served us caviar (unfortunately, being vegetarian, we could not eat it), half-inch-thick real sourdough bread, rice cooked in butter with salad, and tea served with real milk from a china jug; none of your packages of powdered Coffee Mate! This "backwardness" is kinder to the environment.

The air hostesses were less sophisticated and more friendly. When they sold the few duty-free goods that they had, especially the large flower-printed, all wool Russian shawls, they draped them over their shoulders and repeatedly proclaimed their quality and good value as if we were in a bazaar rather than beside the duty-free trolley.

During the flight I read in *The Independent* that a British firm is going to help bring improvements in the supply of consumer goods. A factory will be established in Russia where they will turn wheat into breakfast cereal, inject fruit juice into it, and package it attractively. If I was Gorbachev I would say, "Hands off—keep your progress to yourself! We are quite happy making wheat into bread and drinking the juice separately."

AFTER A FOURTEEN-HOUR FLIGHT, we arrived at Narita Airport. Our friends Nobuo and Kuniko Hiratsuka had driven the forty miles from Tokyo to meet us. We were whisked away over highways busy with countless cars and views obstructed by soundproofing fences on either side.

The Hiratsukas' home is on a small street in central Tokyo, just wide enough for one car and no pavement. Nobuo was a master of driving and could park the car with only a hairbreadth between the car and the wall. It is said that for the same amount of money you can buy a house in London, a flat in New York, or a bathroom in Tokyo. The Hiratsukas, like all Japanese, turn every inch of the available space to use. In their minute garden they had a plum tree, a flowering cherry, herbs, and two chickens.

They are among the growing number of conservation-conscious Japanese who are questioning the unchecked pursuit of material prosperity and living lives that are less damaging to the environment. Solar panels on the roof and neatly tied bundles of old newspapers and magazines waiting to be collected for recycling were the signs of their care and concern. They told us, "Seventy percent of paper in Japan is recycled, but nevertheless, we use too much paper. We should try to use less." By the time we settled in our room, with its traditional tatami-mat floor, we were ready to rest.

In the West we know quite a lot about the Japan of Sony, Sanyo, and Suzuki but very little about the Japan of tradition and spirit. Therefore we went to meet Sori Yanagi, the son of Soetsu Yanagi, the great philosopher and friend of the famous potters Hamada and Bernard Leach. Soetsu Yanagi's book *The Unknown Craftsman* has inspired people of imagination throughout the world. His house is now devoted to exhibitions of traditional crafts, but there is a sad look on the face of his son, who feels that the machine age has overtaken craftspeople. "It is becoming more and more difficult to continue the tradition of crafts. The Japan of my father was very different from modern Japan. Of course we are exhibiting the work of various craftspeople in the museum and selling handmade and traditional goods in our shop, but I also work with industry and design goods which are made by machines. This is my way to attempt to bring some of the spirit of the crafts into the work of machines. By integrating craftsmanship and machines, we might save the crafts and put some quality into machine-made goods." He showed us around the museum. One of the rooms which captured my attention was devoted to a display of urns. Mr. Yanagi explained, "These stone urns were made to house the bones of the dead. That craft has now almost disappeared, which is a shame. The living kept contact with the dead by washing their bones and preserving them in an urn. On the face of the urn there is a small opening, not much bigger than a keyhole, through which the living and the dead could communicate. People in those days believed that the living do not live in isolation, alienated from their ancestors, they live in continuity. The art of making such urns was highly developed: they were beautifully decorated so that the spirits of the ancestors lived in attractive abodes."

Apart from these mysterious and impressive ancient urns, there were many beautiful objects from daily life made by unknown craftsmen, as well as some pots by Hamada and Leach. We were inspired by the realization that this traditional samurai home had come to such good use. It is like an oasis in a desert of modern buildings.

We spent the rest of the day in Tokyo meeting members of the organic movement and sharing with them the experience of eating *izumo soba,* traditional cold noodles served in lacquer bowls stacked on top of each other, accompanying soups, sauces, and dips.

In the evening we went to see Mr. Tokoro, an organic farmer engaged in defending the last undammed river in Japan. The restaurant Tem Ichi, where we met for a *tempura* dinner, specializes in this popular dish. We were asked to take off our jackets, and the waitress tied around us large, white, starched cotton aprons so that we could enjoy our meal without worrying about our clothes.

While June, Kuniko, and I relished the delicious dinner, Mr. Tokoro did the talking. "After the war, we Japanese put all our effort and energy into pulling ourselves out of the ruins of bombing and destruction; work and more work has been the motto of every industry. I am sorry to say that we have gone too far and have forgotten many of our more deeply held values. As a consequence, we have created ecological problems. Only now are we waking up to the excesses of industrial progress, and gradually people are joining the organic, ecological, and antinuclear movements. Recently the state television company conducted an opinion poll and found the great majority of people in favor of phasing out nuclear power stations. This is a good beginning, but we have to go a long way to reverse our so-called progress. Degradation of the environment is causing a great stir in every stratum of society, but the leaders of the government and industry are so entrenched in their ways that they are slow to respond. It is most disheartening that we have to fight so hard to stop the damming of the last undammed river in Japan. It is not the people who want the dam—it is the stalwarts of industry who have such a blinkered view and who think that we need more power, when we already have an excess of electricity."

AFTER A HECTIC DAY we left, with the Hiratsukas, for Kuniko's parents' home on the peninsula of Izu, famous for its views of Mount Fuji. Kuniko's parents had arranged that as soon as we arrived we should enjoy a bath in the hot spring pool, and that is what we did. Communal bathing in the water from hot springs is a unique feature of life in Japan. Because of the volcanic nature of the islands, there is a large number of hot springs up and down the country. Bathing in these mineral-rich waters is considered extremely good for the health.

Kuniko and June went to the ladies' pool, while Nobuo and I went to the men's. As we sat soaking in the hot pool, watching the fishing boats floating in the sea, Nobuo explained, "These baths are not only to clean our bodies but also to clean our minds. Bathing pools like this have always been profitable places for relaxed conversation. We call it 'naked communication.' Here there is no hiding behind smart clothes. When people are exhausted, after a long day of difficult discussions, they go together to the pool. The scene is changed, the tone is transformed, bodies and minds are relaxed; without any fixed agenda and with the ego submerged in water, a meeting of minds can take place." "Perhaps Mr. Gorbachev and Mr. Bush should have their summit meetings in a Japanese bath!" I exclaimed.

Kyoto is fortunate to be one of the few cities that was not destroyed in the war. It was the ancient capital of Japan, and people now consider it the cultural capital. Most arts, crafts, and traditions, such as Noh theater, Tea ceremony, and Zen, have their roots in this ancient city.

We enjoyed wandering through grand temples and shrines, small streets lined with timber houses of old-world charm, rock gardens, and carefully cultivated moss-lined paths under delicate maple trees. Alex showed us the other Japan, hidden in the back streets, behind steel and concrete facades. When we arrived, he packed his bags and moved in with a friend so that we could enjoy the privacy of his flat. But in Oriental fashion, every morning he would come and take us to intriguing places he had discovered during his year in the city while studying Tea. "It is no longer a dying art: thousands of students from all over Japan and from abroad are coming to learn the Way of Tea. This revival is not confined to Tea only—there is also an upsurge of interest, particularly among the young, to learn archery, Kendo, Ikebana, and other traditional disciplines," he said.

One evening, after visiting a Buddhist temple, we were returning to Kyoto by train. Most Japanese rail tickets are bought from automatic machines. As we stood looking confused, trying to work out how much money to put in the machine, a smartly dressed young woman carrying a bouquet of flowers stopped to ask us if we needed any help. She readily pressed the right buttons to produce our tickets. It so happened that we were traveling part of the way together. Her name was Natsumi Inoue, and when she learned that we were on our way to a Tea ceremony, she was delighted. She said, "I also studied the Way of Tea for many years, because I believe that through the Way of Tea one can come close to understanding the true spirit of Japan. After the war we were too much under the influence of American thinking. During those years people felt ashamed of our own rituals and ceremonies, but now we are coming out of our inferiority complex. I feel that now our country is going through a golden age, not only in terms of material prosperity but also in terms of the rediscovery of our identity. If you look at Japan as an outsider, without getting into the spirit of our culture, you will not understand us. Our arts, crafts, ceremonies, and rituals teach us to pay attention to every minute detail so that we can make every movement as beautiful as possible. It is not only what we do but how we do it that is important for us. For this reason, learning the art of Tea is a great discipline."

Natsumi came with us to the taxi stand to act as our interpreter, but the address to which we were going was so obscure that the first taxi driver was unwilling to take us. A second taximan also refused, and even a third. Natsumi was shocked at this behavior. She decided to accompany us to make sure that we didn't get lost, so we all got into the fourth taxi. This young woman was a wonderful example of Japanese courtesy and helpfulness.

Alex, our friend, philosopher, and guide, had arranged for us to go to the mountains of Koya. We took an underground train to Umeda, where Keith Snyder, who was training to be a monk in the tradition of the Seizan School of Pure Land Buddhism, joined us. From Umeda we took a train to Osaka station. Thousands of people were moving in orderly fashion through the underground complex, which was brightly lit, spacious, gleaming, and modern. Not a single cigarette stub on the floor; no one seemed to drop any litter. Uniformed staff by the dozens were reciting a mantra of thanks to the passengers for traveling on this railway.

We were hardly aware of the transition from the station complex to the basement floors of the prestigious department store Takashimaya. Alluring and enticing stalls of food and drink of every variety, packaged to the maximum degree, stunned us. For our journey into the mountains, we purchased *obento,* lunch boxes filled with rice wrapped in fine seaweed and stuffed with pickles and vegetables. At every stall we heard young men and women repeating warm words of welcome and bowing politely to the customers.

We stopped at a bar where two young women wearing white caps, white aprons, and sweet smiles, drew us toward them. They were selling bitter, black coffee with a touch of sweetener if we wanted it. A hot, stimulating drink in their company was a delight to us. This was the world of Takashimaya, the world of eat, drink, and be merry, the world of pleasures and abundance.

We left behind the brightly lit underworld of Takashimaya and took the train heading south. We went up and up and eventually across Paradise Bridge and into the Valley of the Gods. Here the mountains were so steep that the railway line came to an end. We took the funicular to the Land of Ultimate Bliss at three thousand feet above sea level, Mount Koyasan.

This sacred site was found in the ninth century by the famous Buddhist monk, pilgrim, scholar, and traveler, the founder of Japanese Buddhism, Kobo-daishi. Following in his footsteps, other monks and pilgrims came to this holy place and established more than two thousand temples, shrines, stupas, and monasteries. In the days when these monasteries were established, there was no means of easy travel, and therefore once you were here, in the mountains, you were in a world of tranquillity. No worldly distractions could interfere with the meditative mood of this place, far from the madding crowd. The monks lived simply, accumulating no possessions; and women were barred from the mountain for one thousand years. The seekers of enlightenment devoted their time to exploring the inner world, which they believed is as vast as the mountain range.

When they engaged in the world of matter, they used the natural materials of wood, stone, and bamboo and transformed them into objects of exquisite beauty. The temples and monasteries they built, the gardens and courtyards they created, the statues, lanterns, and tombstones they carved were all embodiments of the divine spirit of supreme quality.

Most of the guesthouses in Koya are managed by the Buddhist temples; we stayed in one of them. A fleet of young monks greeted us and led us into a suite of two rooms with tatami mats and gold-painted doors. Apart from a scroll on which words were written in calligraphy to inspire the occupants, the walls were completely free of decoration. In the middle of the room was the *kotatsu,* a low, square table with an electric heating element just under its surface, covered with a large eiderdown. The four of us sat on cushions, with our legs snugly warm under the kotatsu, sipping green tea brought to our room by the bowing young monks. This was an experience of divine simplicity, a world apart from Takashimaya.

While we drank tea in these tranquil surroundings, the rain pattered down on the copper roof. As we had only one afternoon at our disposal, we borrowed umbrellas from the monks and walked through the one-and-a-half-mile-long cemetery under the thick branches of pines and cedars. Here people came to pay homage to their ancestors, to the emperors, shoguns, samurai warriors, poets, sages, and ordinary men and women. Even the modern industrial companies have built memorials for the departed spirits of their workers.

MASANOBU FUKUOKA'S BOOK on natural farming, *One Straw Revolution*, has been an inspiration to many of us, so we could not contemplate coming to Japan and not seeing the author. He lives near Matsuyama on Kyushu Island, which is now connected with the main island of Honshu by the biggest bridge in Japan.

It was nearly one o'clock when we arrived at the entrance to the Natural Farm, where we were greeted by a shaven-headed Zen monk who asked us severely whether we were expected! While we waited, he went through the orange grove to ask Mr. Fukuoka if we could be admitted. On discovering that we were indeed expected, he led the way through wildly flowering mustard and tall white Japanese radish, interspersed with cabbages, eggplants, azaleas, and umpteen other kinds of vegetation. Around us the birds were singing, bees humming, and tranquillity reigned.

After walking along a narrow footpath, we arrived at a one-roomed house, thatched and covered with wisteria that was just coming into flower. Mr. Fukuoka, the seventy-six-year-old sage, with his goatee, balding, short, slim, and somewhat fierce, was sitting on his own on one side of the room. Facing him were a group of young disciples from many countries.

We were asked to join the lunch of brown rice, salted plums, miso soup, noodles, and tofu. The place reminded me of an old Indian ashram in the woods. Here the students spend their time collecting firewood, cooking, building, and doing anything the teacher, Mr. Fukuoka, requires. Fukuoka himself works manually and gives talks twice a day. Although he does not put any label on himself, I could not help comparing him with the traditional Zen masters.

On this farm everyone lives in simplicity; no electricity, no tap water, and earth closets. This is in stark contrast to the rest of Japan, where high technology and life in the fast lane are the order of the day. Fukuoka has had much more influence abroad and very little impact at home. As the saying goes, a prophet is not without honor, save in his own country.

Fukuoka is following an extreme path of "nondoing farming." If he is to have any success in changing the hearts and habits of people, he might have to follow a middle way. But then Fukuoka is not a reformer: he is a seer, a visionary, a purist, a wise man but calls himself a fool.

As we sat in the room, which had been darkened over many years by smoke from the fire, there was an atmosphere of intensity. I was taken aback when Fukuoka asked me, "What is your profession?" I said, "I have no profession." "Then what is the purpose of your life?" It was a rather tense moment—I wasn't expecting such an interrogation. "The purpose of my life is to live," I replied. "What brought you here?" he asked. "I wanted to see your Natural Farm."

Fukuoka said, "I feel like a lonely traveler. I am going in one direction while the whole world is going in the opposite direction. I have been speaking about the return to nature for the last fifty years, but the world has been marching towards artificial ways of farming."

It must be particularly painful for Fukuoka to look down from his farm on the hill and see how his village below and the whole valley have been steadily, day by day, buried in concrete, dams, roads, railways, and overpasses, amid the constant noise of bulldozers, tractors, and traffic. "The world is hurtling downhill, and I alone am making the effort to go up" were the last words we heard from this sad sage.

Simon Piggot, like Alex, is a long-standing reader of *Resurgence*. He is married to a Japanese lady, fluent in the language, and has been living in Japan for many years. He was able to be a perfect bridge between us and the people we met; he accompanied us on our travels and acted as our interpreter for many days, during which time he introduced us to a number of outstanding individuals.

We had heard of the Suzuki method when our children were learning to play the violin, but until Simon told us in Matsumoto about Mr. Suzuki's master classes, we had never dreamed of meeting him. Simon phoned his institute; it was confirmed that Mr. Suzuki was in town and that we would be more than welcome to attend his class at 9:00 A.M.

Simon lived a few miles out of the town. The three of us got on bikes and pedaled to the Talent Education Institute, an international center of music. Mr. Suzuki was already in the hall, so we had a chance to introduce ourselves. One by one the students gathered, some Americans, some English, some Australians, some from Singapore, quite a few Germans and Scandinavians. On the dot, the class began. "I would like to hear the Diamond Tone," declared Mr. Suzuki. "If you produce a glass tone, you won't get high value for it, only the Diamond Tone, please. It is in all of you. You have to find it and bring it out." We watched him walk from student to student listening, and praising, "Good, good, good." We never saw him criticize or put anyone down. In spite of his age of ninety-one, he was full of vigor and moved with flair.

For one hour he coaxed the "Diamond Tone" out of the students with a great sense of humor. It was engaging to watch him perform, like an actor onstage. After his class he took us to his room, as it was "cookies time." "I believe that each and every child is capable of learning music to a high standard, in the same way as all children are capable of learning their mother tongue. There is no such thing as inborn ability: we can achieve the universal playing of music in the same way as the universal use of language. Practice makes perfect. As children learn to speak first, read and write later, I encourage children to play music by ear and by heart. Reading of the notes can come later. The purpose of learning music is to develop as a good human being: this is my message in a nutshell."

Mr. Suzuki gets up at three in the morning and listens to tapes of students playing, sent to him from all over Japan. To each one he adds brief comments. Then at nine he starts to teach and to give interviews, and he does not go to bed until nine in the evening. The idea of retirement has never occurred to him. "I am not ninety-one years old but ninety-one years young!" he joked. Being in the presence of Mr. Suzuki was a singular experience.

Tsuyishi, an organic vegetable merchant from Matsumoto, drove us in his van to the Japanese Alps. The narrow, single-lane road climbed up the edge of the mountain, with hairpin bends at every fifty or sixty yards. Here the drop is absolutely sheer. When we looked down into the valley of Oishika-mura, we shivered, as if we were on the edge of a well three thousand feet deep.

The Japanese mountains often undergo earthquakes, which cause frequent landslides, blocking the roads with earth and rock. In the past people built beautiful retaining walls in stone, which fitted well into the landscape, but the valley of Oishika-mura has been defaced by plastering the mountainsides with concrete; the modern passion for building knows no limit. This valley forms a confluence of five rivers, including the great river Heavenly Dragon. Engineers were engaged in constructing a mammoth hydroelectric plant which will prevent the Heavenly Dragon from flowing free and will force all five rivers into one large pipe to generate electricity. Industry is not prepared to leave the mountains alone.

Our hosts, Etsuko, Jirka, and their daughter, Akebi, live in a traditional farmhouse with a large plot of land. It had stood empty for many years and now they rent it for a mere Y5,000 (£25) a month. Jirka told us, "There are many villages in the mountains with perfectly good houses and good land which are lying empty. In some cases the original inhabitants come during the summer for short periods to maintain the ancestral shrines. They believe that the spirits of their ancestors continue to be present in their family homes. But even that tradition is now weakening. On the other hand, there are families who have come to live here from the city to enjoy the fruits of the good life."

This was no exaggeration. When we sat down to eat with Jirka and his neighbors, we enjoyed a simple feast of mushrooms grown on oak logs, tempura made with tender dandelion flowers, butter bur, horsetail, curled bracken shoots, soup made with homemade miso, home-brewed *sake* (rice wine), homemade tofu, and locally grown brown rice. Everything we ate had the real taste of good food.

Jirka led us up into the mountains. The path went through a natural forest of pine, oak, beech, and maple where deer, monkeys, wild boar, bears, and foxes roam freely. A lonely but happy bumblebee singing the praise of purple mountain azalea flowers caught our attention. Who needs to be in the crowd when solitude can be so glorious? Catching the spirit of this passing yet eternal moment, Jirka sang an old song:

> *And today again we are crossing*
> *The mountains of living*
> *Carrying a false dream seriously.*

In the valley was the beautiful village of Okawara. Once upon a time a claimant to the Imperial title had escaped to the valley with some of his samurai warriors and thereafter lived in obscurity. Wooden-framed houses, darkened by time, were scattered asymmetrically on irregular terraces among paddy fields, fruit orchards, and vegetable gardens.

Toshio Kobayashi, a friend of Jirka's, was born into a farming family of this village and now lives on the outskirts. As we approached his house, we stopped at a stone basin which held spring water. We rinsed our mouths and hands, a familiar ritual at the approach to a temple, Tea house, or family home.

The Kobayashis' ideas about organic farming were not popular with their conventional neighbors, but they made a good living by selling cheese to customers who came to the house. This way of selling cheese brings them in touch with the world beyond the valley. Friendship with their customers has become as important to them as the business of selling cheese.

Within minutes of our arrival, green tea was poured, followed by *soba* (buckwheat noodles) placed in square bamboo frames containing a bamboo mat on which the soba sat in six small circles. Finely chopped onion, grated white radish, and green *wasabi* mustard were served in a small dish. We added this garnish to a sauce of soy, sake, and sugar and dipped our noodles into it. This simple food was presented with grace and refinement. Works of art were not hung on the walls but appeared on the table.

Everything we ate was grown, picked, prepared, and cooked by the family. Even though such a life of self-sufficiency is hard work, the Kobayashis do it with style and without sign of strain.

Our four weeks in Japan passed quickly, without a dull moment. Motoe and Yoshinari Komatsu, with whom we spent our last day in Tsukuba city, drove us to the airport. As a parting gesture they gave us a huge bottle of Gold Sake, boxed in a wooden case. We were able to share this delicious liquor with many friends on our return to Hartland.

Kozo Nakamura, who rightly considers himself and his associates "Schumacher people," came all the way from Tokyo to bid us farewell, bringing a box of Japanese sweets which proved to be a delicacy for some weeks to come. Kazu Okui, an old friend of June's, managed to catch us and spend the last hour with us at the airport. Her present was a *furoski,* an ingenious Japanese invention of a carrying cloth which serves as a bag, a suitcase, or a basket. This particular square cloth was printed with the face of a geisha from an old painting. The giving of gifts comes to the Japanese as naturally as offering a cup of tea.

Laden with these presents, and many more that we had been given throughout the journey, we left Japan not saying good-bye but feeling that we would return.

CHAPTER 16

The College

ONE SPRING MORNING IN 1988 I was visiting my friend John Lane at his home in Beaford. He looked a bit gloomy, which was rather unusual for him. "The reason is that we have decided to close the school at Foxhole. It has been a painful decision. The school has been the very soul of Dartington, but the experience of the past year has proved that it cannot carry on." "Every crisis is an opportunity," I said. "When old doors close, new ones open. If you are unable to run the school, why not start a university? Dartington would be an ideal site for the study and practice of ecological and spiritual values. Why not see the closure of the school as an opportunity to start something new?"

Since my coming to live in north Devon, John and I have taken a serious interest in each other's projects. John had been acting as the art editor of *Resurgence* and a board member of Green Books. I had been down to Dartington on numerous occasions to help with conferences and courses. This way we had built up a good working relationship with each other, and when I made the suggestion to turn Dartington into a university, he did not take it lightly.

John was of the opinion that, to some extent, Dartington had fallen into a rut and needed some new input to reinvigorate the place. He said, "Say something more." "The medieval times are described as the age of religion: everyone studied theology. Then came the age of reason, when studies were approached in a rational, scientific, and analytical way. Now we are going through another transition, and the new age will be the age of ecology and spirituality. New institutions are needed to give expression to this transformation, and I would like to see Dartington giving a lead," I replied. "I am not convinced yet. What other arguments have you got up your sleeve?" said John laughingly. "Take, for example, the Gaia hypothesis of James Lovelock. No university will touch it, whereas this is perhaps the most significant idea of our time. Similarly, Rupert Sheldrake's idea of morphogenetic fields is viewed by the establishment with great suspicion, as you know. *Nature* said that if there was ever a case for burning a book, Rupert Sheldrake's *A New Science of Life* would be a prime candidate. None of the universities is interested in the spiritual underpinning of intellectual inquiry. Therefore, where can one go to study these ideas in depth? The closing of Foxhole—and all those empty buildings—gives you the opportunity and the space to begin something big!" "This is all very well, and sounds interesting, but how can we take the idea forward?" John wondered. After a moment's thought he said, "I will get the key people from Dartington together—you try to convince them." This was quite a challenge, but I agreed to do it.

A FEW WEEKS LATER, in the comfortable morning room of the Elmhirst Center, all the departmental managers of the Dartington Estate and some of the trustees assembled. In his brief introduction John Lane said, "Every age has been shaped by a few radical and powerful thinkers like Descartes, Marx, Freud, Jung, and Einstein. Satish has a big idea. He wants Dartington to provide a base for the powerful thinkers of our time whose ideas are going to shape the future. I have invited him here to explain his vision to us."

I said "Dartington has been in the avant-garde of change, but change cannot come overnight. We have to lay firm intellectual, philosophical, and practical foundations for a new kind of society. At present there is no place in Britain where this kind of work is being done. I would like to see a university established at Dartington which would be fully devoted to an ecological worldview of sustainable economics, agriculture, and industry." "How will you do it?" I was asked. "We will invite eminent thinkers, scientists, philosophers, and activists, such as James Lovelock, Wendell Berry, Hazel Henderson, David Bohm, Rupert Sheldrake, Fritjof Capra, and others who are doing pioneering work in their fields, to come and teach here. Students will come from around the world and live here for two or three years. Work, meditation, scholarship, and a sense of community will be the four essential aspects of this university."

Much discussion followed. How could such a project be financed? What kind of student would come? Would they be given degrees and certificates? Everyone appeared to be excited by the idea. Beneath all the questions and comments there was a sense of ambivalence, and also astonishment. No one was prepared to say yes, and no one was prepared to say no.

John Pontin, chairman of the trust, commented, "The idea of a university and students coming for two or three years may be too ambitious to begin with. It may be better to think in terms of shorter courses. However, I would like you to prepare a more detailed paper and a proposal which we can consider seriously."

For me this was a very encouraging reaction. John Pontin offered me a fee of £1,000 to write the proposal. I took this as a proof of his firm commitment to the idea. I was given six weeks to write the proposal, and a weekend conference was organized to discuss it.

Two days of deliberations concluded that offering degrees and getting accreditation would involve too many problems. We also conceded that instead of attempting to establish a university we should begin with a college which would offer courses of four to five weeks' duration. These courses would be led by a scholar in residence, who would be chosen for his or her outstanding contribution in the areas of ecology and spirituality and for the ability to teach and communicate. A small steering group, comprising John Lane, Anne Phillips, Brian Nicholson, and myself, was appointed to prepare a formal application, including a budget, to present to the Dartington trustees at their next meeting, which was to take place in October 1989.

The steering group met throughout the summer. I traveled down from Hartland to Dartington almost every fortnight for our meetings. We wrote and rewrote, rejected and revised draft after draft of the prospectus. Every word and line was worked over with a fine-tooth comb.

The final draft of the budget and the prospectus was ready by the end of September, and it was agreed that this would go to the trustees for their decision at their next meeting, which would take place while I was running a course at Cortijo Romero. The steering committee agreed that we must get together immediately after the trustees' meeting to prepare the launch of the college. This involved me flying back from Spain a day early and in a state of great excitement.

As arranged, Brian met me at the station. I got into his car anxiously waiting to know what the outcome of the trustees' meeting was, and whether they had approved the proposal and the budget. Brian said not a word. He kept driving for half an hour while we talked about my time in Spain and other casual matters. Eventually I could wait no longer and asked, "What was the decision of the trustees?" "I was waiting and wondering when you would ask me this question," replied Brian. "I am sorry to say that the decision has been deferred, and the proposal will go to the trustees at their next meeting in six months' time."

It was a moment of grave disappointment for me, but we went ahead with our meeting at John Lane's house in Beaford, as planned. In my heart I was grumbling, saying to myself, "Things take so long at Dartington!"

We were working feverishly, but this deferral injected some doubts in me. We were working on the assumption that the trustees would eventually say yes, but in my heart of hearts I knew this was by no means certain. Of course, John Lane was totally committed to the idea, and behind the scenes he was working on every trustee, but how they would vote at the meeting was anybody's guess.

AT LAST the day of decision came. On March 29, 1990, Brian, Anne, and I were invited to the premeeting lunch with the trustees, and I was asked to make my final case for the college. Evoking the names of Tagore and the Elmhirsts, I said, "The idea of this college is entirely in the spirit of the founders of Dartington Hall, and by approving this proposal you, the trustees, will be making a courageous response to the crisis of our time. If you do not take such initiative, who will?"

I spoke for about ten minutes, and I could sense the atmosphere was such that my plea had been well received. The trustees withdrew to their meeting room, and we waited anxiously for their decision.

At about 5:00 P.M. John Lane came out and announced, "We have the college, and Maurice Ash has come up with a name. He said, 'Why not call it Schumacher College, since we take so much inspiration from the work of E. F. Schumacher?' And you, Satish, are invited to be the director of this new college." This was a moment of great delight!

Between April and December we appointed the core faculty, arranged the scholars in residence, and advertised the program. We opened the college on January 13, 1991, with James Lovelock as the first scholar in residence.

By a strange coincidence, on the very opening day of the college the Gulf War broke out, which deterred some would-be participants from abroad. Considering this situation, we all felt relieved to find that there were twenty-five participants for the first course. And after that the college went from strength to strength. Within the first year of its operation, people from thirty different nations came to participate.

Editing *Resurgence* and directing Schumacher College feels like doing two jobs simultaneously. But I also feel that this challenge has given me a new sense of service. Being involved in the creation of an educational center which is responding to the crisis of Western culture is a great challenge. Working for the college and *Resurgence* replenishes my soul.

Schumacher College is the culmination of my life's work. Here it is possible to bring together the spiritual foundation of the monk's life, the social concerns of the Bhoodan movement, the ideals of peace which I pursued during my walk around the world, and the ecological concerns of *Resurgence*. This is a convergence of the values and aspirations by which I have been guided throughout my life.

CHAPTER 17

—❀❀❀—

Mount Kailas

"Three miles above sea level,
Tibet is the roof of the world, and the
sacred Mount Kailas is the
ladder to heaven."
　　　　　　—An old Indian saying

T HAT WAS A COOL EVENING in Beaulieu, in southern France, when June and I were guests of our friend Rosalie Basten. We were enjoying a delicious feast under a canopy in Rosalie's garden. My eyes were set on the horizon of the calm Mediterranean Sea. Suddenly, and out of the blue, Rosalie asked, "For your fiftieth birthday you went on a pilgrimage around Britain; how do you wish to celebrate your sixtieth?" I had not thought of this, so my answer surprised me. I said, "I don't think I can afford it, but I have always dreamed of making a pilgrimage to Mount Kailas in Tibet. It is rather inaccessible, but many of my ancestors have gone on foot and I wish to do the same."

Without any hesitation Rosalie said, "You should do it! And take June with you. May I come with you, too?" Imagination was flying. In seconds the future was being spoken. "It will be my pleasure to cover all the costs of this journey as a birthday present!" I could not believe my ears, and now there was no excuse not to do it.

This was the summer of 1995. In the summer of 1996 Rosalie came to England and we three went on a practice walk over the hills and valleys of Dartmoor. There Rosalie realized that for her, walking across the Himalayas would be physically impossible. So with regret in her voice she said, "I cannot come, but you two must go." And we accepted her wish and her gift. It took us a year's mental and physical preparation before we could set off in September 1997.

OUR JOURNEY BEGAN in Kathmandu, which literally means "a great wooden temple." In the center of the city there stands the ancient temple from which the capital takes its name. There is an age-old tradition: a young girl from a noble family is chosen to live in this temple until she reaches puberty. She is revered as the soul of the city and worshiped as the virgin goddess. This was a good place to start our pilgrimage. A glimpse of this young divinity as she leaned out from an intricately carved wooden balcony was mysterious and inspiring.

We stayed at a newly built Jain guesthouse. The white marble temple in the courtyard demonstrates how all the sects of the Jain religion work together in harmony. On the first floor is the shrine of the *shwetambaras,* the white-robed monks. Downstairs is the shrine of the sect of *digumbaras,* the sky-clad, whose monks wear no clothes. The third order, the *terapanthis,* who worship no idols and build no temples, use the great hall of the guesthouse for their gatherings. All three sects worked together to build this center, overcoming their historic disagreements and divisions. Every morning we were woken by beautiful bells, sweet songs, and the chanting of mantras.

For Jains, as for Hindus and Buddhists, Mount Kailas is most sacred. Their first prophet, Adinath, died there in meditation. Legend has it that the Hindu god Shiva and the Jain prophet Adinath are one and the same. For Hindus, Shiva never dies but lives eternally at Kailas. In fact, Kailas is Shiva.

Shiva is also called Pashupathinath, the god of animals. His temple accommodates pilgrims in the thousands from Nepal and from India. Some come to die and be cremated here on the banks of the sacred river which eventually merges into the most sacred river, the Ganges in India. We saw a corpse on a funeral pyre in full flame "releasing the soul from the body and uniting it with the spirit of Shiva."

For Buddhists there are two great temples, Bodhnath and Swayambhunath, but there is no exclusivity here. Buddhists visit Pashupathinath, Hindus visit Bodhnath, Jains visit Swayambhunath and find no contradiction. The Nepalese we met claim to be Hindu as well as Buddhist.

When it comes to birth, death, marriage, and other rites of passage, they observe Hindu rituals, but for the practice of meditation and compassion they take Buddha's teachings as their guide.

Buddhists, Jains, and Hindus find a common source of spirituality in Mount Kailas. For thousands of years pilgrims have made arduous journeys to that sacred site. Although the Chinese occupation made it hard to enter Tibet, since 1993 the rules have been relaxed. A quota of 450 Indian pilgrims are allowed each year to cross the border. Other nationals are allowed either from Lhasa, which takes five days of driving in a Land Cruiser on a dirt road, or on foot through the protected district of Humla in northwestern Nepal.

WE CHOSE THE Humla route, which starts from Simikot, a mountain town with an airstrip where small planes fly in and out, weather permitting. We took a helicopter of Gurkha Airlines, flying along the river valleys with steeply forested mountains on both sides.

From Simikot it was seven days of walking to cross the Himalayas. Five sherpas accompanied our party of nine. The tents, food, kerosene, sleeping bags, and the rest of the gear were carried on yaks, mules, and horses driven by a group of herdsmen. We started climbing on a steep path immediately out of town. It was up and up and up, a good taste of the climbs to come. We followed the Humla Karnali River, which was flowing fast. At night we found either terraces or tiny meadows by the river to camp. This part of Nepal is one of the most remote and requires a special trekking permit. People live here in small settlements. The houses were beautifully built with earth and wood. Terraced villages clung to the mountain slopes. Hardworking mountain men, women, and children were bringing down brushwood and grass for the winter. Wild herbs, apricots, walnuts, and gooseberries lined the slopes in between the maize and millet, marijuana and hemp.

People wore beautifully knitted and woven clothes and heavy necklaces of silver with huge turquoise and coral beads. Their faces were weathered by sun, wind, and hard work, yet they radiated laughter in abundance.

We followed the traditional trade route, along which sheep and goats carry loads of ten kilograms each in handmade wool and leather pannier bags. They also carry grains to Tibet and bring back much desired and precious Tibetan salt. This was the middle of September, nearly the end of the trading season. The shepherds and goatherds were returning from Tibet with salt.

The paths were so steep that even the goats were panting and flopping down to rest. So you can imagine us, the unaccustomed travelers. The steepest of them all was Nara Lagna Pass, a continuous ascent reaching a huge rock cairn festooned with prayer flags at an altitude of 15,000 feet. Even though we had been walking for days and were somewhat acclimatized, every few minutes we had to stop to catch our breath. The pace of walking had to be extremely slow, but then neither speed nor time was any object.

THUS WE REACHED TIBET. It is a great country, covering an area as large as Western Europe. At the border post, the Chinese flag was flapping furiously in the wind. The presence of Chinese soldiers and their power were evident everywhere. Chinese control over Tibet may not be legal, but it is complete. As we progressed over the vast expanse of the Tibetan plateau, we encountered checkpoint after checkpoint manned by Chinese soldiers numbering half a million.

We spent our first night in the small town of Purang. Here the hideous un-Tibetan architecture of Chinese modernism imposes itself. Traditional Tibetan dwellings painted with pleasing earth colors are dwarfed. Not only the Tibetan houses but also the Tibetan people are overshadowed. They appear to feel second-class citizens in their own land. Tibetans have been reduced to a minority; large numbers of Chinese immigrants, 7 million, have been settled here. They control most of the trade and other economic activity. After the serenity and tranquillity of Humla, we were shocked at the signs of political tension and the creeping squalor of "development." Any idea of the Dalai Lama returning to Tibet seemed fanciful. In fact, thank goodness the Dalai Lama escaped when he did; otherwise he would almost certainly have been killed. His escape brought Tibetan Buddhism and culture out into the world, and that could be seen as a blessing in disguise, but those who are left behind are in a perilous predicament.

But the Chinese cannot take away the sacred lakes and the holy mountains. Curiously and amazingly, at three miles above sea level, in the desolate and desertlike landscape, on the roof of the world, there are two great lakes side by side. One is called the Demon Lake (Rakshastal), 140 square miles in area; the other, the Divine Lake (Manasarovar), is 200 square miles. The Demon Lake has salty water, and the Divine Lake fresh water.

Demon and Divine are like yin and yang. Both are essential and complementary, but pilgrims have preferred Manasarovar. It is more sheltered, and has easier terrain, and its form is round. Eight monasteries are built on the shores of this lake, and there are numerous caves where ascetics have practiced penance.

As we approached Lake Manasarovar, a great peak rose on the horizon. "Here it is, here it is, here it is," everyone shrieked. It was Mount Kailas, mysterious, majestic, and monumental. We stood still, looking at it in stunned silence. No words can describe the experience of seeing this towering temple of nature.

Mount Kailas is the Mount Meru of myth and story, the *axis mundi,* the backbone of the Earth, the upholder of the universe, the ladder to heaven. It is the jewel in the crown of the Himalayas.

Camping at Manasarowar was magical. Clear sky at night with billions of stars; the waning moon and the wild water wrapped us in the realms of pure nature. Everything was undisturbed, uncluttered, uninterrupted, and uncorrupted. No wonder that for thousands of years seekers of the spirit and pilgrims of the soul have found refuge on the shores of this lake. We broke the thin ice of the lake to take a dip, remembering the words of the Hindu poet Kalidasa: "When Manasarowar touches your body, you shall go to paradise and shall be released from the sins of one hundred births."

From the lake we traveled to Darhan to arrange for yaks and prepare for our long-awaited circumambulation of Mount Kailas. The name Darhan is derived from the Sanskrit word *darshan,* which means sacred view. We left half of our gear here and fitted the possessions of both of us into one bag. Even so, our party needed nine yaks, herded by two women and two men, to carry our equipment! So much stuff!

At 16,000 feet we began what the Tibetans call *kora,* the Greeks call *temenos,* and the Hindus call *parikrama;* the circumambulation of the sacred space. A river valley made a perfect path for us to encircle Mount Kailas. We went clockwise from south to west and came to the first of four prostration stations, where Tibetans kneel and then lie on the earth, chest, forehead, and arms touching the ground. This is the act of humility to the mountain and to the countless great teachers, yogis, mahatmas, rinpoches, and ascetics, including the sage Milarepa, who disseminated their teachings and sang their poetry here.

Kailas is unusual in that it can be circumambulated on foot within twenty-four hours. And even if you are not an accomplished trekker, you can do it in two or three days. We saw scores of Tibetan men, women, and children, including babes in the arms of their mothers, circumambulating the mount. Old and young, peasants and city dwellers, farmers and nomads, with their rosaries and prayer wheels in their hands, proclaiming the mantra *Om mani padme hum,* were moving along the path at a great pace, passing us by.

On our first day of the kora, the weather changed. Ferocious cold winds accompanied by sleet drove into our faces. If this was the condition in a valley, what was to come on the high pass of Drolma La, we started to wonder. Thermal underwear, woolen jumpers, down jackets, four seasons sleeping bags, and hot water bottles were not enough to keep us warm that night. We were provided with a half tablet of Diamox each to keep the altitude sickness away. But even that did not stop several of us from developing a high-altitude cough, which stayed with us for the rest of the journey. That night hardly anybody was able to sleep.

Next day the cold weather continued until about midday, but then the sun came out and we were able to have a clear view of the north face of Kailas. We ascended to Shiva-Tsal, where Tibetans place an article of clothing or a drop of blood, or hair or a stone, as part of leaving their prejudices behind them. We followed their example and left some hair and a stone which we had carried from our home in Hartland. "Leave your fear, your ego, your anxiety, and your meanness here," said our Tibetan guide. The evening turned severely cold again.

We camped at the foot of the high pass. A passing pilgrim said, "This is not a good place to camp. You will freeze at night." But we were too tired to contemplate climbing the highest and most arduous pass at that time of the evening. The pilgrim was right. We shivered all that night. Little rest, no sleep. Next morning, when we looked at our yaks, they were covered in frost.

As we warmed ourselves up with hot tea and porridge, we saw Tibetan pilgrims, clad in long sheepskin coats, heading fast toward Drolma La. That sight inspired us to set off on the steep, rocky path. The ascent was daunting. Every few steps, we were so short of breath that we needed to sit down, and we could only proceed by pulling each other along. Would we ever make it to the top? We kept doubting, but there was some force which drew us inexorably onward; perhaps it was Mount Kailas itself calling us.

At 18,600 feet, we reached the highest point, the Drolma La itself. We came to the great boulder of the goddess Tara. The stone was covered with long strings of prayer flags left by pilgrims. "When you leave a prayer flag here, you also leave behind your anger, your desire and attachments. This is your second chance to unburden yourself. You will be reborn into a new life if you can allow your old self to die," the Tibetan guide reminded us.

We felt a great sense of relief, of accomplishment. We were blessed with a cloudless blue sky. The sun shone upon us even though a strong wind was trying to sweep us away. Sometimes pilgrims complete the kora while Mount Kailas is completely obscured by dense white clouds. They get not a single glimpse of the mountain during the entire journey. But we were able to see the peak from all four sides and complete thirty-two miles of circumambulation.

ALONG THE ROUTE there are *mani* walls built with stones which are carved with sacred mantras. Pilgrims place these stones on the walls as offerings, symbols of their commitment to the way of the Buddha. On these walls are also placed the horns of yaks as signs of the impermanence of life. Yaks, once strong and sturdy, are now dead and gone. Similarly, we will all pass away, however rich and powerful we may be. So we should live humble lives and not become proud of our achievements, even the achievement of a pilgrimage.

When we arrived back in Darhan, we met an Indian swami who has been going around Mount Kailas every year since the border was opened in 1993. He carries no special equipment, walks barefoot, and stays in the monasteries along the route. He took us to a Tibetan tea shop, saying, "Your cough is partly due to the mountain water, which lacks mineral salts. Water in Tibet is melted ice since there is very little rain in this country. That is why Tibetans add salt and yak butter to their tea, to make up for the mineral deficit." Initially, we found the taste of such tea unpleasant, but we drank it as medicine. The Hindu swami said, "It is an acquired taste, but after a few days you will like it," and so we did. As time passed we became "addicted" to Tibetan tea.

From Darhan we went to Tirthapuri, one of the resting places on the pilgrimage route from India. Pilgrims stop here because of the delightful hot springs. They bathe and clean themselves after the long journey across the Himalayas and the dusty Tibetan plateau. This is a sacred site, and pilgrims lead their horses around the monastery, the hot springs, and the hillside. But then every hill, every river, every being is sacred for the Hindus, the Buddhists, and the Jains.

During the Cultural Revolution, the monastery at Tirthapuri was destroyed, in common with thousands of other monasteries throughout Tibet. Some of them are now being restored and opened for religious activities. Others are kept under lock and key, to be opened only for visitors or tourists. Wonderful frescoes of Tibetan iconography, as we saw in the town of Tsaparang, are left to decay. These sacred paintings and sculptures, which were sources of great religious inspiration, are treasures of Tibetan culture, but for the Chinese they seem to carry little value. By neglecting this evidence of a great tradition, the Chinese are effectively destroying Tibetan culture.

As the Native American Indian culture has more or less disappeared from America, and as the Aboriginal tradition has been reduced to a minority interest in Australia, we fear that very little of Tibetan tradition will be left if the present trend continues. The Chinese are imposing their ideas of modernization, progress, secularization, development, civilization, and education on the land of Tibet. But Tibetan artists and religious teachers are flourishing in Nepal, Bhutan, and India. Those who wish to support Tibetan culture should support the efforts of the Dalai Lama and other Tibetan leaders in exile.

—∞∞∞—

CHAPTER 18

Influences

MY BODY, MY MIND, MY SOUL, and my self are made up of many influences, as a river is made up of many tributaries. I am not a separate, isolated, individual being. I am indivisible, interbeing. The thoughts, ideals, visions, and attitudes I embody have come from a multitude of sources.

A Vedic prayer says:

> *Let the noble thoughts come to me*
> *From all corners of the universe.*

The reverse is also true. Let us send our noble thoughts to all corners of the universe. Thoughts are not in our heads, thoughts are all around us, we live in thoughts.

There is nothing new under the sun; I am not looking for an original thought. Nothing can emerge out of nothing, and something cannot disappear into nothing. Matter and spirit are in continuous motion of change, transformation, and recycling. I am part of that wheel of life, which is continuously turning and returning.

However, there are certain influences on my life which I can acknowledge. In previous chapters I have talked about my mother, my guru Vinoba Bhave, and others, but there is one prominent figure who stands out like a beacon, and that is Mahatma Gandhi. I was born in a Jain family surrounded by Hindus; Gandhi was born in a Hindu family surrounded by Jains. That Jain influence made him an adherent of nonviolence. In turn, he influenced many Jains, including myself, reminding us of the strength and depth of our own roots. Thus a circle was complete. Gandhi was a living example of the kind of life to which I have aspired. He dissolved the division between action and thought, practice and theory, and silence and speech.

I never met Gandhi: I was eleven when he was assassinated. So I learned from Gandhi's writings as well as from his associates that politics and principles are two sides of the same coin. It is no good to leave the world and live in caves or monasteries, thinking that the world is a trap and the only way to be liberated is to escape from it. On the other hand, the majority of people believe that spirituality is only for saints and that it cannot be practiced in everyday life. Gandhi took it upon himself to show that people can engage in politics truthfully and nonviolently. Economics and ethics are indivisible. Religion must permeate everyday activity. When agriculture, business, industry, education, arts, crafts, homemaking, family life, human relationships, and our interaction with the natural world are built on a spiritual foundation, then human beings are able to find the true meaning of life.

Some of Gandhi's contemporaries were absorbed with the single-issue campaign for the independence of India. But Gandhi himself presented the big picture. He knew that independence would come sooner or later, but the real point was not just to replace the white sahib with the brown sahib and continue on the same path of modernity, industrialization, materialism, and rule from the center. He wanted to develop a new vision of statecraft, so that independent India would be very different from British India: it was a vision of total transformation.

In order to create such a holistic and integrated nation, he proposed eleven principles on which the social order should be built. Before the whole of India, and for that matter the rest of the world, could adopt these principles, Gandhi established hundreds of ashrams. These small communities were experimental; in them willing volunteers came together to explore, modify, and refine the principles. Gandhi's interest in experimentation was legendary. He even subtitled his autobiography *The Story of My Experiments with Truth.*

These communities were and are models of a sustainable, convivial, frugal, ecological, self-reliant, and spiritual society. Gandhi composed a chant which strung together these principles and was sung collectively morning and evening by the members of the ashrams, in one of which Gandhi himself lived.

I chanted this enchanting chant twice a day while I lived in the ashram. Composed of deeply meaningful Sanskrit words, it is like a rosary of moving mantras. I still chant it and find myself entranced whenever I do.

> *Ahimsa, satya, asteya,*
> *Brachmacharya, asangraha,*
> *Sharirashram, aswada,*
> *Sarvatra, bhaya varjana,*
> *Sarva dharma samanatva,*
> *Swadeshi, sparsha bhavana,*
> *Vinamra vrata nishtha se,*
> *Ye ekadash sevya hain.*

It translates as follows:

> *Nonviolence, truth, nonstealing,*
> *Sacred sex, nonconsumerism,*
> *Physical work, avoidance of bad taste,*
> *Fearlessness, respect for all religions,*
> *Local economy,*
> *and respect for all beings,*
> *These eleven principles*
> *Should be followed with humility, care, and commitment.*

These principles are not dos and don'ts. They are not vows; they are aspirations and inspirations. They are like resolutions which are made on the eve of the new year. In this case the resolutions are made daily. They are guidelines for conduct, a framework to be interpreted by each individual and society according to its own context. They could be used as resolutions for the new millennium.

Let me explain these eleven points of reference one by one, with my own interpretation.

1. Nonviolence (Ahimsa)

Ahimsa, or nonviolence, is a universal first principle of nonoffensive living. Hindus, Buddhists, Jains, Jews, Muslims, Christians, and followers of all other religions, one way or another, have to a greater or lesser extent proclaimed this to be fundamental. Nonviolence should underlie all relationships among humans and between humans and the nonhuman world. Nonviolence is part of the perennial philosophy. But Gandhi made it more relevant to our time by using it as a weapon of resistance to social injustice, to British colonialism, to economic exploitation of the weak by the strong, and to caste discrimination in India.

Nonviolence goes much further than not killing. On a personal level it begins with nonviolence of mind. At the ashram I was taught to cultivate the skill of restraint from any aggressive, offensive, damaging thought. If by any chance I had entertained violence in the mind, I was to cultivate the skill of not expressing it in speech. Words which wound or insult or debase another can precipitate a cycle of violence. I learned to express my opinions about politics, politicians, or people with whom I disagreed in a respectful manner. If I lost control of my speech then, of course, I was to avoid physical violence at all costs. If I was attacked verbally or physically, then I was to respond through the techniques of nonviolent defense.

The nonviolent way is the way of the strong and the brave. This is not passivity and not weakness. Gandhi always kept a Chinese miniature of the three wise monkeys on his desk. One covers its eyes with both paws, one covers its ears, and one covers its mouth. This figure symbolizes see no evil, speak no evil, and hear no evil.

At the social and political level, nonviolence means opposition to institutional and structural violence. I learned from Gandhi not to be shy of engaging in constructive criticism but to approach opponents in person or in writing with a kind heart, because the aim is always to bring about a change of heart and mind in the person or society. This technique continues to impress me deeply, especially when I see much of the media engaged in inciting violence between politicians, nations, and ethnic or religious groups. We have to learn to live with people and nature nonviolently, which means giving up the desire to impose our will, to subjugate, to dominate, and to control other people, animals, and the natural world for the fulfillment of our own ambitions and our own egos. The more I have seen and thought, the more I have realized that nonviolence is the essential ground on which a sustainable future for humanity as well as for the Earth can be envisioned and built.

It seems to me that the strife and conflict which are so prevalent in the world today are the results of our belief in the power of violence. In spite of all the wars, conquests, colonialism, and imperialism, humanity has learned nothing. We still believe in violence as the ultimate sanction. From newspaper articles to nuclear weapons, we follow the path of violence. Hindus and Muslims in India, Jews and Palestinians in the Middle East, Catholics and Protestants in Northern Ireland are too ready to believe that ultimately they will find a solution through violence. For me this is not an option.

At the ecological level, humanity has been at war with nature. Our desire to conquer nature has led to destruction of wilderness, reduction of biodiversity, production of poisonous chemicals, construction of megacities, megadams, megaindustries, and megacorporations. This has resulted in polluted seas, polluted rivers, polluted air, depleted foods, and eroded land. Our cruelty to animals, our disregard for traditional tribal cultures and their rights, our relentless drive to extract oil and other minerals without limit are all part of the same story.

We need to change this story. The story of violence is too old and boring. Humanity and the Earth have suffered enough. Let the new millennium begin with a new story, the story of nonviolence. In this story all relationships are embedded in the spirit of mutuality and reciprocity, the spirit of reverence for all life—human life, animal life, plant life, the life of rock, soil, and water. Only by living in a story of the sanctity of life can life be sustained.

In our arrogance we humans have assumed that we are the masters of nature and that we can cause havoc and devastation all around us yet somehow escape harm ourselves. When we do not impose violence on others, others will not impose violence on us, but if we live by the sword, we will die by the sword. The result of nonviolence is peace at all levels. Personal peace, world peace, and peace with nature.

Without inner peace, no other peace can be realized. If I have achieved a degree of peace of mind within myself, then I will not fear others, but if I have not been able to overcome my personal fears, then it is easy for political and military leaders to create in me fear of an external enemy. Every day on the radio and television and in the newspapers I hear or read about "enemies." We are all divided into different groups and fear somebody. So many of the world's resources are spent on armaments, which are connected with our inner insecurity. War and violence begin in our minds. So unless I start with myself and make peace with myself, I cannot achieve peace in the world.

This inner peace should be translated into world peace. I cannot retire into the serene space of my inner peace and leave the world as it is. I cannot sit calmly meditating while nuclear weapons pile up. So nonviolent action to bring peace in the world is a natural consequence of inner peace.

World peace is a building block to making peace with nature. When nations fight, when bombs are dropped, it is not only human beings who are killed; natural habitats are also destroyed. But no one counts the cost of nature's demise. Making peace with nature is important even if there is no war, because war with nature leads to war between nations. Most wars are fought over resources and to protect markets. Wars are less and less political and more and more economic. All wars are wars against nature since they involve a tremendous amount of air pollution, sea pollution, and land pollution; land mines are a case in point. So the nations of the world have to agree unanimously that, whatever their dispute, diplomatic and nonviolent methods will be the only course they will follow; under no circumstances will violence be used.

Of course, this will not happen overnight, but if this could be a new millennium resolution and if, step by step, the world could work toward this goal, then one day we might establish a nonviolent social order. In the wake of nuclear, biological, and chemical warfare, and in the wake of global warming, ozone depletion, and world hunger, the stark choice is between nonviolence and nonexistence.

2. Truth (Satya)

Satya, or truth, means seeing reality as it is. Although we can never be sure of the nature of ultimate reality, it is right and proper to seek it. There is no one truth which can be described, explained, and defined in language. Buddha, Jesus Christ, Mahavir, Mohammed, and Socrates have all been seekers of truth. Poets, saints, and mystics like Kabir, Tulsidas, Rumi, Hildegard of Bingen, Mother Julian of Norwich, and St. Francis experienced the divine and the sacred in all things. For them that was the truth. But we cannot live on the wealth of our ancestors. We must seek our own treasure and take up the quest to find our own truth.

Truth is multifaceted and pluralistic. Seeing existence in all its mysterious diversity yet realizing its wholeness prevents me from imposing a monolithic belief system onto it. The quest for truth is a liberating journey; it liberates me from dogmas, both religious and political. There is no final point at which I could say that I have found the truth, this is the truth, and this is the truth for everyone. The moment truth is imprisoned in a belief system, the truth is lost. As long as the experience and the techniques of other seekers are used as pointers, as signposts, then those disciplines and methods can be of some help. But the signpost is not the real thing. Truth cannot be preached; it can be communicated, if at all, only in dialogue and conversation and, more important, through living example. Truth is not a commodity which can be dished out from temples and churches. Truth is not something which can be conceptualized or extracted from holy books. It has to be lived and experienced.

Seekers of truth are free from all kinds of fundamentalism. It is easy to see the fundamentalism of others but more difficult to recognize one's own. So Christians may criticize Muslim fundamentalism without recognizing their own fundamentalism. Similarly, capitalists may criticize socialist fundamentalism and forget that the fundamentalism of the free market is no less oppressive. Those who preach the superiority of Western democracy are in as much danger of undermining the community-based tribal cultures as those who preach the politics of the one-party state.

The fundamentalism of the global economy suppresses ideas and information in the name of trade secrets, intellectual property rights, patenting, and copyright. Monopoly businesses create monoculture economies as well as monoculture of the mind. Such monoism is the bedfellow of dualism and blocks the search for and discovery of multifaceted truth.

To follow the way of truth is to have no preconditions, no prejudice.

It is a way to face things as they are. Truth is the "isness" of Zen. The pursuit of truth is unconditional and open-minded inquiry and exploration, up to the last moment of our lives.

3. Nonstealing (Asteya)

Asteya, or nonstealing, means not taking what does not belong to you, but it goes far beyond the conventional concept of theft. According to the Upanishads, all and everything, from a blade of grass to Mount Everest and from an earthworm to a human being, is imbued with the divine. Earth, fire, air, and water are sacred elements. All beings take from the Earth for the continuity of life. Babies take milk from their mothers' breasts, deer take water from the stream, birds eat fruit from the trees, humans take the produce of the Earth. Gandhi said that there is enough for everybody's need but not enough for anybody's greed.

When humans use resources not out of need but out of greed, they are consuming what other inhabitants may need or they are depriving future generations of their livelihood. When humans clear-cut forests, they are stealing from the birds, animals, and insects who inhabit those forests.

The humanism of the last few hundred years has given birth to an ideology which states that human beings are at the pinnacle of evolution; they are a superior species, they are masters of nature, and they have a God-given right to use nature and other lives for their convenience. This is a false philosophy. As a result, industrial technology has been developed to plunder nature and exploit the weak. The land has been stolen from the aboriginal and tribal peoples all over the world.

Asteya is more than illegal theft: when family farms are destroyed by agribusiness, it is theft of the countryside; when crafts are destroyed by industry, that is theft of skills; when big trawlers overfish the oceans and thus destroy small fishing villages, that is theft of livelihood. Legal or illegal, these are all ways of stealing. To follow the way of Asteya is to use and consume only what nature can replenish. It is a way to consume only to meet our vital needs, knowing that other peoples and creatures also need to meet their vital needs, and therefore I take only my share of things. Asteya is a way of living simply so that others may simply live. Asteya is a way of generosity. Asteya tells me that meanness, hoarding, accumulation, and overconsumption are thefts of nature and stealing from God.

4. Sacred Sex (Brahmacharya)

Brahmacharya, or sacred sex, means appropriate sexuality within a healthy human relationship. In the wake of the population explosion, restraint and care in sexual relationships are required. Human sexuality, appropriately practiced, is part of love of God. Love for God begins with human love. This is the microexperience of macrolove, the intimate realization of ultimate love. Unconditional love between two individuals leads to universal love.

Trivialization of sex, media- and film-induced temptation to seek temporary gratification, pornography, rape, sadism, masochism, physical violence, and sexual abuse all stem from our disrespect for the sanctity of sex. Sacred sex is based on the foundation of commitment, responsibility, sacrifice, celebration, and joy.

All Hindu gods are married. Rama with Sita, Krishna with Radha, Shiva with Shakti, Vishnu with Lakshmi—these mythological icons are the models of the man-woman relationship. In them sensuality, dance, music, color, flowers, perfume, food, and all other aspects of good living and religiosity play their full parts. Everything in proportion, in the right place, at the right time, with wisdom and common sense. The man-woman relationship is the ultimate fulfillment of yin-yang balance, the Shiva-Shakti principle: it is the union of matter and spirit, the world and God, body and soul, nature and culture. In such unions all opposites are transformed into complements.

5. Nonconsumerism (Asangraha)

Asangraha, or nonconsumerism, means nonacquisition, nonaccumulation, and nonconsumption of goods and services which are inessential, wasteful, harmful, and unnatural. Excessive possessions are a trap; they bind us, imprison us, and enslave us. If I were caught in the trappings of wealth and power, I would be unable to live a truly comfortable, creative, and compassionate life. Much of my time would be absorbed in taking care of houses, cars, household gadgets, furnishings, paintings, silverware and china, computers, yachts, and umpteen other things. I would need to work hard to earn enough not to meet my needs but to service these possessions. A stage would come when my possessions would possess me rather than my possessing them. I would be in the knot that is *graha.* When that knot is pulled tight, it becomes *sangraha,* but when I am free from the noose I am practicing *asangraha.*

In our modern times possessions have become signs of status, of success, of position, and of power. No wonder that modern society has been named the consumer society. Unlimited economic growth has become the ideal of every nation in the world. In order to achieve this individual lives, families, the social fabric, and our relationship with the natural world have been destroyed. We have passed the point of increasing human well-being by increasing material wealth.

Many surveys have found that in the Western world a reasonable living standard was reached in the 1970s, but since that time there has been a downward curve, more cars have meant more pollution and more congestion in the cities, waste disposal has reached levels at which landfills are poisoning the earth and water. In spite of enormous wealth and economic success, poverty has by no means been abolished; a small percentage of people control a large percentage of wealth, which affects social cohesion and harmony negatively. Increasing crime and a large prison population, drug trafficking, unemployment, homelessness, and social exclusion are acute problems in most Western nations.

There is total confusion about the aims of society and the meaning of life. Material wealth is only a means to an end—and that end is living a good life: spiritually, psychologically, socially, and artistically. Living the good life entails good human relationships throughout. But in our present culture means have become ends. Human societies are pursuing the accumulation of wealth for its own sake. Having has become more important than being. We value people not for who they are but for what they have, what kinds of status, power, position, and possessions they have. We have lost the sense of meaning, we are holding on to an empty form.

However, there is increasing awareness of this state of affairs; movements of voluntary simplicity, downshifting, local economy, and local currency are growing. Ordinary people reacted against the stranglehold of state-controlled socialism in the countries of the former Soviet bloc; now, in the West, the signs of revolt against the dictatorship of the market and the rule of money are evident. Such new economics, based on the principle of sustainability, give me hope of a transformation from acquisition to asangraha.

Nonconsumerism is not asceticism, it is not a principle of denial; it is knowing the limits and enjoying the abundant gifts of nature without possessing them. Nonconsumerism is integral to a life which is simple in means and rich in ends.

Obsessive attachment to acquisition leads to poverty of spirit and of imagination. Nonconsumerism is a way of finding the critical balance between material and spiritual wealth. If in balance, material wealth can be helpful to the society in service, sharing, and generosity. Therefore, nonconsumerism is nothing to be afraid of; with it life will be more enjoyable, not less. A nonconsumerist society is a no-poverty, no-affluence society. Such a society is worth aspiring to and worth working for.

For the last few hundred years we have been working for the creation of a consumer society, and its promise of utopia. All drudgery and chores were to be done by machines, and people would have plenty of time to pursue spiritual, artistic, and creative activities. Now there are cars and computers, faxes and phones, washing machines and central heating, and shops are filled with all conceivable kinds of goods, but where is the time? Where are the creativity and spirituality? Where is the utopia?

6. Physical work (Sharirashram)

Sharirashram, or physical work, means the practice of daily manual labor. Society the world over is divided into two parts: those who work with their hands and those who enjoy the fruit of other people's work. Peasants, farmers, craftsmen and women, factory workers, and other laborers work hard but get little in return. Lawyers, professors, accountants, managers, bankers, stockbrokers, landowners, and aristocrats use only their brains and are highly paid.

There is always a deep tension between the managers and the managed, the intellectual workers and the manual workers, between those who manipulate the market and those who are their victims. Such a divided society is unhealthy. The purpose of physical work is to heal that division. It gives an opportunity to all to use their hands as well as their heads. We may not be able to achieve complete parity in this field, but the goal for intellectuals, managers, and members of the middle class is to include a certain amount of manual work in their everyday lives.

I was deeply inspired to know that Gandhi, however busy he was, always incorporated some spinning, cleaning the toilets, and nursing the sick into his day. He made the spinning wheel a symbol of India's political independence and economic self-reliance.

Working with one's hands is much more than making or producing things. Physical work is a form of worship. It is a spiritual practice. It is a healing process, a therapy. It is an activity essential to ignite our imaginations and an antidote to alienation and exclusion.

Our hands have a tremendously transformative power. A lump of clay is turned into a beautiful pot, a block of stone into a sculpture, a pile of bricks into a home, a heap of wool into a tapestry. Sacrificing hand skills at the altar of technology can only bring disenchantment and mental confusion. A deskilled society is a degraded society.

We need to begin at the beginning. We need to restore the place of manual work in our schools. Together with reading, writing, mathematics and science, languages and literature, we need to teach children gardening, cooking, building, pottery, smithying, carpentry, animal husbandry, music, dance, and other crafts of life. Children leaving school should know what to do with themselves in very practical terms, and the industries which destroy manual jobs must be made to pay a heavy tax, which should be spent on encouraging handiwork. However sophisticated the technology, it cannot fulfill the deep urge of the body to act and to make.

Even when we have a good income from our professional work, that is no substitute for engagement with our hands. Gandhi wrote, "It is a tragedy of the first magnitude that millions of people have ceased to use their hands as hands. Nature has bestowed upon us this great gift which is our hands. If the craze for machinery methods continues, it is highly likely that a time will come when we shall be so incapacitated and weak that we shall begin to curse ourselves for having forgotten the use of the living machines given to us by God. Millions cannot keep fit by games and athletics; and why should they exchange the useful, productive, hardy occupations for the useless, unproductive, and expensive sports and games?"

All of us should be able to bake bread with whole flour. Dependence on denatured, mass-produced bread causes the loss of home culture.

What value has a home without a proper kitchen, where members of the family cook creatively and imaginatively and celebrate food, work, and life together?

When I have engaged in manual labor, I am satisfied with less. The work itself is a source of satisfaction. But when I have not engaged in the process of making, I am hungry for something, and I do not know what I am hungry for. And so I want more—I seek satisfaction in shopping, yet I remain dissatisfied. I realize that true satisfaction cannot be derived from things; it comes only when mind and body join in bringing out the potential of matter by interacting with it.

A purely materialistic and utilitarian mind-set pursues one, and only one, aim—continuous and endless production through mechanical means. This has resulted in the loss of a sense of beauty. We have created an ugly world, and the tragedy is that we no longer have the ability to discriminate between what is ugly and what is beautiful. Furthermore, with mechanized modes of production, things such as paper plates and polystyrene cups are made to be used once only, so that human hands are not required even to wash them. And of course built-in obsolescence is the curse of our time; it is always easier and cheaper to buy new rather than mend the old.

When craftsmen or women make things by hand, they unselfconsciously combine heart, head, and hands. As a result, whatever they make is beautiful, useful, and durable (the BUD principle). Tribal people in many parts of the world, traditional craftspeople, the illiterate peasants of the past and present, make artifacts, build houses, erect stone walls in their fields, and these are items of exquisite beauty. They make these things for practical purposes or for aesthetic purposes or for ritual. And these objects are durable; they last until their natural end. The older they become, the more attractive they look. They are always repairable. Making and mending are part of the same continuum. The BUD principle is the source of true satisfaction, spiritual, sensual, and physical.

7. Avoidance of Bad Taste (Aswada)

In the case of food, aswada, or avoidance of bad taste, means not eating unhealthy food. This includes junk food, fast food, convenience food, processed food, imported food, and too much food. We are what we eat. With good food, body and mind function well. Bad food contributes to mental breakdown, cravings, and ill health. A good life cannot be built on a bad diet.

Food should be pleasing to the eyes, pleasing to the nose, pleasing to the tongue, but above all, it should nourish body and soul. Food is sacred. It is a gift of nature, and we should take it in its natural form or as close to that as possible. Playing politics with food or profiteering from food is an insult to our common sense. Tampering with food through genetic engineering and patenting shows a desire to dominate natural processes. Food patenting is a kind of theft. It has been called biopiracy and rightly so. The dominant nations and corporations have devised laws and regulations to suit their purpose in the name of nutrition.

Indian science classifies food into three types: *satvik, rajsik,* and *tamsik.* Satvik food is associated with true food. It is simple, natural, seasonal, and local. Fruit, vegetables, grains, pulses, nuts, and herbs come in this category. Relishing the natural taste, the original flavor of food with the least interference and processing has been considered the highest form of cuisine by Indian nutritionists and Ayurvedic doctors. Those who eat satvik food need no other medicine. This is the diet of gods and angels, sages and sadhus, mothers and babies. Natural spring water; fresh and untreated milk and yogurt; pure boiled rice; potatoes baked in their skins; beans and peas; salads of all kinds; thyme, rosemary, sage, cardamom, cumin, turmeric, basil, coriander, chives, and other herbs; and mangoes, apples, bananas, and every local fruit are satvik foods.

It is not just what you eat but how you eat it. Preparing with care, sharing and celebrating, being unhurried and relaxed in a convivial ambience contribute to making food satvik. Preparing and eating satvik food is a spiritual practice.

Rajsik food is associated with Raja the king. It is spicy, stimulating, exciting, lavish, and elaborate. It is complicated, preserved, and processed. Onions, garlic, chili, spices, pickles, mature cheeses, salt, sugar, canned food, alcoholic drinks, tea, coffee, chocolate, ice cream, foreign food, and frozen food out of season come in this category. Rajsik food has been promoted by soldiers, merchants, and people who prefer taste above nutrition, pleasure above satisfaction, and design above delight.

Tamsik food is associated with malevolent forces that cause lethargy, depression, anger, cruelty, and intoxication. Tamsik food is artificial, violent, and addictive. Hard spirits, hard drugs, tobacco, meat, stale food, overcooked or burned food, and stolen food come in this category. Overeating is also tamsik.

Some readers may object to having meat included in this class, but modern methods of raising animals in factory farms and slaughtering them in huge mechanized abattoirs involve an immense amount of pain and suffering for the animals. Meat production on this scale takes up vast amounts of land, causing extinction of wildlife. Huge quantities of grain are grown in countries where local people are malnourished and living below the poverty line so that grain can be exported to feed animals of the rich, industrialized countries to provide cheap meat. Furthermore, virgin forests are being cleared to create farms to rear stock so that meat eaters can buy cheap meat burgers. All this for what benefit? Meat eating causes heart disease, cancer, and other illnesses. Then billions of dollars are spent on health care. The medicines themselves are the results of cruel experiments on animals.

An ecologically balanced, environmentally sound, and economically sustainable future has to be largely vegetarian. Such food needs to be produced through organic methods. In the future we will have to return to small-scale farming, in which people in greater numbers are working the land, cultivating the soil with simpler tools. Farming will be more like gardening than like agribusiness. Poisoning the land with massive inputs of chemicals for short-term gain is in itself a tamsik act and against the ethos of good food. Methods of permaculture, biodynamic agriculture, forest farming, and natural farming are in tune with the quality of satvik food. The essential point of good food is to practice moderation in all circumstances.

The categories of satvik, rajsik, and tamsik are not watertight. They provide a frame of reference so that we can consider moving from tamsik to rajsik to satvik as far as possible. They are helpful indicators of where our priorities should lie. A satvik state is an aspiration rather than a rule.

These three qualities can also be applied in other spheres of life. For example, inspiring, poetic, educative, nonviolent films will fall in the satvik category; romantic, entertaining, high-budget films are rajsik; violent, pornographic, or depressing films are tamsik. Similarly, a simple, beautiful, and appropriate-sized home, made with natural and local materials, is satvik. Opulent, expensive, palatial, exhibitionist, plush, showy homes are rajsik. High-rise, high-tech homes built with plastic, asbestos, and other unnatural materials are tamsik. Castles built to dominate the landscape and people are also tamsik. These qualities can be applied to cities, transport, dress, sport, and other areas of life. In each case, in meditating on the three qualities one attempts to turn oneself toward the practice of good taste.

8. Fearlessness (Sarvatra Bhaya Varjana)

Sarvatra bhaya varjana, or fearlessness, means freedom from fear always and everywhere. Our lives are ruled by fear. Fear of death, fear of old age, fear of illness, fear of unemployment, fear of failure, fear of superiors, fear of inferiors, fear of responsibility, fear of commitment, and numerous other fears cause us continual anxiety. Fear leads to violence and war; fear prevents us from seeking and speaking the truth; fear forces us to steal, stops us from loving, makes us accumulate things. Fear is at the root of all evil. Fear is the cause of inner and outer insecurity. Because of fear we want to control, dominate, and rule others. Fear erodes personal as well as social harmony.

The cure for the problems created by fear is unconditional trust in the workings of the universe. As we trust that the sun will rise, water will quench thirst, fire will cook food, boats will sail the seas, so we have to trust that each life, including our own, will fulfill its destiny.

Most of our fears are artificially induced. They are induced at school, in the family, by our peer groups, by politicians, by the media, by religions, and by our own ignorance. The greatest task is to be free from all fears.

In many religious traditions and mythologies, dissolution of ego has been spoken of as a hero's journey or a warrior's path. When I am able to leap to help someone without fearing my own death, I become a hero, because at that moment I am unaware of my own self. If that moment of emptiness, that experience of egolessness, that bliss of enlightenment can become a way of being for always and everywhere, then I am free from fear.

A hero is not a special kind of person; every person is a special kind of hero when he or she is without fear. Every life is a hero's journey. When I trust in the universe, I am not afraid to take risks. If I am afraid of taking risks, is life worth living?

All human beings are part of the tapestry of the universe, part of a pattern which connects. Nothing exists in isolation, in separateness.

When I realize this network of grand relationships, I lose the illusion of my separate self, I lose the ego, I lose the sense of "I" and "my." When there is no ego, who is afraid of whom?

When I am no longer self-concerned or self-seeking, then I am also not so critical and judgmental of others. I am able to get on with living life rather than worrying about it. I get up in the morning, I clean my teeth, I eat a piece of fruit, I dig the garden, I answer letters, I shop for myself and for my neighbor who is ill, I cook lunch and share it with my family, I clean the dishes, and I rest, I read, I write, I go for a walk, I attend a meeting, I make a few phone calls, and I go to bed at night. The next day is another day. Whatever needs to be done, I do it. Without always questioning, complaining, criticizing, doubting, and, above all, fearing.

In Gerald Jampolsky's words, "Love is letting go of fear." I always seek love but am unable to love because I am unable to let go of fear. Love is all I need. Love is the source of joyful living. Love is my true destiny. In love I find the meaning of life. Love is the ground of all relationships. I am longing for love, but fear stops me from giving and receiving, from being fulfilled.

When I have been able to cultivate fearlessness in my everyday life and have accomplished solid trust from which all activities flow, then I am able to act socially, politically, and collectively without fear and to follow a truthful and right course of action. When I am faced with an unjust law, I am prepared to break it and stand for justice, freedom, and integrity; I am not afraid of the consequences, including imprisonment or death, as Emile Zola, Henry David Thoreau, Martin Luther King, and Mahatma Gandhi showed.

9. Respect for All Religions (Sarva Dharma Samanatva)

Sarva dharma samanatva, respect for all religions, means appreciation of all religious traditions and tolerance of beliefs with which we may disagree. A religion stems from a particular historic condition, or a specific geographic context, or a unique social need. A religion gives expression to a spiritual quest through a set of formulations and principles and stories. Following the original revelation, scholars, philosophers, theologians, and writers create theories, interpretations, and commentaries. Priests and preachers turn the original teachings of a great prophet into dogma, which is followed in a literal, inflexible, and rigid manner. As a consequence the spirit and the meaning of original teachings are forgotten and the empty shell is worshiped. Ritual takes over and becomes an end in itself. The challenge for a spiritual seeker is to clear away the clutter and search for his or her own experience. Deep down, all religions are pointing toward the same wisdom: the wisdom of love and compassion, peace and generosity, service and serenity, egolessness and self-realization.

To put it simply, different religious paths are like different cuisines. The ingredients are the same: rice, wheat, potatoes, pulses, vegetables, herbs, et cetera, but in the hands of Chinese, Indian, French, Italian, and Arab chefs, these ingredients are transformed. They smell, taste, and look so different, but they are all able to satisfy hunger. Similarly love, truth, compassion, and charity put in the religious traditions of Christians, Hindus, Muslims, Jains, Buddhists, and Jews may appear different, but if practiced sincerely they all bring about a transformation of consciousness leading to equanimity and peace.

Of course there are different beliefs emerging from these different traditions—belief or no belief in God, in reincarnation, in hell and heaven, life after death, the soul, good and evil, sin and virtue. These beliefs are like theories of food; some people believe that chamomile tea will help you to sleep, garlic is an aphrodisiac, an apple a day keeps the doctor away—no one can ever determine for certain whether such theories are ultimately wrong or right, or work for everybody. Therefore there is no point in fighting, quarreling, and killing each other in the name of one theory or another. Hindus and Muslims could happily coexist, as Chinese and Italian restaurants can coexist. If people prefer Chinese to Italian food or vice versa, let them enjoy whichever food they like.

Let us cultivate respect for the diversity and plurality of religions. If the whole world had only one religion, it would be no better. People would invent religions within the religions, sects within sects. Not all Christians have been renowned for living in peace and harmony, nor all Buddhists. So the principle of sarva dharma samanatva is to let the thousand flowers bloom. As we have many languages with their own specific excellences and insights, so it is wonderful that we have so many religions. The world is richer for it. If we do not wish to discard small languages like Hungarian or Tibetan in the name of convenience, why should we wish to make Christianity or Islam or any other religion the only valid religion for the whole world?

Religion is not in the Koran or the Bible, it is in our hearts, in our actions, and in our practice. Religion is not in a church, a mosque, or a temple, it is in the way we relate to other humans, to animals, to forests, to the poor and oppressed, to the ill and dying. Belief in this or that is to some extent speculative, though interesting. Healing the wounded, sharing ourselves with others, listening to them, being gentle, open, and humble are immediate and practical expressions of true religion. So I should be free to practice whatever religion I like, but I must be free of the burden of arrogance and exclusivity.

10. Local Economy (Swadeshi)

Swadeshi, or local economy, means developing a sense of your own place and loving it. All of us have a mother and a father who have given birth to us. In the same way, we all have a place where we live. That place sustains us, and we should sustain it. A nation-state can have a centralized government, but the better form is a confederation of self-governing, self-reliant communities, neighborhoods, districts, townships, and bioregions, where people fulfill their lives from the products of their own localities. When all people are looking after their own patches of land, then every place will be looked after. Where a local economy prevails, people derive maximum benefit from the bounty of their own locality and refrain from desiring, obtaining, and controlling the resources of other localities. They do not permit any damage to the people and to the local environment. "Not in my backyard" is a perfect formulation, as every yard is somebody's backyard. If every backyard is protected, no yard will be damaged.

This means local apples, local butter, local vegetables, local cheese, local crafts, local industry, local shops, local schools, local hospitals, and in all other matters turning to local goods and services before others. Maximum economic and political power, including the power to decide what is imported into or exported from the local community, remains in the hands of the local government.

For thousands of years before the industrial revolution, mass transportation, and cheap energy, people all over the world lived in relative harmony with their surroundings, weaving homespun clothes, eating homegrown food, caring for the countryside, building homes, temples, and churches with local materials. And yet ideas, cultures, arts, and religions spread far and wide, creating a universal consciousness. Thinking globally and acting locally has been practiced for millennia.

But in modern times minds have grown narrow while markets have expanded. There used to be freedom for people to move and freedom for ideas to spread while goods and services were local. That was a much healthier state of affairs and less damaging to the environment. Now all governments put severe restrictions on immigration of people, but they allow the dumping of goods in countries where the same goods are plentifully available. For example, New Zealand butter is dumped in England while English butter is turning into a butter mountain. Californian wine is pushed into the French market while France knows not what to do with its wine lakes. Japanese cars are forced on the American people while American cars are lying unsold, occupying vast acres of parking lots. Meanwhile transportation of butter, wine, cars, and other goods is causing depletion of the ozone layer and global warming. Who, other than the giant corporations, benefits from this massive movement of goods? Small and local businesses, shops and industries are closed down, throwing people on the unemployment heap and making them dependent on state benefit.

Recently the Wuppertal Institute in Germany asked a question. How many miles does a container of strawberry yogurt travel before it reaches the kitchen table of a German household? They discovered that the yogurt, including the plastic container, the label printed on it, the sugar, milk, and strawberries, had traveled eleven hundred miles. If that yogurt was part of the local economy, it would hardly travel at all.

Once E. F. Schumacher related an incident to me. He observed a large truck bringing biscuits made in Manchester to London. A few minutes later he observed another truck taking biscuits made in London to Manchester. Now Schumacher was an economist, so he started to ponder the economic rationale behind a truck full of biscuits coming from Manchester to London and vice versa. What could it be? If the specialty of a Manchester biscuit was desired in London, the biscuit manufacturer could send the recipe to London on a postcard. The Manchester manufacturer could even send someone to London to teach the art of biscuit making. Schumacher could not understand what benefit was derived from using a fleet of trucks, congesting the highways, polluting the air, and making the drivers sit alone for several hours day after day for the best part of their lives in the service of moving around biscuits. In the end, in some desperation, he said to himself, "Oh well, I am a mere economist and not a nutritionist. Perhaps the nutritional value of these biscuits is increased by transportation!"

Schumacher was not against trade altogether. If there was something in Manchester which could only be made there, then it was reasonable to exchange it for something which could only be made in London. But to ferry identical goods around in the name of free trade is economic insanity. The trade between nations and regions should be minimal, like icing on a cake.

This observation was narrated to me in the early 1970s, before globalization of the economy, the stranglehold of GATT and NAFTA, and obsession with world trade were strong. Now, under the regime of liberalization, biscuits are carted around not just from Manchester to London but from Manchester to Moscow, from London to Los Angeles, and from Tokyo to Toronto.

If people think that the global economy is based on rationality, then they need to have their heads examined! World trade is the most irrational system yet devised. Everyone loses except the global corporations, and the environment suffers most of all. The globalization of the economy is colonialism pure and simple, wearing the mask of free trade, progress, development, science, technology, modernity, the promise of utopia tomorrow. Today there is a net flow of resources and wealth from the poor countries of the South to the rich countries of the North.

The answer to globalization is swadeshi. Whatever is made or produced in a locality must be used first and foremost by the people of that locality. Every local community should have its own carpenters, potters, shoemakers, builders, mechanics, farmers, engineers, teachers, weavers, doctors, bankers, merchants, musicians, artists, and priests. In other words, each local community should be a microcosm of the macroworld.

The principle of swadeshi is not against cities, but it is against sprawling suburbs and megalopolies. If there were cities of one to two million people, flanked by greenbelts and sufficient amounts of supporting farmland, then New York would not depend on lettuce imported from California and London would not depend on potatoes imported from Egypt.

Swadeshi is concerned not with personal self-sufficiency or family self-sufficiency but with self-sufficiency of the bioregion. In conjunction with the principle of manual work, the economy should be based not on centralized and mechanized modes of production but on decentralized, homegrown, handcrafted modes of production. In other words, not mass production but production by the masses.

Mass production is concerned with the product, whereas production by the masses is concerned with the product, the producers, and the process. The industrial system depends on impersonal, alienating, and soul-destroying structures, whereas small-scale methods of production for, by, and within the local area encourage neighborliness and human relationships. People take care of each other and of animals, land, and forestry. A healthy economy is a local economy, and a local economy is a healthy economy.

The champions of globalization are mostly from the United States and Western Europe. These countries profess to believe in democracy, but democracy and the global economy are a contradiction in terms. Industrial bureaucrats operate anonymously. Their power and wealth is so enormous that many small and poor nations, not to mention local communities, are unable to stand up to them. Multinational corporations can use their money and muscle to bribe officials, can hire clever lawyers to interpret laws in their favor, can spend large sums of money to entertain and impress politicians, and can use their cunning to overpower any opposition.

If the companies were small and local, they would have to work within the bounds of local support, local culture, and local accountability. They would be obliged to serve the local community since they would be making a profit out of it. Ethics and economics would be twinned. There would be more chance to implement the triple bottom line—financial profitability would be required to match with social responsibility and environmental sustainability. Within the local economy, profit has a place, but it is kept in its place. In the matrix of society, profit, culture, nature, and spirituality together make the complete picture.

11. Respect for All Beings (Sparsha Bhavana)

Sparsha bhavana, or respect for all beings, means that caste, color, class, creed, sex, age, race, and other similar distinctions are no reason for putting people down or up. In India the caste system makes some people outcasts or untouchables. In Britain the class system divides society. In Northern Ireland religion keeps communities apart. In the United States color causes segregation. Then there is the divisiveness of sexism, ageism, and racism. In subtle or not so subtle ways, discrimination is practiced in most societies. In many cultures men treat women as second-class citizens. The rich turn their noses up at the poor; the clever and educated look down on the illiterate. City people look at country folk with disdain. Civilized societies consciously, or subconsciously, consider primitive and tribal societies to be dispensable. Industrialized societies look at agrarian societies as backward.

Of course attitudes are changing, racial harmony is improving, untouchability in India has been outlawed, and in the United States civil rights have been restored. However, we are a long way from establishing equal and unqualified respect for all human beings. We are even further from looking at speciesism. To some extent the concept of human rights has been brought into public discourse, but animal rights and the rights of wildlife, including the whole animate and inanimate world, have hardly been expressed. I wonder whether you, my reader, even grasp the concept of species rights. But sparsha bhavana requires a deep respect for all species and acceptance of the intrinsic value of all beings.

Most people think and act as if God created animals for the benefit of human beings and therefore human beings consider it their birthright to hunt them, kill them for sport, ride on them, and of course slaughter them to eat. This attitude to animals is comparable to past attitudes to slaves and to servants. It has been and still is argued that animals have no souls and are therefore of no value other than their usefulness for human beings. This collective myopia is at the root of the present-day ecological crisis. Millions of species are becoming extinct because of human encroachment on their habitats. This human colonialism is ever expanding over the territories of the nonhuman species.

We don't think that nature exists in its own right. If there is a piece of land, we automatically assume that some individual or government owns it; if a piece of land is not being used either for farming or for building, people think that that land is being wasted. If we are to cultivate respect for all beings, then we need a radical change, almost a revolution in our attitudes. We need to learn to rejoice in the beauty and the mystery of existence as it is and not look at it as a source for economic activity.

Of course we have to take things from nature for our use. We have to take wood for the house, food for the body, wool and cotton for our clothing, but we must take these things not as a right but as a gift and feel gratitude toward nature. If we have that kind of attitude, then we will take with care and restraint because we will think that if we cut down a tree, we are not only taking the life of that tree, but also taking away a whole environment, the home of many birds and insects, shade and food for all kinds of creatures. So if we are taking one tree away, we should plant five trees in its place.

Basically it is a question of attitude. The attitude which allows people to kill animals and clear forests is the same attitude which allows stronger nations to attack weaker nations. We are at the threshold of a new century and a new millennium. I wish to see an emergence of the century of ecology. We humans need to rediscover our humility and learn to practice sparsha bhavana toward all species. There is a built-in instinct in all species to live. We need to respect their instinct, their right to live and flourish.

THROUGHOUT GANDHI'S ELEVEN PRINCIPLES there is a common thread—there can be no such thing as freedom without limit, restraint, and responsibility. Understanding and accepting the limit is a guarantee, a protective shield of freedom. My body has a protective skin; the skin forms the boundary of the body. Within the bounds of the skin, my senses, my heart, my veins, my bones, and numerous organs, cells, and bacteria can function freely. Similarly my house has a boundary, a limit. Within the four walls of the house, I live freely, reading, writing, cooking, cleaning, caring for my family and friends, and undertaking numerous other activities. My society also has limits. I function within laws and regulations. My rights and responsibilities are defined by those laws. Freedom of speech, freedom of assembly, freedom of movement, and all the other aspects of civil liberty I exercise within the law of the land. But as there are laws of the body, of home, of society, and of nations, there are laws of nature.

Some of the eleven principles, such as nonviolence, are stated in the negative. The aim is not to tell me what to do—that would be too prescriptive—the aim is to show where my limits are and to make clear that by stepping out of those limits I will endanger my freedom. But if I stay within my limits I am free to act as I choose. In terms of nonviolence, I am free to live as long as I let others live. In terms of nonconsumerism, if I tread lightly on the Earth, the Earth will continue to sustain life; if I live simply, then others can simply live.

If we accept that the body has a limit, the house has a limit, the nation has a limit, then why do we have difficulty in accepting that there is a limit to economic growth? Since the publication of *Limits to Growth,* I have participated in numerous environmental gatherings, particularly in the UN conference on the environment in Stockholm in 1972 and the UN Earth Summit in Rio de Janeiro in 1992. Lip service is paid to protecting the environment and conserving energy, forests, biodiversity, and wildlife, but there is a strong drive to continue on the path of unhindered economic growth. The debate has been continuing for decades, but the penny has not yet dropped. The Western way of life, based on economic expansion, is not yet open to negotiation, to paraphrase George Bush when he was president of the United States.

The idea of limit is very simple. A child is born, grows for about twenty years, very slowly, almost without being noticed, then reaches her or his full height of five to six feet. For fifty years or more that person remains the same height. This principle of scale is built into each and every natural phenomenon. An organization, a business, an industry, a national economy, and a world economy should be no exception. But this theory of scale has been constantly ignored by the powers that be.

In the context of such a dominant culture of growth, the eleven principles may appear pious thinking at best and irrelevant at worst, but I am not so pessimistic. The Roman Empire did not last forever. The British Empire, over which the sun never set, came to an end. Communist control of the Soviet bloc, once so powerful, has disappeared into history. Slavery ended, apartheid ended, and there is no reason to believe that the ecologically unsustainable and personally dissatisfying forces of materialism manifested in money-dominated economies will last forever. Once human consciousness has changed, once we have a new awareness of our place in the scheme of things, once we have realized that there is more to life than the unending chase for material possessions, and once we focus on the importance of being rather than having, we will see a dramatic transformation all around us. Then we will take to these eleven principles as ducks to water.

CHAPTER 19

⚯

Realization

Performing penance as a monk, experiencing ecstasy in love, engaging in revolutionary land reform, walking for world peace, being imprisoned in France, facing a bullet in America—the many dimensions of my life have led me to ponder one question above all: What is Good and what is Evil? Or, indeed, do Good and Evil exist?

Again and again I have come to the conclusion that there is ignorance, there is ego, there is wisdom, there is humility, but there are no static states of Good and Evil. There are negative and positive, winter and summer, day and night, but for me none of these opposites is necessarily good or bad. Sometimes, what appeared to be good turned out to be not so good, and what seemed bad proved to be a blessing in disguise. More often than not, I have been trapped by my own language, which I have inherited from others. I have been imprisoned by concepts, perceptions, and prejudices.

But whenever I have kept flowing, I have found my natural state of being, beyond the chains of mental abstractions. At those times I have felt like water: no specific color, no particular taste, no solid structure, but natural and fluid. Sometimes water stagnates, but this is overcome when its natural state of motion is resumed; water finds again its own true nature. In the same way, by letting go of attachments to ideologies, places, and people, I have found my own true nature. My life has been a quest for self-realization.